The MICHIGAN Guide
to English *for*
Academic Success
and
Better TOEFL®
Test Scores

The MICHIGAN Guide
to English *for*
Academic Success
and
Better TOEFL®
Test Scores

Catherine Mazak

Lawrence J. Zwier

Lynn Stafford-Yilmaz

Ann Arbor
University of Michigan Press

TOEFL® is a registered trademark of Educational Testing Service.
This publication is not approved or endorsed by ETS.

Copyright © The University of Michigan 2004
All rights reserved

ISBN 0-472-08991-9

Published in the United States of America by
The University of Michigan Press
2007   2006   2005   2004   4   3   2   1

No part of this publication may be reproduced, stored in a retrieval system, or transmitted in any form or by any means, electronic, mechanical, or otherwise, without the written permission of the publisher.

The test directions and sample questions printed in this book are not actual TOEFL® Test materials. This book consists of training materials with information provided in its entirety by the University of Michigan Press. No endorsement of this publication by Educational Testing Service should be inferred.

ACKNOWLEDGMENTS

We would like to thank the following people for their contributions to this book: Matthew Weltig; Clair Brown, Professor of Economics, University of California, Berkeley; Clark McKown, Ph.D. Faculty Fellow in the Department of Psychology, University of California, Berkeley; Toby Bradshaw, Professor of Biology, University of Washington; Amori Yee Mikami, Lecturer in the Psychology Department, University of California, Berkeley; Dr. Jerry W. Sanders, Lecturer, Department of Peace and Conflict Studies, University of California, Berkeley; E. David Ford, Professor, College of Forest Resources, University of Washington; Raleigh Wilson, Manager, Black Lightning Lecture Notes, University of California, Berkeley; Greg Walsen, student, University of Washington; Guillermo Ortiz Colón, Michigan State University, for his expertise in adipose tissue; Debra Shafer and Sarah Murphy for their help with permissions; and Sarah Briggs and Rita Simpson for their assistance with selections from the MICASE. We wish to thank all of the students who participated by allowing their written and spoken responses to be included in this book.

Grateful acknowledgment is made to the following authors and publishers for permission to reprint previously published materials.

Lerner Publishing Group for "A Revolution in Healing: Biotechnology in Medicine" in *The New Biotechnology: Putting Microbes to Work* by Cynthia Gross, copyright © 1988.

James W. Russell for "Contemporary Societies and the World Economy" from *Introduction to Macrosociology, Second Edition,* copyright © 1996.

The University of Michigan Press for excerpts from: *The Cat and the Human Imagination: Feline Images from Bast to Garfield* by K. Rogers, copyright © 1998; *Beyond Complementary Medicine: Legal and Ethical Perspectives on Health Care and Human Evolution* by M. Cohen, copyright © 2000; *Adoption in America: Historical Perspectives,* E. W. Carp, ed., copyright © 2002; *Ruin and Recovery: Michigan's Rise as a Conservation Leader* by D. Dempsey, copyright © 2001; *The Woman Who Knew Too Much: Alice Stewart and the Secrets of Radiation* by G. Greene, copyright © 1999.

Thanks to the following individuals for agreeing to appear in photos in this text: Mary Bisbee-Beek, Giles Brown, Chris Hebert, Deborah Kopka, Mike Landauer, Allison Leefer, Sarah Murphy, Jim Reische, Julia Suarez, Kristin Thomas, and Yune Tran. Thanks to Kerri Kijewski for photographs.

Thanks to the following individuals for voice talent on the accompanying audio: Anna Marie Alvarez, Stephanie Browning, Zineb Chraibi, Lee Crooks, Charles Gerace, Susan Perdue, Sean Reid, Brian Schmitzer, and Lisa Taylor.

CONTENTS

INTRODUCTION

Communicative techniques have prevailed for many years in the teaching of English to speakers of other languages (ESOL)—and the testing world is finally catching up. Students once saw little connection between solid ESOL courses and such high-stakes tests as the TOEFL® Test. The advent of communicative testing, which asks students to work across the four language skills, changes all of that. The purpose of this book is to make this connection clear, and to help students to work on the skills that will actually improve their English—not just for test preparation, but for academic purposes as well.

This book can be used as a core text in multi-skills English for Academic Purposes (EAP) classes and in dedicated communicative-test preparation programs (such as a TOEFL®-prep class). This book **builds** academic English language skills, **practices** those skills, and finally **tests** them. This volume works well as a classroom text and can also be used by students for self-study (see the section How to Use This Book: For Students on page xiv).

Using This Book for Test Preparation

The complete revision of the TOEFL® Test released in 2005 (referred to in this book as the 2005 TOEFL®) makes earlier test-preparation materials obsolete. Consequently, this book does not look like a traditional test-preparation book. It works on the skills that students develop in EAP classes because these skills are now, in themselves, valuable preparation for important tests like the 2005 TOEFL®. These tests reward students who have worked hard to develop their communicative abilities in English, not just students who have spent a lot of time in test-prep classes. Students cannot memorize grammar rules or vocabulary lists in order to improve their tests scores because discrete-point grammar and vocabulary questions are no longer part of the TOEFL® Test. Although other tests may continue to use the discrete-point test format, the TOEFL® Test remains the most widely used English language admissions test, and other tests can be expected to follow its lead in becoming more communication-oriented.

Other TOEFL®-preparation materials are software-based and awkward to use in classroom situations. Even if you have an excellent computer lab at your disposal, it is hard to teach from software. This book was written **by EAP teachers for EAP teachers and students.** We focused on making it as teacher friendly as possible. We look at test preparation through an EAP teacher's eyes. We are delighted by the new legitimacy that communication-oriented tests give to the testing process and to the efforts of EAP teachers. As teachers, our principle goal is for students to improve their language skills. Fortunately, *these efforts now constitute test preparation* (as they always should have).

To adequately prepare for the 2005 TOEFL®, students must tackle both longer readings (600–700 words) and more substantial listening passages (three to four minutes) than on previous versions of the test. Such readings appear in print in this guide, and such listening passages are on the accompanying

CDs and in the audio script (in the back of the book). Whereas in an actual testing situation TOEFL® Test questions will be answered at a computer, these questions can be presented just as well in print. The computer is just a tool; the 2005 TOEFL® is not a computer-adaptive test.

To help students preparing to take the 2005 TOEFL® Test, this book contains extensive sections on how written and spoken responses will be rated. These include sample essays and spoken responses that are broken down and explained for students. Of course, this helps students see which features can improve their performance. It also encourages true skill improvement through self-editing and working to understand the reactions of native-speaker listeners and readers.

The answer key is provided in the back of this book. We believe that having access to answers improves students' ability to monitor their progress and ultimately prepare for the test itself. Students serious about raising their TOEFL® scores will only use the answer key to check answers *after* full effort has been made to answer the questions independently. In addition, a book can never truly mimic a test administered by computer. That said, in the listening and practice test sections, it's possible for more advanced students to read and answer the questions as they listen to the lectures and conversations. As a result, teachers may want to ask students to close their books as they listen so they can focus their attention on understanding and taking notes about the passages.

Using This Book for Building EAP Skills

This book focuses on academic tasks across the four main skill areas: *reading, listening, writing,* and *speaking.* Within each chapter, key academic skills are identified, explained, and practiced in the **Building Skills** sections. These academic skills are then worked across the four language skills. For example, Building Skills: Identifying the Main Idea is introduced in the *reading* section, then applied to the context of a lecture in the *listening* section. The *writing* section explains how to write a main idea in thesis statements and topic sentences, and finally the skill is applied to *speaking* with hints about how to clearly state the main idea in a spoken response. This book takes key academic skills, breaks them down, gives examples and lots of practice, and shows how they might be tested—all while connecting them across the four language skills. The result is ***true multi-skills EAP practice*** that will improve students' success in academic work in English.

The book's many exercises offer ample opportunity for classroom activity. Working with the sample student responses, students can develop their skills as editors and reviewers of their own writing and speaking. There are many opportunities for simulated test practice throughout each part of the book.

Organization of This Book

After a short description of communication-oriented tests, this book is organized on a skill-by-skill basis. There are four skill-related sections: reading, listening, writing, and speaking. The skills developed in each part depend on those that were developed in previous parts; the book is meant to be completed in order from beginning to end. Other possible sequencing can work, but students may find that they will want to study previous sections as they work through the exercises. There is cross-application of skills because many writing and speaking tasks depend on reading and listening input.

Within each skill section, sequenced activities move from short-context exercises to full-length review activities. Answers for all of these exercises are provided either in the part (with discussion and analysis) or in the answer key at the end of the book. A complete practice test modeled after the 2005 TOEFL® is included. This can be used by students in part or as a whole, and by teachers as extra homework practice or as a whole simulated test.

A Note about the Use of Authentic Materials

The majority of full-length readings are taken from authentic college-level textbooks and academic books published by the University of Michigan Press. All the lectures in the listening section are authentic, taken from university first- and second-year general education classes. However, we have slowed the pace of the listening passages to more closely simulate a testing situation. The pace, lecture to lecture, will vary in an attempt to expose students to more true-to-life listening experiences and to improve students' overall listening comprehension skills. Because of these decisions, some lectures practiced on the audio program are longer than four minutes proscribed by the TOEFL®. To achieve the necessary focus, shorter skill-development passages have been constructed by the authors. Writing and speaking items, because of their nature, were constructed by the authors. The sample student writing and speaking responses found in the How Your Response Will Be Graded sections were collected from international graduate and undergraduate students at a large state university. The non-native speakers contributed their responses in a proctored, timed session simulating test conditions. By keeping the materials in the book as close to authentic as possible, we hope to prepare students for the types of academic tasks that they will encounter in a university context.

How to Use the Audio Component for This Book

The two audio CDs packaged with the text include: all of the lectures, conversations, and practice exercises in the Part 2: Listening; the lectures and sample prompts that are integral to the integrated writing task in Part 3: Writing; the conversation and lecture prompts on which speaking responses are based in Part 4: Speaking; and all the material on the Practice Test that requires listening. The sample student responses to the speaking prompts are not included on these CDs. Because these samples were not recorded in a studio and were recorded by having students record their responses into a microphone on a computer—in order to replicate the testing situation—the responses can be found on the University of Michigan Press ESL website: *www.press.umich.edu/esl/testprep*. You will need to have a media player plug-in installed on your computer to listen to these audio files. However, access to the Internet is not necessary to use this book. Students preparing to take the 2005 TOEFL® can gain much insight into the speaking responses by reading each written version of the response, viewing the score of each response, and understanding the analysis of the response.

The 🎧 icon indicates a new track on the audio CDs. For some activities, the listening material requires listening to more than one track. Instructions as to when to **Press Play** are provided in the text for each item on the audio. To make it easier to move through the audio, press **Pause,** not Stop, when the narrator says "Stop the audio." A list of items on the audio can be found on the very last page of the book (opposite the audio CDs).

How to Use This Book: For Students

This book contains exercises and narrative explanations about the exercises. This book is arranged in a specific order by skill (reading, listening, writing, and speaking) and is then divided into smaller skills such as Identifying the Main Idea. The book is meant to be completed from beginning to end, since the later parts heavily rely on skills that are developed and practiced earlier.

The answer key will assist you as you progress through most exercises. However, there are some tasks, like writing a timed essay, for which there is no one right answer. For items such as these, we provide extensive sample responses at different levels. These passages are authentic student writing. Each of these was rated by a panel of experts. There is an explanation of why each response received its score. You should read through these sections and compare your work to that of other students to get an idea about how responses are scored.

If you are using this book in preparation for the 2005 TOEFL®, you should give yourself plenty of time to practice. If you do not have access to a teacher or tutor, forming a study group with friends who are also going to take the test will help. And remember, as you are practicing for the test, you are also practicing vitally important academic skills that will serve you well in your university life.

What to Expect on the 2005 TOEFL®
Physical Conditions

You will take the 2005 TOEFL® by computer. However, the computer is simply a tool for transmitting your test answers to the Educational Testing Service. The format of the test is not dependent on high technology and could just as easily be done with a piece of paper and a tape recorder. Unlike the CBT®, the 2005 TOEFL® is *not* computer-adaptive (all questions are the same for every test-taker).

The entire test takes about four hours.

What to Expect: Skill-by-Skill
Reading

1. The reading test will present three readings (about 600–700 words each), one at a time, in a long bar on one side of your computer screen. You have 25 minutes to read each passage and complete about 13 questions related to it. You will be able to view the reading while you answer the questions related to it.

2. In most reading questions, you will choose the best answer by clicking on an oval. If the question requires more than one answer, you will click two boxes.

3. To answer other questions, you will move pieces of text into place in tables or a summary box.

4. After choosing your answer to a reading question, click a Next button near the top of the screen to move to the next question.

5. In the reading section only, you may go back to change your answers as long as the 25-minute limit has not expired and you have not clicked a button to move to the next reading.

Listening

1. For the listening part of the test, you will wear headphones connected to your computer. This section takes about one hour.

2. The listening section contains six listening passages—two conversations and four lectures. The shortest of these is about two and one-half minutes long, and the longest is close to five minutes. There are about 35 questions total for these six passages.

3. As you listen to each passage, one or more pictures representing the listening situation will appear on your screen.

4. While you listen, you can take notes.

5. There are two types of listening passages.

   a. *Conversations* (two passages): Conversations involve typical, academic-setting topics and speakers—advisor-student, student-student, professor-student, and so on. Most conversations involve two speakers, but some may involve more.

   b. *Academic lectures* (four passages): Academic lectures are usually monologues, with a professor speaking on an academic or classroom-related topic. Some academic lectures may include interaction between lecturer and students.

6. Each listening passage is followed by five or six questions that focus on two main types of understanding:

   a. *The comprehension of facts*—questions about main ideas and details in the passage

   b. *Pragmatic understanding*—questions about the speaker's attitude, purpose, or feelings

   Once you have started to answer the questions about the passage, you cannot go back to listen to any part of the passage again.

Break

There will be a ten-minute break after the listening section of the TOEFL® Test.

Speaking

1. The speaking section is similar in form and content to the TAST® (TOEFL® Academic Speaking Test). It contains six questions: Two of these ask you to draw on your own

knowledge and experience to speak about a topic. In the next four questions, you will listen to short conversations and lectures or read about topics before you speak about them.

2. The use of several skills in answering the speaking questions is intended to help you integrate skills.

3. You will be allowed to take notes during the speaking section.

4. For each question, you will have some preparation time (15 to 30 seconds), and 45 to 60 seconds in which to respond. Note that the timer on the computer will monitor your response time for each question and will stop recording from the microphone at the designated time limit.

5. Once you have started to answer the questions, you cannot go back to listen to the passages again.

Speaking Section Question Types				
Question Number	Question Types	Preparation Time	Response Time	Expected Response
1	*Independent speaking. Choose something and explain your choice*	15 seconds	45 seconds	opinion
2	*Independent speaking. Tell about a preference.*	15 seconds	45 seconds	opinion
3	*Short reading and short listening about a general topic related to university life.*	30 seconds	60 seconds	summary
4	*Short reading and short lecture on an academic topic.*	30 seconds	60 seconds	summary
5	*Listen to a conversation about a school-related problem or topic.*	20 seconds	60 seconds	summary and opinion
6	*Listen to a short lecture.*	20 seconds	60 seconds	summary

Writing

1. Your written answers on the 2005 TOEFL® will be typed on a keyboard and displayed on a computer screen.

2. You will also have some sheets of scratch paper at hand for taking notes.

3. There are two types of writing on the 2005 TOEFL®.

   a. *Independent task:* a 30-minute opinion or preference essay

   b. *Integrated task:* a 20-minute response to a reading and a lecture about the same topic

4. The 30-minute independent task is much like that on the TWE® (Test of Written English).

5. The integrated reading-listening-writing task involves summarizing and integrating the information from the reading and the lecture. The reading remains on the screen for five minutes and then will disappear. You will hear the lecture (about three minutes long) through your headset. You will only be able to listen to the lecture once.

Scoring

At the time this book went to press, possible points on the 2005 TOEFL® Test totalled 120, 30 points per section. For updated scoring information, please visit the ETS website *(www.ets.org)*.

PART 1

Reading

Four General Test-Taking Strategies for the Reading Section

A few general test-taking strategies will improve your performance on all questions in the reading section of the 2005 TOEFL®.

1. Look back at the reading as often as you need to. A copy of the reading will appear on screen as long as you are answering questions about it.

2. Use key words from the question to help you find the answer. Scan for capital letters, numbers, percentages, and other easy-to-find material.

3. Ask yourself: "How would this question-writer try to trick me?" Watch for negatives, words that look like other words, etc.

4. Answer the hard questions last. In the reading section, you can go back to questions you missed or skipped. A question that seemed hard the first time through might not seem so hard after you've answered the rest of the reading questions.

Reading in English is the best way to become a better reader of academic material and to prepare for the reading sections of communication-oriented tests like the 2005 TOEFL®. Reading broadens your vocabulary and helps make English a more important part of your academic and personal life. Do a lot of reading in English, and do it regularly. Include non-fiction works written for university-level readers, not simply popular fiction.

If you have an English for Academic Purposes (EAP) class that involves reading, work hard at your assignments, ask your teacher about things that are unclear to you, and make a special effort to build your academic vocabulary. Building a solid academic vocabulary will help you in your academic work and on communication-oriented tests.

Building Skills: Identifying Main Ideas and Understanding Content

Basic Skills	Some Related Academic Tasks	Related Tasks on Tests like the 2005 TOEFL®
1. **Global comprehension:** identifying the main ideas of a reading 2. **Understanding other elements of content and relating them to the main idea**	• writing essays on tests • writing reports about materials you've read • answering multiple-choice questions on tests • participating in classroom discussions about readings	• comprehending the passages as a whole (global comprehension) • completing summaries (called *prose summaries* on the 2005 TOEFL®) • completing concept tables (called *schematic tables* on the 2005 TOEFL®) • answering multiple-choice questions about main ideas • choosing the best paraphrase of an original sentence • writing an essay about the ideas in a reading passage • speaking about the main ideas in a reading

Understanding a reading includes *global comprehension* of what you have read. This helps you see how several smaller ideas come together to create **main ideas.**

In academic classes, an ability to identify and understand main ideas helps you:

- learn more efficiently from what you read
- write well-focused reports
- answer questions on tests
- see important relationships among readings from various sources
- stay in touch with the influential ideas in your field of study

In the 2005 TOEFL®, this is a heavily tested skill. Earlier versions of the TOEFL® did not emphasize *global comprehension.*

Recognizing Levels of Generality

To identify main ideas, you must recognize relationships among many ideas in a text; in particular, you have to see which ideas are more general than others. The relationships among certain words might indicate such **general-specific patterns.** Read the following passage.

> Human dependence on plant products is older than civilization. Even before humans learned to fashion the crudest shelter out of wood or hew the simplest boat, they were plucking fruits from trees or pulling vegetables from the ground for dinner. The fruits made perhaps the easiest targets, with bright apples or cherries announcing their edibility from the branches of a tree, or green bananas occasionally cracking from their stalks and attracting more animals as they yellowed on the ground. Indeed, humans probably knew which fruits were edible by noticing which ones attracted other animals.

Consider the following vocabulary items, and write them inside or near the circle diagram to show their relationships. The largest circle is for the most general, and the smallest circle is for the most specific.

apples

bananas

cherries

fruits

plant products

vegetables

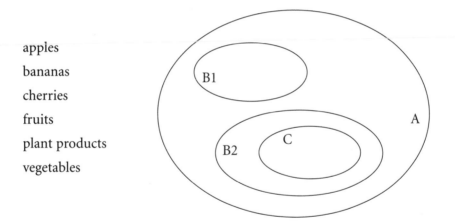

This diagram shows a general-specific relationship among vocabulary items in a passage. *Plant products* is the most general term, so it should go in area A. *Vegetables* (in area B1) and *fruits* (in area B2) are one level more specific. Finally, *apples, bananas,* and *cherries* should go in blank C because they are kinds of fruits—at a level even more specific than the "B" level.

A passage will probably *mention* ideas at many different levels of generality. The main idea is found at only one of those levels. More general ideas might be in the passage only to introduce the topic, whereas more specific ideas might be in the reading as support for the main idea.

Understanding Repeated Reference

There is no magic formula for finding the main idea. Common sense tells you, however, that a concept appearing very often in a passage is likely to relate to the main idea. Do a large number of sentences in a passage contain a noun phrase or pronoun with a similar meaning? Do a large number of sentences contain a verb with a similar meaning? If so, the idea indicated by that set of noun phrases/pronouns or by that set of verbs could be part of the main idea. One common tool in **repeated reference** is the use of pronouns—*this, it, they,* etc.

On the 2005 TOEFL®, questions about pronoun reference are very common. Practice with a short passage.

> Most people's homes will continue to rely on mechanical security systems, such as lock-and-key systems or numeric-combination systems. Industrial security will be dominated by biometric systems. These use such physical features as fingerprints, iris patterns, voice profiles, or facial features to identify the person seeking entry. Biometrics have their drawbacks—such as complete uselessness when no electricity is available—but they are far less vulnerable to theft or co-option than mechanical systems. They are also remarkably accurate. Voiceprint machines, for example, may be the crudest of biometric security systems, but they have been shown to operate with more than 90% accuracy even when the user's voice has been altered by a cold or by surgery.

What is this paragraph's main idea? A diagram of the ideas in the passage follows. Circle the word or group of words that best states the main idea.

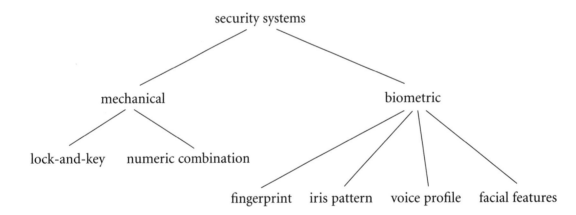

You should have circled *biometric*. Ideas at other levels are mentioned, but they are not the main point. One clue to the main idea is that the phrase *biometric security systems* or other words/phrases with that meaning can be found in almost every sentence. This is a case of **repeated reference:** the passage refers to the same concept many times, even though it does not always use the same words for that concept.

EXERCISE 1

*Re-read the short passage and underline every word or phrase that means **biometric security systems**. (Hint: Be sure to consider pronouns!) See the answer key at the back of the book to check your answers.*

In Exercise 1, you were told to pay special attention to pronouns. There are two main reasons for this.

1. They often set up a pattern of repeated reference by substituting for nouns.

2. Many questions on communication-oriented tests ask you to identify what a pronoun refers to. We will practice with pronoun-reference questions in all parts of this reading section.

Recognizing Relationships among Ideas

Some questions on the 2005 TOEFL® require you to choose the best paraphrase for a sentence from the passage. This means you must find the sentence that best uses other words to say the same thing. To do so, you must see the proper relationships among ideas in the original.

For example, consider this sentence:

> *Boundaries between watersheds typically follow the ridgelines of hills or run through arid regions that contribute little runoff.*

Which of the four options below is the best paraphrase of the original?

    a. A watershed is a hill where very little rain falls.

    b. The dividing line between one hill and another is called a watershed.

    c. Dry regions are often very hilly.

    d. Hills and dry regions often divide one watershed from another.

The best option is **d**. The original contains the idea of a "boundary," which is found only in *b* and *d*. Option *b*, however, makes a watershed sound like a boundary between hills. The original passage doesn't contain this idea. The original speaks of *boundaries between watersheds*—an idea that we find only in *d*.

Exercises with Short Passages

The following section contains some very short readings to help you develop your skill in finding main ideas. These passages are shorter than those on the 2005 TOEFL® where the readings are at least 600 words long. These practice readings, though short, are difficult. They are written at an advanced level of English, so don't be discouraged if you have to work hard to find the main ideas.

After each short passage, circle the letter of the best answer to each question. Check your answers with your teacher or in the answer key at the back of the book.

EXERCISE 1

➡   Liberals (as distinct from socialists or communists) believe that the free market and private ownership of property are beneficial to society. They diverge from conservatives on the issue of how much trust to put in unfettered capitalism. In the liberal view, government must regulate capitalist enterprise to keep the moneyed forces of society from exploiting labor unfairly and from appropriating too many resources unto themselves. Government has a duty to oversee banking, the credit system, and the mechanisms for trading securities. The liberal believes in the great game of capitalist production but sees government as a sort of referee who must constantly cite the most powerful players in the game—the biggest and richest industries—for violating the rules.

1. Which of the following best expresses the main idea of this passage?

    a. There are many differences between liberals and conservatives.

    b. There are many ways in which capitalist society is like a game.

    c. The government has several ways of regulating capitalist enterprises.

    d. Liberals believe that capitalism needs regulation.

2. In the line with ➡, the word *They* stands for

    a. liberals

    b. socialists or communists

    c. the free market and private ownership of property

    d. society

3. The author mentions a referee in order to explain liberal beliefs about

    a. the mistakes government has made

    b. the proper role for government in the economy

    c. the bad influence of big business

    d. the value of capitalism

4. "In the liberal view, government must regulate capitalist enterprise to keep the moneyed forces of society from exploiting labor unfairly and from appropriating too many resources unto themselves."

    What is the best paraphrase of this sentence?

    a. Liberals think government should control itself.

    b. Liberals think businesses should control government.

    c. Liberals think the government should control businesses.

    d. Liberals think they should control the government.

EXERCISE 2

The chemical composition of ink is one indicator of authenticity in a map or drawing, but it's not the only one. It is certainly not dependable enough to be the sole factor in deciding whether a work is genuine or a forgery. The detection of fakes is a complex mixture of science and art, of laboratory work and human discretion. History is full of cases in which chemical analysis has been misleading. For example, a chemical analysis might discover titanium dioxide—introduced as an ink additive only in the early 20th century—and this might appear to disprove the authenticity of a map ➡ supposedly drawn in the 15th century. Then again, it may simply be detecting a compound that crept naturally into the ink or paper. Other elements of the map—the world view it reflects, its consistency with similar works by the same purported cartographer—must be taken into consideration. If these seem right, it is worth being skeptical about laboratory results.

1. Which of the following best expresses the main idea of this passage?
   a. Chemical analysis of ink can indicate whether a map or drawing is fake.
   b. Chemical analysis of ink is not always an accurate indicator of authenticity.
   c. Chemical analysis of ink cannot indicate whether a map or drawing is fake.
   d. Chemical analysis of ink is only one of many ways to indicate authenticity.

2. In the line with ➡, the word it stands for
   a. ink
   b. chemical analysis
   c. map
   d. titanium oxide

3. According to this passage, titanium oxide
   a. was not put into ink until the 20th century
   b. did not exist until the 20th century
   c. does not exist in nature
   d. often misleads people trying to decide whether a painting is authentic

4. "The detection of fakes is a complex mixture of science and art, of laboratory work and human discretion."

    What is the best paraphrase of this sentence?

    a. Finding copies of paintings involves scientific factors and the opinion of art experts.

    b. Science can tell when a person has copied a famous work of art.

    c. Most artists appreciate the complexities of a well-copied painting.

    d. The more complicated a painting is, the harder it is to tell whether it's original or a copy.

EXERCISE 3

Traditionally, bioethics, the study of legal and ethical issues arising in health care, has centered on four essential values: respect for patient autonomy, nonmaleficence, beneficence, and justice. Although some commentators have criticized overreliance on such broad principles for ethical decision-making, others believe that the four principles describe common, core values. Autonomy refers to the patient's self-rule and the opportunity to make meaningful choices; nonmaleficence, to the physician's obligation to do no harm; beneficence, to contributing to patient welfare; and justice, to fairness and equity. These moral principles establish ideals for relationships between physicians and their patients. In addition, emotional responsiveness—the caregiver's feeling response to the patient—enhances the moral quality of the relationship in a way that transcends ethical principles and rules.

Adapted from Michael H. Cohen, *Beyond Complementary Medicine: Legal and Ethical Perspectives on Health Care and Human Evolution* (Ann Arbor: University of Michigan Press, 2001).

1. Which of the following best expresses the main idea of this passage?

    a. The four traditional bioethical principles are not important if the physician shows emotional responsiveness to the patient.

    b. Physicians have focused too much on only four bioethical principles.

    c. The traditional bioethical principles provide a good basis for relationships between patients and physicians.

    d. Common core values held by most patients are better than the four traditional bioethical principles.

➡ 2. In this passage, the word boxed[others] refers to

    a. commentators

    b. principles

    c. decision-makers

    d. values

3. The author of this passage probably believes which of the following about autonomy?

    a. Patients should be allowed to make important decisions about their own treatment.

    b. Physicians, not patients, should make important decisions about treatment.

    c. Rules set by the government should guide patients' choices.

    d. Patients can get effective treatment only from physicians who demonstrate a "feeling response" to the patient.

4. "Traditionally, bioethics, the study of legal and ethical issues arising in health care, has centered on four essential values: respect for patient autonomy, nonmaleficence, beneficence, and justice."

    What is the best paraphrase of this sentence?

    a. These four beliefs used to be important in bioethics, but they aren't important anymore.

    b. These four beliefs are very important in bioethics.

    c. Bioethics is the study of whether a certain health-care practice is right or not.

    d. Four new centers for bioethics have been established.

EXERCISE 4

    Evidence from various sources points to a significant climatic role for solar
➡ disturbances, particularly for the absence of boxed[any]. Much attention has focused on a period from 1645 to 1715, known as the Maunder minimum (named for E. W. Maunder, a late 19th-century astronomer), when sunspot activity was virtually nil. For some time, researchers wondered whether this period of marked inactivity might simply have been a period of poor record-keeping. That issue seems settled, and most historical astronomers accept that reliable observers were watching the sun regularly and that a remarkable paucity of sunspots truly did characterize this long period. The years of the Maunder minimum correspond to tree-ring evidence of higher-than-normal concentrations of carbon 14, which would be consistent with a

period of very little solar flaring. Evidence from the late 17th century also reveals a period of colder-than-average global temperatures. This has thrust the issue of solar variability into one of the most intense debates of the 21st century, the contest over the extent and causes of global warming.

1. Which of the following best expresses the main idea of this passage?
    a. Periods of low sunspot activity can cause a lot of damage to trees.
    b. The Maunder minimum may be one of the causes of global warming in the 21st century.
    c. Periods like the Maunder minimum probably have significant effects on Earth's climate.
    d. Many astronomers claim that the Maunder minimum was not really a time of low solar activity.

➡ 2. In this passage, the word any refers to
    a. attention
    b. solar disturbances
    c. climatic role
    d. evidence

3. The author mentions high concentrations of carbon 14 in tree rings as evidence of
    a. low solar activity during the Maunder minimum
    b. climate change
    c. the damaging effects of solar variability
    d. the value of tree rings in scientific inquiry

4. "Much attention has focused on a period from 1645 to 1715, known as the Maunder minimum (named for E. W. Maunder, a late 19th-century astronomer), when sunspot activity was virtually nil."

    Which is the best paraphrase of this sentence?
    a. Scientists are very interested in the period known as the Maunder minimum because it contained almost no sunspot activity.
    b. The large amount of sunspot activity during the Maunder minimum makes it interesting to scientists.
    c. Scientists have not adequately considered the sunspot activity during the Maunder minimum.
    d. No one except E. W. Maunder paid much attention to sunspots during the Maunder minimum.

EXERCISE 5

Shakespeare viewed the cat no more imaginatively than did Shylock in *The Merchant of Venice*—merely as "a harmless necessary" animal. Benedick, the hero of *Much Ado about Nothing*, refers with callous jocularity to the pastime of hanging up a cat in a leather bottle (bag) to shoot at it. Lysander rebuffs Hermia by calling her a cat, in reference to the female cat's claws and aggressive amorousness *(A Midsummer Night's Dream)*. The cat's dominance over mice can be presented both negatively, as when Tarquin hears Lucrece's prayers like a cat dallying with the mouse panting under his paw *(The Rape of Lucrece)*, or positively, as when Westmoreland in *Henry V* compares England to a cat preventing Scottish mice from plundering England.

Adapted from Katherine M. Rogers, *The Cat and the Human Imagination: Feline Images from Bast to Garfield* (Ann Arbor: University of Michigan Press, 1998).

1. Which of the following best expresses the main idea of this passage?
   a. In Shakespeare's plays, cats are usually referred to as unimportant animals that fit certain stereotyped images.
   b. Shakespeare was one of the first playwrights to mention cats in his plays.
   c. Shakespeare's plays show that cats were important in the culture of England at the time Shakespeare lived.
   d. Shakespeare tried to present a balanced view of cats in his plays—sometimes positive, sometimes negative.

2. According to the passage, why did people of Shakespeare's time put cats in leather bags and shoot at them?
   a. because cats were considered dirty and dangerous
   b. because cats were aggressively amorous
   c. because cats dominated mice
   d. because they thought it was fun

3. According to the passage, Lysander wants Hermia to do what?
   a. marry him
   b. leave him alone
   c. save him from another woman
   d. make him laugh

4. "Lysander rebuffs Hermia by calling her a cat, in reference to the female cat's claws and aggressive amorousness . . . ."

   Which is the best paraphrase of this sentence?

   a. Lysander liked Hermia because she was like a cat.

   b. Lysander gave Hermia a cat that had sharp claws and liked to fight.

   c. In telling Hermia to go away, Lysander said she had some of a cat's bad characteristics.

   d. By calling Hermia a cat, Lysander was trying to make her feel good.

EXERCISE 6

Our image of physical change as normally incremental and gradual has to be left behind as we consider superconductivity. Superconductivity is all about critical points—of temperature, current density, and magnetic field strength—where sudden changes occur. This became clear long ago, when Heike Kamerlingh Onnes (Nobel laureate in physics, 1913) first achieved virtually zero electrical resistance in a mercury wire cooled to 4.2 K and named the state of the metal "superconductivity." As far as we know, not every material can become superconductive, but any material that can do so has its own Critical Temperature (T_c). For pure metals, this is typically very low, under 20 K. For many newly developed ceramics, T_c is much higher—near or even above 100 K. Critical Current Density (J_c) refers to the fact that, at a given temperature, a material can carry only so much electrical current and stay superconductive. If the current density exceeds J_c the material will suddenly lose its near-zero resistance and flip to its normal resistive state. Most complex of all is the third factor, Critical Magnetic Field (H_c), which refers to a critical point in the strength of the magnetic field around the superconductor. Superconductors have a unique ability to prevent an external magnetic field from penetrating the superconductive material. In one kind, called type I or "soft" superconductors, the material reverts to its normal resistive state if the external magnetic field reaches or surpasses H_c.

1. Which of the following best expresses the main idea of this passage?

   a. The superconductive state of a material depends on three critical points having been reached.

   b. Superconductive materials have promoted great changes in many industries.

    c. If you cool a metal enough, it suddenly has almost no electrical resistance and becomes a "superconductor."

    d. Onnes's discovery of superconductivity changed the way scientists think about the physical world.

➡ 2. In this passage, the shaded word this refers to

    a. material

    b. Critical Temperature

    c. pure metal

    d. ceramic

3. Which of the following does the author imply by using the phrase as far as we know ?

    a. Scientists are sure that not every material can become superconductive.

    b. Some day, scientists may discover that every material can become superconductive.

    c. Every material now known is superconductive, but new materials may be discovered that are not.

    d. Scientists in other countries have not been sharing their data about superconductivity, so there may be facts about it that we don't know.

4. "Our image of physical change as normally incremental and gradual has to be left behind as we consider superconductivity."

    Which is the best paraphrase of this sentence?

    a. Superconductivity helps us recognize which changes are normal and which are not.

    b. Gradually, people came to realize that superconductivity is a normal process in nature.

    c. Like most natural processes, superconductivity takes place in small stages.

    d. Superconductivity forces us to consider physical changes in an unusual way.

EXERCISE 7

By 1960, when Stanley Kramer's *Inherit the Wind* was released, the issues central to the Scopes "Monkey Trial" of 1925 (which the film fictionally portrayed) had become slightly quaint, at least for mainstream U.S. society. The general outlook for real science at school was somewhat brighter in those days (despite all the drills about how to crouch at your desk during a nuclear attack). Kramer could get away with sympathetically portraying evolutionism as progressive and with lampooning Bible-toting creationists.

➡️ It's an open question whether a film with that point of view —and with such unflattering characterizations of creationists—could long endure in today's film market. It's amazing enough that the basic issue is still with us: Should public schools teach natural selection as scientific fact or should the Bible's story of creation get equal billing? We've been at this for at least eight decades. We should have nailed it by now, and kids throughout the land should be examining the fossil evidence. What's doubly amazing is that the creationists have grown in strength and number, they dress better, and some of them have unidentifiable accents. Many of them head federal agencies, which in itself erodes the separation of Church and State and helps drive secular humanism to the closet. If an updated *Inherit the Wind* were released today, it might still be nominated for four Academy Awards as the original was in 1960 (left-leaning Hollywood insiders make those nominations), but no teacher in heartland America would risk showing it at the local middle school on film night.

1. Which of the following best expresses the main idea of this passage?
    a. A film that positively portrays creationism would probably be unpopular in modern America.
    b. A film that positively portrays creationism was unpopular in America in 1960.
    c. A film that negatively portrays creationism would be less popular in modern America than in 1960.
    d. A film that negatively portrays creationism could not be shown in a modern American theater.

➡️ 2. In this passage, the phrase that point of view refers to the belief that
    a. science should be taught in public schools
    b. religion should be taught in public schools
    c. creationism explains human origins better than evolutionism
    d. evolutionism explains human origins better than creationism

3. With which statement would the author of this passage be most likely to agree?
    a. There are no good movies being produced in the U.S. anymore.
    b. It's important for Americans to continue debating whether evolutionism or creationism is more accurate.

    c. It's unfortunate that creationists are more powerful in the U.S. now than they were in 1960.

    d. Creationism should be taught in public schools.

4. "If an updated *Inherit the Wind* were released today, it might still be nominated for four Academy Awards as the original was in 1960 (left-leaning Hollywood insiders make those nominations), but no teacher in heartland America would risk showing it at the local middle school on film night."

    Which is the best paraphrase of this sentence?

    a. A new version of the movie would probably be unpopular among average Americans.

    b. A new version of the movie would be very popular among average Americans.

    c. A new version of the movie would make the old one look bad.

    d. A new version of the movie would probably not be allowed by the government.

Practicing with Longer Readings

In your academic classes you will read passages much longer than one or two paragraphs. You'll read them for main ideas and you'll need to connect ideas. On the 2005 TOEFL®, the typical passage is between 600 and 700 words—longer than the readings on earlier versions of such tests. You need to practice understanding main ideas of longer passages as well as those of shorter readings.

To understand the main idea of a longer passage, you must apply, to a far larger text, the skills you practiced with shorter passages:

- finding the right level of generality
- looking for repeated reference
- balancing the importance of ideas

Also, with longer passages, you must be aware of certain features that usually do not show up very clearly in shorter passages. These include:

- the author's apparent purpose
- the relationship of two or more large ideas, each of which is explained in some detail
- tying together ideas that appear quite far from one another in a text

In your academic coursework, you may be asked to do various tasks after reading a longer passage:

- answer comprehension questions
- discuss the meaning of new vocabulary
- show how various ideas in the reading are related to one another

- show how the ideas in one reading are related to those in other readings
- summarize the important parts of a passage
- sort information into categories

For communication-oriented tests like the 2005 TOEFL®, you will have to perform several tasks that are similar to academic activities:

- answer multiple-choice questions
- choose the best sentences to complete a summary of the passage
- sort information from the reading into tables
- choose the best paraphrase for a short passage from the passage
- write an essay based on the main ideas from the passage

In this section, we will give you practice with the first four types of tasks. Practice with the fifth can be found in the Writing section.

Following are two longer passages, nearly the size of the readings that occur on newer communication-oriented tests. The correct answers to these questions are discussed briefly after each practice reading.

Because we are now working with longer passages, you will see a kind of multiple-choice question that wasn't asked in shorter passages. This question is in the following form:

Look at the 4 triangles (△) in the reading (numbered 1–4). Which triangle shows the best place to insert (add) the following sentence?

The question will be followed by a sentence that fits well at one spot in the passage but not very well elsewhere. This "inserting-a-sentence" type of question appeared on earlier versions of communication-oriented tests but in relation to shorter readings. On newer communication-oriented tests like the 2005 TOEFL®, you have a longer context to scan in order to place the sentence correctly.

Following the section of practice passages is a set of four review readings, each followed by some questions related to main ideas. These give you more practice with long passages like those on the 2005 TOEFL®. Test yourself by answering the questions for each passage. Then check your answers by asking your teacher or by looking in the answer key at the back of the book.

Practice Reading 1 (with Answer Analysis)

Read the following passage and answer the questions that follow it. You may re-read parts of the passage as often as you like.

Endocrine disorders (malfunctions of the human hormone-producing mechanisms) can have serious consequences. Hormones like insulin or human growth hormone (hGH) are crucial physical messengers, regulating and coordinating such functions as digestion and the balance of serum minerals. Severe shortages of hormones can mean a virtual shutdown of essential bodily processes. Endocrine disorders are routinely treated by administering hormones obtained from sources outside the body of the person suffering the disorder. The supply of such chemicals in nature, however, is far short of that needed in modern medicine. Since hormones are proteins, they are perfect candidates for production by genetically engineered bacteria. △1 This production represents one of the most useful and widespread applications of rDNA (recombinant DNA) technology.

More than 5 million people worldwide take the hormone *insulin* each day to control some form of diabetes. Most of the insulin sold comes from cow or pig pancreases collected at abattoirs as a byproduct of meat production. While insulin from these sources is generally safe, it has slight structural differences from the human form. Rather than slipping comfortably past the immune defenses of the recipient, these insulin molecules are easily recognized as outsiders. Consequently, a few people taking *bovine or porcine* insulin develop allergic reactions as their immune systems reject the foreign intrusion. This problem is avoided by substituting human insulin, which, to be available in significant quantities, must be manufactured by genetically altered bacteria.

bovine or porcine: cow or pig

Insulin was the first therapeutic rDNA product approved by the FDA for sale in the United States. △2 It went on the market in 1982 under the brand name Humulin. The development work had been done by the pioneering biotech firm Genentech; Eli Lilly and Company produced and marketed Humulin.

The biotechnology used in making insulin is more complicated than that used in making human growth hormone. The insulin molecule is made up of two polypeptide chains (linked strings of amino acids), which join to make the active form of insulin. In the production of genetically engineered insulin, the DNA that codes for the A chain is introduced into one batch of *E. coli* bacteria and the DNA for the B chain into a different one. The bacterial cells are induced to make the two chains, which are then collected, mixed, and chemically treated to make them link. **△3** The resulting insulin molecules are identical to those secreted by the human pancreas.

Human growth hormone (hGH) was another early target of rDNA approaches to hormone deficiency. HGH controls the growth of bones and regulates weight gain. In some children, the pituitary gland fails to produce enough hGH for normal development, and this is evidenced by markedly short stature (perhaps only 60%–70% of normal height for a given age) and other growth deficencies. The condition can be ameliorated, but only if hormone supplementation takes place during the growth years of childhood. Beyond this critical period, many bones (such as the femur) lose their ability to elongate.

Early in the development of hGH therapy, the only sources of the hormone were the pituitary glands of human cadavers . Suppliers and marketers worried that drawing a chemical from the glands of the dead might eventually create a public relations problem. But a more serious problem was that the source was not prolific enough. First of all, the number of cadavers from which the pituitary gland could be harvested was very limited and not easily increased (within the bounds of the law). Secondly, each cadaver yielded a very small amount of the hormone—only about 4 mg, whereas one week's treatment for an individual deficient in hGH requires about 7 mg. No successful animal sources were found. Clearly, new sources were needed.

The supply of human growth hormone is maintained by applying rDNA techniques and achieving high-volume synthesis. A gene for hGH production is spliced into *E. coli,* which are cultured and exploited in very large amounts. **△4** A 500-liter tank of bacterial culture can produce as much hGH as could have been derived from 35,000 cadavers. Growth hormone produced by this technique was approved for human use in 1985 and is now commonplace.

Adapted from Cynthia S. Gross, *The New Biotechnology: Putting Microbes to Work* (Minneapolis: Lerner, 1988).

QUESTIONS ABOUT PRACTICE READING 1

*The following are similar to two kinds of **content/main-idea** questions asked in communication-oriented tests like the 2005 TOEFL®—multiple choice and summary. Follow the directions to answer each question. Then look at the correct answers and discussion that follow.*

Multiple Choice

1. Which sentence best expresses the essential information of this passage?
    a. Hormones produced by rDNA techniques are critical tools in the treatment of endocrine disorders.
    b. Most importantly, rDNA techniques produce hormones that don't cause allergic reactions.
    c. Endocrine disorders are among the most serious health problems people face.
    d. Producing hGH is much easier than producing insulin.

2. Why does the author mention cadavers ?
    a. because they can be a source of *E. coli*
    b. because they can be a source of hGH
    c. because they are produced by rDNA techniques
    d. because they are produced by *E. coli*

3. In the first paragraph, the word that refers to
    a. body
    b. disorder
    c. supply
    d. nature

4. "Consequently, a few people taking bovine or porcine insulin develop allergic reactions as their immune systems reject the foreign intrusion."
    Which is the best paraphrase of this sentence?
    a. Most insulin from pigs or cows comes from other countries.
    b. Insulin from pigs and cows is safe for animals but not for humans.
    c. Some people get sick if they take insulin from pigs or cows.
    d. Some people think it's wrong to put animal insulin into their bodies, so they refuse to take this insulin.

5. Look at the 4 triangles (△) in the passage (numbered 1–4). Which triangle shows the best place to insert (add) the following sentence?

The linked elements form a whole, usable molecule.

The sentence could best be added at

    a. △ 1

    b. △ 2

    c. △ 3

    d. △ 4

Summary

An introductory sentence for a brief summary of the passage is provided below. Complete the summary by selecting the three answer choices that express the most important ideas in the passage. Some sentences do not belong in the summary because they express ideas that are not presented in the passage or are minor ideas in the passage. In each blank, write the letter of one of your choices.

<u>Note:</u> In academic courses, you may be asked to build a summary yourself or to arrange information, as this exercise asks. On tests like the 2005 TOEFL®, which uses a computer, you may be asked to drag your answer to the blank or to indicate it in some other way. According to information from the Educational Testing Service, the order of your summary choices does not affect your score. As this book went to print, ETS said it plans to award partial credit for partly correct answers.

> Hormone supplementation therapy depends greatly on hormones produced by recombinant DNA techniques.
>
> • _____
>
> • _____
>
> • _____

    a. A single cadaver can yield only about half of the hGH needed by one person for a week's treatment.

    b. The *E. coli* used in rDNA techniques can sometimes cause death or injury among people being treated.

    c. One of the earliest successes in rDNA-produced hormone treatments involved the production of human insulin, which could not be gathered in sufficient amounts from other sources.

    d. Producing human growth hormone (hGH) by splicing genes into *E. coli* made it possible to produce sufficient quantities of the hormone.

e. Hormones can help cure human endocrine disorders.

f. Producing hormones by rDNA techniques can overcome the problems posed by trying to find natural sources of these hormones, such as short supply and possible rejection by the human body.

ANSWER ANALYSIS OF PRACTICE READING 1

The following section explains the correct answers to the questions about Practice Reading 1.

Multiple Choice

1. Which sentence best expresses the essential information of this passage?
   a. Hormones produced by rDNA techniques are critical tools in the treatment of endocrine disorders.
   b. Most importantly, rDNA techniques produce hormones that don't cause allergic reactions.
   c. Endocrine disorders are among the most serious health problems people face.
   d. Producing hGH is much easier than producing insulin.

The best answer to this question is **a**. Not every passage has a clear thesis statement (a statement of its main idea), but this one does. The last two sentences of the first paragraph form this thesis statement, and choice *a* in this question is very close in meaning to this thesis statement. Choice *b* is a true statement, but it expresses only one of the many advantages of hormones produced via rDNA techniques. It's too specific to represent the main idea of the passage. Choice *c* is very far from the main topic of this reading; this passage is clearly not about the seriousness of endocrine disorders. This seriousness was mentioned early in Paragraph 1 only as a way of leading into the topic of the passage. Choice *d* is a true statement, but—like choice *b*—it expresses only one of many details that add up to a larger idea—the idea expressed in choice **a**.

2. Why does the author mention cadavers?
   a. because they can be a source of *E. coli*
   b. because they can be a source of hGH
   c. because they are produced by rDNA techniques
   d. because they are produced by *E. coli*

The best answer to this question is choice **b**. The cadavers (bodies of dead people) are mentioned because, though hGH could be obtained from them, they were not a sufficient source. Choice *a* is an unlikely one, because the paragraph involving cadavers contains no mention of *E. coli*. The two are not spoken of in this reading as being at all connected. Once you know the meaning of *cadaver*, both choice *c* and choice *d* become unattractive. Dead bodies are not produced by either means.

3. In the first paragraph, the word that refers to

 a. body

 b. disorder

 c. supply

 d. nature

Choice **c** is best because it is the closest singular noun to the pronoun *that*. This closeness alone makes it very likely for the two to refer to the same thing. Also, logically, a supply of something is the most likely to be *needed in modern medicine*.

4. "Consequently, a few people taking bovine or porcine insulin develop allergic reactions as their immune systems reject the foreign intrusion."

 Which is the best paraphrase of this sentence?

 a. Most insulin from pigs or cows comes from other countries.

 b. Insulin from pigs and cows is safe for animals but not for humans.

 c. Some people get sick if they take insulin from pigs or cows.

 d. Some people think it's wrong to put animal insulin into their bodies, so they refuse to take this insulin.

Only option **c** mentions sickness as a result of taking insulin. *Allergic reactions* lead to illness. The other options fail to contain this idea, which is a crucial point in the original.

5. Look at the 4 triangles (△) in the reading (numbered 1–4). Which triangle shows the best place to insert (add) the following sentence?

 The linked elements form a whole, usable molecule.

 The sentence could best be added at

 a. △ 1

 b. △ 2

 c. △ 3

 d. △ 4

The best answer is choice **c**. Triangle 3 occurs immediately after a sentence that talked about linking two chains. The sentence after triangle 3 discusses a molecule that results from this linking. The sentence in the question creates a bridge between these two ideas.

Prose Summary

> Hormone supplementation therapy depends greatly on hormones produced by recombinant DNA techniques.
>
> - **f** Producing hormones by rDNA techniques can overcome the problems posed by trying to find natural sources of these hormones, such as short supply and possible rejection by the human body.
>
> ---
>
> - **c** One of the earliest successes in rDNA-produced hormone treatments involved the production of human insulin, which could not be gathered in sufficient amounts from other sources.
>
> ---
>
> - **d** Producing human growth hormone (hGH) by splicing genes into *E. coli* made it possible to avoid dependence on cadavers and to produce sufficient quantities of the hormone.

    a. A single cadaver can yield only about half of the hGH needed by one person for a week's treatment.

    b. The *E. coli* used in rDNA techniques can sometimes cause death or injury among people being treated.

    c. One of the earliest successes in rDNA-produced hormone treatments involved the production of human insulin, which could not be gathered in sufficient amounts from other sources.

    d. Producing human growth hormone (hGH) by splicing genes into *E. coli* made it possible to avoid dependence on cadavers and to produce sufficient quantities of the hormone.

    e. Hormones can help cure human endocrine disorders.

    f. Producing hormones by rDNA techniques can overcome the problems posed by trying to find natural sources of these hormones, such as short supply and possible rejection by the human body.

The best three sentences to add to this summary are **c, d,** and **f.** Choice **f** summarizes the passage as a whole and is therefore a good element in this summary. Choice **c** summarizes the ideas of paragraphs 2, 3, and 4 in the passage. Choice **d** summarizes paragraphs 5, 6, and 7. Choices *a* and *b* don't belong in a summary of this passage, since they are very specific illustrations of larger ideas in the passage. Choice *e* is a very general statement, more general than the topic of the passage as a whole. It would be out of place in a summary of this passage.

Practice Reading 2 (with Answer Analysis)

Read the following passage and try to answer the questions that follow it.

Developing societies contain within them 85 percent of the world's population. Between the poorest and relatively most prosperous, there are more differences in average living conditions than among developed societies. The ratio between average incomes in the relatively poorest developed country and the richest is about one to three. In contrast, the ratio between average incomes in the poorest developing countries and the relatively most prosperous is about one to twelve. **Δ1**

It is also worth remembering that people in any given developing country are likely to have a sense of pride in their own system and may not focus on those systemic problems that would cause an economic theorist to classify it as "developing." The people of a given developing country may also take great offense at being grouped with another country whose circumstances they consider vastly inferior to their own. Even an attempt to address these issues from a value-neutral, science-based perspective can cause considerable offense. **Δ2** Caution must therefore be exercised in drawing generalizations about developing countries. Nevertheless, it can be concluded that certain characteristics are common to most of them.

One defining characteristic is an economic profile that includes low GNP per capita, a low average income, and very limited accumulations of capital. A history of having been a colony is also typical, although the same could also be said for several of the world's developed countries (e.g., the U.S., Singapore, and Australia). Nevertheless, the proportion of former colonies among the developing societies is great (and the proportion of them among developed countries small). Some economists, as we shall see below, see causality in this pattern. A third characteristic of most developing societies is that a relatively high proportion of the labor force is still in agriculture. **Δ3** Also, the typical developing country imports not only significant amounts of finished goods, but also significant amounts of *capital* in the form of loans and foreign investment, while it exports a limited number of raw materials and/or goods that have been assembled in foreign-owned factories.

capital: money for development or to finance production

The typical developing country has a foreign-dominated economy, with its economic functioning being dependent on continual infusions of foreign investments, loans, and aid from developed countries, for which it pays a high price in profit repatriations, interest payment, and economic sovereignty. Their economies thus function at, and are integrated into, a lower level of the world economy and division of labor.

5 ➡ There is considerable debate among social scientists regarding the historical origins of Third World inequality. Dependency theorists, such as Baran (1957), Frank (1969), Wallerstein (1974), and Amin (1980), hold that as the capitalist world economy developed, European countries seized control through conquest, colonialism, and other forms of domination of large parts of the economies of Asia, Africa, and Latin America. They forced Third World economies into molds which served their own development interests. The agriculture of Caribbean island countries, for example, was oriented toward production of sugar for export rather than all-around production for domestic needs. Modernization theorists, such as Rostow (1960), Hagan (1962), and Eisenstadt (1966) hold that the causes of Third World poverty and misery are primarily domestic, lying in pre-capitalist and pre-industrial institutional structures which are antithetical to development needs. △4 Still other social scientists blame rising population growth rates for continuing poverty in the developing countries (an argument that will be treated in detail in Chapter Eleven).

Virtually all these development theorists agree that agricultural efficiency is the primordial first step toward development. The more technologically efficient the agriculture of a country, the more the agricultural workers can be shifted to industrial and service occupations. The more developed a country, the proportionally fewer agricultural workers in its labor force and the smaller the contribution of agricultural production toward its economic production. Hence, the World Bank (1994, p. 6) has reported that agricultural production accounts for only 3 percent of the total gross domestic product of developed countries (in aggregate), compared to 29 percent for all low-income countries combined—nearly 10 times as high.

Adapted from James W. Russell, *Introduction to Macrosociology, 2d ed.* (Upper Saddle River, NJ: Prentice Hall, 1996).

QUESTIONS ABOUT PRACTICE READING 2

*The following are similar to two kinds of **main-idea** questions asked in the academic coursework and in communication-oriented tests like the 2005 TOEFL®—multiple choice and concept table. Follow the directions to answer each question. Then look at the correct answers and discussion that follow.*

Multiple Choice

1. Which sentence best expresses the essential information of this passage?

    a. Economists do not know why some countries remain poor while others become rich.

    b. The typical differences between a developed country and a developing country are numerous and may have developed from a variety of causes.

    c. Foreign interference is the main reason why developing countries remain poor.

    d. The countries we call "developing" are very different from one another, so it is wrong to make generalizations about them.

2. Why does the author mention sugar production on Caribbean islands (Paragraph 5 ➡)?

    a. to support one belief held by dependency theorists

    b. to support one belief held by modernization theorists

    c. to name one belief that all development theorists hold

    d. to name one belief that is based on inaccurate information

3. In this reading, the term the same refers to

    a. "They were once a colony."

    b. "They have a history."

    c. "They have low GNP."

    d. "They are developed."

4. "They [colonial powers] forced Third World economies into molds which served their own development interests."

    Which is the best paraphrase of this sentence?

    a. Colonial powers helped the people of the Third World have better lives.

    b. Colonial powers re-shaped Third World economies to make them profitable for the colonizers.

    c. Colonial powers prevented Third World farmers from being able to sell their crops.

    d. Colonial powers were forced to give up their colonies in the Third World.

5. Look at the 4 triangles (Δ) in the reading (numbered 1–4). Which triangle shows the best place to insert (add) the following sentence?

> *This difference results, to some degree, from the size of the category (there are more developing countries than developed ones), but some commentators attribute it to a sort of "critical income level," below which a country is forced to live poor even if it seems wealthy in comparison to its neighbors.*

The sentence could best be added at

   a. Δ 1

   b. Δ 2

   c. Δ 3

   d. Δ 4

LEARNING ASSISTANCE CENTER
ST. MARY'S UNIVERSITY
ONE CAMINO SANTA MARIA
SAN ANTONIO, TX 78228-8554

Schematic Table

Complete the table by classifying each of the answer choices according to whether, according to the passage, *it is characteristic of most (1) developed countries or (2) developing countries. Two of the statements will not be used. Write the letter of each of your choices in the proper blank.*

Developed countries	_____ _____ _____
Developing countries	_____ _____ _____

   a. have a history of being colonized by foreigners

   b. suffer from constantly changing governments, often as a result of military coups

   c. not much difference in income between the richest and poorest

   d. agricultural products make up a very small part of gross domestic product

   e. import a lot of capital in the form of aid or investment

   f. have weather and soil conditions unsuitable for agriculture

g. have capital reserves large enough so they don't have to depend on loans, aid, or foreign investment

h. a large proportion of the labor force works in agriculture

ANSWER ANALYSIS OF PRACTICE READING 2

Multiple Choice

1. Which sentence best expresses the essential information of this passage?

    a. Economists do not know why some countries remain poor while others become rich.

    b. The typical differences between a developed country and a developing country are numerous and may have developed from a variety of causes.

    c. Foreign interference is the main reason why developing countries remain poor.

    d. The countries we call "developing" are very different from one another, so it is wrong to make generalizations about them.

The main point of Practice Reading 2 is to give characteristics of developing economies and to briefly mention some schools of thought about why developing economies are as they are. Answer **b** best covers all these main ideas. Option *a* is not a good choice, because *causes* is too narrow a focus and because the idea of uncertainty is not really emphasized by the author. Option *c* is not a good choice because it states an idea that appears in the passage only as support for one larger idea—the beliefs of dependency theorists. Option *d* is not a good choice because it takes an idea mentioned in the introduction but then draws an inaccurate conclusion from it. Most of this passage *does* make generalizations about developing countries.

2. Why does the author mention sugar production on Caribbean islands (Paragraph 5)?

    a. to support one belief held by dependency theorists

    b. to support one belief held by modernization theorists

    c. to name one belief that all development theorists hold

    d. to name one belief that is based on inaccurate information

Option **a** is the best, because (as you can see by looking back at the passage) the comment about sugar production is linked by the phrase *for example* to a description of the belief, held by dependency theorists, that foreigners forced colonies to produce goods valuable in the economies of the colonizers. It is not linked in this way to either modernization theorists or development theorists, so choices *b* and *c* are not good choices. There is no mention of *inaccurate information* in connection with sugar production, so choice *d* is not a good one.

3. In this passage, the term the same refers to
   a. "They were once a colony."
   b. "They have a history."
   c. "They have low GNP."
   d. "They are developed."

Option **a** restates the point that was just made about Third World countries—that they had a colonial history. Option *b* is too general to be meaningful. Option *c* mentions an idea made much earlier in the passage, an idea that is therefore hard to link with *the same*. Option *d* gives a statement that was not previously made.

4. "They [colonial powers] forced Third World economies into molds which served their own development interests."

   Which is the best paraphrase of this sentence?
   a. Colonial powers helped the people of the Third World have better lives.
   b. Colonial powers re-shaped Third World economies to make them profitable for the colonizers.
   c. Colonial powers prevented Third World farmers from being able to sell their crops.
   d. Colonial powers were forced to give up their colonies in the Third World.

The author clearly has a negative attitude toward colonization, so *a* is wrong. Option **b** contains a crucial idea of the original sentence—*re-shaping*. In the original, this idea is stated in the phrase *forced . . . into molds*. Also, the original expresses something bad that happened to the Third World economies. Options *d* and *c* both express something bad, but *c* talks about farmers. This idea is not in the original.

5. Look at the 4 triangles (△) in the reading (numbered 1–4). Which triangle shows the best place to insert (add) the following sentence?

   This difference results, to some degree, from the size of the category (there are more developing countries than developed ones), but some commentators attribute it to a sort of "critical income level," below which a country is forced to live poor even if it seems wealthy in comparison to its neighbors.

   The sentence could best be added at
   a. △ 1
   b. △ 2
   c. △ 3
   d. △ 4

The best place for this sentence would be at △1. The context is one of difference, income levels, and categories. That makes the sentence a good fit at this point.

Schematic Table

Developed countries	c. not much difference in income between the richest and poorest (*see Paragraph 1, sentences 3 & 4*) d. agricultural products make up a very small part of gross domestic product (*Paragraph 6, sentences 3 & 4*) g. have capital reserves large enough so they don't have to depend on loans, aid, or foreign investment (*is implied in Paragraph 3, last sentence*)
Developing countries	a. have a history of being colonized by foreigners (*see Paragraph 3, sentence 2*) e. import a lot of capital in the form of aid or investment (*Paragraph 3, sentences 1 and the last sentence; see also all of Paragraph 4*) h. a large proportion of the labor force works in agriculture (*see Paragraph 3, sentence 5 and Paragraph 6, sentence 3*)

The following choices should be omitted, because the passage contains no such ideas:

- suffer from constantly changing governments, often as a result of military coups
- have weather and soil conditions unsuitable for agriculture

The other choices can be supported from the passage. In the preceding schematic table answer key, a paragraph number and a sentence number are given; these can help you match the statement with part of the passage.

Review: Identifying Main Ideas and Understanding Content

This section contains three long passages for extra practice. Each passage is followed by some content/main idea questions similar to those asked in academic courses and on communication-oriented tests like the 2005 TOEFL®. (Vocabulary-oriented questions will be practiced later in this part of the book.)

This section of practice passages does not include any writing or speaking questions. Such questions are practiced in the Writing and Speaking parts of this book and in the Multi-Skills Practice Test at the end of the book.

Main Idea Review Passage 1

(1)   When President Bill Clinton's approval ratings plummeted in 1994, the cartoonist Herblock drew him staring in shock at his cat, Socks, who was resolutely walking out of the White House with his possessions in a bundle on his shoulder. This image would have been inconceivable a century ago. It is based on the assumption that a cat can be a valued friend, who can be counted on to provide solace during affliction.

(2)   Four centuries ago, few people could have conceived of a cat as a friend at all. Common English-language expressions from long ago make clear that our ancestors viewed the cat as a hunter of rodents and did not approve of its methods. **△1** Instead of forthrightly chasing down its prey, like a dog, a cat lies in wait, stalks, and pounces on its unsuspecting victim; instead of immediately killing its prey and wolfing it down, it may prefer to defer eating and play with its catch. Accordingly, *catty* means slyly spiteful, and *feline* connotes stealth. To *play cat and mouse with* is to toy heartlessly with a victim in one's power, and the children's game *puss in the corner* involves surrounding and teasing one of the players by offering and withdrawing opportunities to escape.

(3)   Only in recent times, as we have come increasingly to like and value cats, has the English language begun to reflect any appreciation of the animal's beauty, coordination, poise, and style. Although a woman would still object to being called a *cat,* she may like to be praised for feline grace and seductiveness. **△2** The great baseball player Johnny Mize, a large but well-coordinated man, was called "the big Georgia cat"; and "Harry the Cat Brecheen" was a particularly lithe and graceful pitcher.

(4)   In the 1930s, African-Americans began to describe a smart man who appreciates swing or jazz music as a *cat* or *hepcat*. This sense has been extended to refer to any streetwise, self-assured, stylishly dressed man-about-town—one who has the cool sophistication suggested by the cat's poise and elegant detachment, along with the defiance of mainstream social conventions suggested by its refusal to conform. **△3** A *cat* may also be a member of the *avant-garde* that defies traditional artistic conventions.

(5)   Finally, a whole family of expressions reflects a general perception of the cat as fortunate and superior: if something is really special, it is described

avant-garde: leaders of fashion

as *the cat's whiskers, the cat's meow,* or *the cat's pajamas. Fat cats* enjoy luxury and special privileges, and *the cat that swallowed the canary* is a proverbial example of triumphant satisfaction. One who sits *in the catbird seat* is in an enviable or controlling position.

(6) In contrast, dog terms are almost invariably used to demean. A *dog* is a despicable man or a crude woman, a worthless thing or an utter failure. **△4** *Bitch* has almost lost its primary meaning of female dog as it has become a handy term of abuse. A *bitch* can also be an ill-tempered complaint or an unpleasantly difficult task; *to bitch* is to gripe or grumble. A *puppy* is a pert, conceited, empty-headed young man. A *dog-eat-dog* competition is particularly destructive and ruthlessly self-interested. A *yellow dog* (a mongrel of undistinguishable ancestry) is the type of abject cowardice.

(7) Even when the terms are based on actual canine behavior, they are used negatively. To *dog* or *hound* is to pursue remorselessly. A human who behaves in a *hangdog* manner is browbeaten and abject, and usually guilty and ashamed as well. Even if we admire the fidelity and self-abnegation implied in *doglike devotion,* we find something contemptible in [its] uncritical, subservient nature and would not like to see our own love characterized in this way. Another set of expressions—to *lead a dog's life, it shouldn't happen to a dog, in the doghouse,* and *die like a dog*—suggest that dogs lead a substandard life because they are inferior beings. Why should the animal that is most loved by people be so negatively presented in our language? Why should cats, which despite their popularity are neither so beloved nor so morally esteemed, fare so much better? Probably it is because dogs are closer to us, both from our warmer attachment to them and from their constant efforts to be part of our world. We therefore think of them as second-class humans; we judge them by human standards and assume they are entitled to fewer privileges.

Adapted from Katherine M. Rogers, *The Cat and the Human Imagination: Feline Images from Bast to Garfield* (Ann Arbor: University of Michigan Press, 1998).

1. Which of the following best expresses the main idea of this passage?

    a. English expressions about animals indicate that cats have become more popular than dogs.

    b. Changes in English expressions indicate changes in attitudes toward cats.

    c. Changes in English expressions indicate changes in attitudes toward dogs.

    d. Even though some English expressions involving cats are positive, most people don't like cats as much as they like dogs.

2. Someone called a "cat" in the sense described in Paragraph 4 is most likely

    a. stylish

    b. African-American

    c. conformist

    d. conventional

3. According to the passage, dogs are negatively presented in the English language because

    a. cats are now presented more positively

    b. most people don't have warm feelings toward dogs

    c. English words are based on actual dog behavior

    d. humans judge dogs according to standards that are too high

4. In the last paragraph, the shaded word its refers to

    a. a dog

    b. abnegation

    c. the phrase *doglike devotion*

    d. love

5. "*Bitch* has almost lost its primary meaning of a female dog as it has become a handy term of abuse."

    Which is the best paraphrase of this sentence?

    a. *Bitch* is now a kind of insult, but it used to mean only "female dog."

    b. *Bitch* now usually means "female dog," but in earlier times it used to be an insult.

    c. In modern times, almost no one knows what *bitch* means.

    d. Someone who is angry at his or her dog will call it a *bitch*.

6. Look at the 4 triangles (△) in the reading (numbered 1–4). Which triangle shows the best place to insert (add) the following sentence?

> *Public figures who projected a tough, straightforward image*
> *began to enjoy having cat-related nicknames.*

The sentence could best be added at

    a. △ 1
    b. △ 2
    c. △ 3
    d. △ 4

Schematic Table

Complete this table by classifying each of the answer choices according to whether, according to the passage, it is an image of cats from (1) the English of long ago or (2) recent English. Two of the statements will <u>not</u> be used. Write the letter of each of your choices in the proper blank.

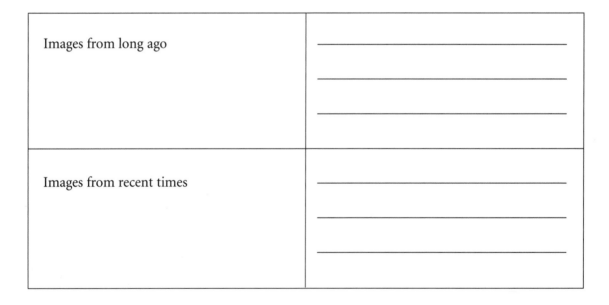

Images from long ago	_____
	_____
	_____
Images from recent times	_____
	_____
	_____

a. a fortunate animal

b. a killer that dishonorably plays with its victims

c. an animal that feels guilty and ashamed

d. a lithe and graceful pitcher

e. a poised and elegantly detached animal

f. a sneaky animal

g. a graceful animal

Main Idea Review Passage 2

(1) Herbal medicine is perhaps the fastest growing category of complementary and alternative medicine. Most patients do not tell their physicians about use of dietary *supplements,* and relatively few physicians presently inquire about such use or are versed in herbal medicine. A few herbs have become more popular and/or proved more effective than their synthetic counterparts, while others have raised concerns about potential adverse herb-drug interactions. △1

supplements: things you eat to get more nutrients than your food contains

(2) Regulation of dietary supplements presents perhaps the greatest area of regulatory controversy in complementary and alternative medicine regulation today. Ongoing efforts by one agency of the federal government, the Food and Drug Administration (FDA), to increase enforcement efforts have generated intense debates among lawmakers, consumers, providers, and supplement manufacturers.

(3) In addition, the complementary and alternative medicine practices involving dietary supplements illustrate the clash in paradigms alluded to earlier: while herbal medicine is being widely researched and efforts are being made to understand herbs from a strictly pharmacological perspective, many complementary and alternative medicine practitioners regard herbs as sacred, having properties beyond those conferred by their chemistry. △1 In Native American traditions, for example, the relationship between humans and herbs involves profound relationship exchange; in traditional oriental medicine, herbs are chosen to influence *chi,* the Chinese notion of vital energy, rather than produce specific pharmacological responses. Even researchers recognize that many herbs, particularly in Chinese and Tibetan medicine, have multiple active ingredients that may have a synergistic effect

on the body. And some herbal formulas have effects that are not understood—for example, research has shown *that* but not *why* St. John's wort elevates mood. Whether herbs have a biofield effect—for example, the consciousness of the herb (such as a property relating to happiness) interacting with the consciousness of the human being—has not been extensively considered.

(4) The starting point for current debate regarding regulation of dietary supplements in the United States is the federal Dietary Supplements Health and Education Act (DSHEA), enacted in 1994. One of the major justifications the statute provides for its enactment is the need to "protect the right of access of consumers to safe dietary supplements . . . in order to promote wellness." Δ3 This justification is amplified in the report of the Senate Committee on Labor and Human Resources on the DSHEA. The committee specifically found that the FDA had "pursued a regulatory agenda which discourages . . . citizens seeking to improve their health through dietary supplementation" and that "[i]n fact, the FDA has had a long history of bias against dietary supplements . . . [and] pursued a heavy-handed enforcement agenda against dietary supplements for over 30 years."

(5) In light of these findings and comments, the DSHEA has had enormous popular appeal yet has generated controversy among regulatory authorities. Δ4 Since the statute's enactment, various regulatory proposals have circulated to further restrict consumer access to dietary supplements. Rather than devoting detailed analysis to one or more such specific proposals, I will address a broader and more pervasive question—namely, ideally, how should the government regulate dietary supplements? In setting controls on the dietary supplement market, should regulation tip toward restriction or freedom? How do underlying beliefs about consumer health and intelligence shape regulatory values, policies, and rules? In what ways do the paradigmatic differences between conventional medicine, on the one hand, and complementary and alternative medicine, on the other, suggest the way that underlying belief systems ultimately influence the regulatory stance and resulting legal rules?

Adapted from Michael H. Cohen, *Beyond Complementary Medicine: Legal and Ethical Perspectives on Health Care and Human Evolution* (Ann Arbor: University of Michigan Press, 2001).

1. Which of the following best expresses the main idea of this passage?

    a. The government's regulation of dietary supplements has been too strict and is opposed by a large number of social groups.

    b. Dietary supplements are potentially dangerous because they are poorly regulated and poorly researched.

    c. Dietary supplements offer a perfect illustration of the conflicts between conventional medicine and alternative (or complementary) medicine.

    d. The degree to which the government can regulate dietary supplements is made uncertain by factors such as popular opinion, lack of research, and many others.

2. According to the boxed section of this passage, who criticized the actions of the FDA?

    a. a group of journalists

    b. a group of doctors

    c. another part of the U.S. government

    d. people who worked for the FDA

3. In Paragraph 4, the word its refers to

    a. the law's

    b. the government's

    c. the debate's

    d. the justification's

4. "In light of these findings and comments, the DSHEA has had enormous popular appeal yet has generated controversy among regulatory authorities."

    Which is the best paraphrase of this sentence?

    a. Most regulators and most other people dislike the DSHEA.

    b. Most regulators and most other people like the DSHEA.

    c. Many regulators like the DSHEA, but most other people don't.

    d. Most people like the DSHEA, but many regulators don't.

5. Look at the 4 triangles (△) in the reading (numbered 1–4). Which triangle shows the best place to insert (add) the following sentence?

    This could put governmental regulators in the awkward position of seeming to restrict religion or culture as they try to regulate herbs.

The sentence could best be added at

    a. △ 1

    b. △ 2

    c. △ 3

    d. △ 4

Prose Summary

An introductory sentence for a brief summary of the passage is provided below. Complete the summary by selecting the three answer choices that express the most important ideas in the passage. Some sentences do not belong in the summary because they express ideas that are not presented in the passage or are minor ideas in the passage. In each blank, write the letter of one of your choices.

> Efforts to regulate the use of dietary supplements have sometimes been difficult or unpopular.
>
> • _____
>
> • _____
>
> •

    a. Herbs and other supplements often have cultural implications beyond their pharmacological properties, so regulators risk violating religious or cultural rights of herb users.

    b. Most patients don't tell their physicians that they are using dietary supplements.

    c. Some elements of U.S. law, particularly the DSHEA of 1994, specifically aim to give consumers easy access to dietary supplements and would likely conflict with a strict regulatory program.

    d. Research has shown that St. John's wort elevates mood, but no one is sure why it does so.

    e. Some herbal formulas have effects that are not yet well understood, so it's difficult to evaluate their risks and benefits.

    f. Government regulation frequently makes items too expensive for ordinary people to afford them.

Main Idea Review Passage 3

(1) Adoption touches almost every conceivable aspect of American society and culture. Adoption commands our attention because of the enormous number of people who have a direct, intimate connection to it—some experts put the number as high as six out of every ten Americans. Others estimate that about one million children in the United States live with adoptive parents and that 2 to 4 percent of American families include an adopted child. According to incomplete 1992 estimates, a total of 126,951 domestic adoptions occurred, 53,525 of them (42 percent) kinship or stepparent adoptions. Because of the dearth of healthy U.S. infants for adoption, 18,477 adoptions in 2000 were intercountry adoptions, with slightly more than half of those children coming from Russia and China. **△1** In short, adoption is a ubiquitous social institution in American society, creating invisible relationships with biological and adoptive *kin* that touch far more people than we imagine.

kin: relatives

(2) Any social organization that touches so many lives in such a profound way is bound to be complicated. Modern adoption is no exception. That is why it is so important to have a historical perspective on this significant social and legal institution. Newspapers, television news shows, and magazines frequently carry stories about various facets of adoption. Numerous online chat rooms and list-serves focus on issues related to the subject. There is a reason for this prominence of adoption. While raising any family is inherently stressful, adoption is filled with additional tensions that are unique to the adoptive relationship. **△2** From the moment they decide they wish to adopt a child, couples begin to confront a series of challenges. First comes the problem of state regulation. A host of state laws govern every aspect of legal adoptions: who may adopt, who may be adopted, the persons who must consent to the adoption, the form the adoption petition must take, the notice of investigation and formal hearing of the adoption petition, the effect of the adoption decree, the procedure for appeal, the confidential nature of the hearings and records in adoption proceedings, the issuance of new birth certificates, and adoption subsidy payments. Second, since World War II, the entire edifice of modern adoption has been enveloped in secrecy. Records of adoption proceedings are confidential, closed both to the public and to all the parties involved in the adoption: birth parents, adoptees, and adoptive parents. Third, in a nation that sanctifies blood kinship, adoptive families and adoptees are stigmatized because of their lack of biological relationship. **Δ3**

(3) With the onset of World War II, a revolution began in the world of adoption that only a historical perspective can explain. A few examples will illustrate this point. In reaction to the stigmatization, rationalization, and secrecy associated with adoption, the adoptee search movement emerged and began to demand the opening of adoption records. Opposing these adoptees, some birth mothers argued that they were promised secrecy when they relinquished their children for adoption and that abrogating that promise constituted an invasion of privacy. Since World War II, intercountry adoptions have increased tremendously, but critics have denounced such adoptions as a shameful admission of a nation's inability to care for its own people, exploitative of its poorest class, destructive of children's cultural and ethnic heritage, and riven by baby-selling scandals.

(4) Since the mid-nineteenth century, formal adoption—the legal termination of the birth parents' (traditionally defined as a heterosexual couple) parental rights and the taking into the home of a child—has been the way Americans have created substitute families. **Δ4** But nontraditional families are becoming more common. Thirty percent of adoptive parents are single mothers, and gay and lesbian couples are increasingly winning the legal right to become adoptive parents. And as an outgrowth of in vitro fertilization technology, researchers have developed "embryo adoption" where an infertile couple can adopt a donated frozen embryo, bringing into question the very meaning of the institution of adoption. The embryo is implanted into the uterus of the adopting mother, who then gestates and gives birth to the baby. Embryo adoption obviates the need for legal adoption because many state laws maintain that a woman who gives birth to a child is the biological parent. The growth of assisted reproductive technologies, along with almost every aspect of modern adoption—whether the state's intervention into the family or removal of children from their country of origin—raises profound emotional and ethical considerations that only the history of adoption can begin to illuminate.

Adapted from E. Wayne Carp, ed., "Introduction: A Historical Overview of American Adoption" in *Adoption in America: Historical Perspectives* (Ann Arbor: University of Michigan Press, 2002).

1. Which of the following best expresses the main idea of this passage?

    a. Because society makes adoption of a child so difficult, very few adoptions now occur in the United States.

    b. Couples wishing to adopt a child face a series of challenges.

    c. Adoption touches many parts of American life and involves complicated interactions among the government, adoptive parents, and adoptees.

    d. After many years of secrecy, adoptees are finally claiming their right to know who their birth parents are.

2. The author of this passage mentions World War II in order to

    a. give a time in the past when important changes occurred

    b. show the seriousness of adoption

    c. explain why so many countries were unable to care for their own children

    d. illustrate the kind of conflict that exists between pro-adoption and anti-adoption groups

3. In Paragraph 3, the word its refers to

    a. a country whose children are being adopted by Americans

    b. a country from which adoptive parents come

    c. a country that invades the privacy of its citizens

    d. a country that does not permit adoptions

4. "Records of adoption proceedings are confidential, closed both to the public and to all the parties involved in the adoption: birth parents, adoptees, and adoptive parents."

    Which is the best paraphrase of the sentence above?

    a. The parties involved in an adoption can read the records, but the public can't.

    b. The public has a right to know what is said at an adoption hearing.

    c. The records of an adoption hearing are kept secret even from the parties involved in the adoption.

    d. The government does its best to protect the parties in an adoption from being publicly identified.

5. Look at the 4 triangles (△) in the reading (numbered 1–4). Which triangle shows the best place to insert (add) the following sentence?

    Through most of the twentieth century, the adoptive parents were assumed to be middle-class couples who wanted children in order to fill out a more-or-less traditional family.

The sentence could best be added at

    a. △ 1

    b. △ 2

    c. △ 3

    d. △ 4

Schematic Table

Complete the table by classifying each of the answer choices by whether, according to the passage, *it is (1) something that makes adoption easier for parents who want to adopt a child or (2) something that makes adoption harder for parents who want to adopt. Two of the statements will <u>not</u> be used. Write the letter of each of your choices in the proper blank.*

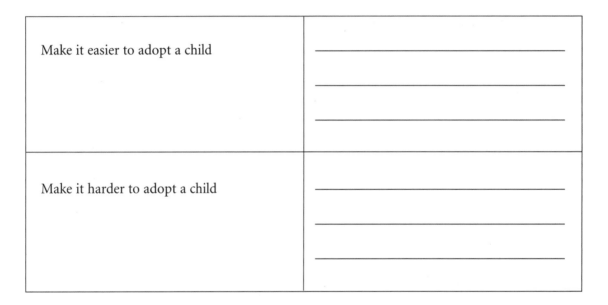

Make it easier to adopt a child	_____ _____ _____
Make it harder to adopt a child	_____ _____ _____

    a. The adoptee search movement began to demand the opening of adoption records.

    b. Gay and lesbian couples are increasingly winning the right to become adoptive parents.

    c. Raising any family is inherently stressful.

    d. State laws govern such things as who may adopt, who may be adopted, and who must consent to the adoption.

    e. There is a dearth of healthy U.S. infants for adoption.

    f. As an outgrowth of in vitro fertilization technology, researchers have created embryo adoption.

    g. According to incomplete 1992 estimates, a total of 126,951 domestic adoptions occurred.

Building Skills: Vocabulary

Basic Skill	Some Related Academic Tasks	Related Tasks on Tests like the 2005 TOEFL®
Understanding the meanings and roles of vocabulary items in a reading	• writing essays on tests • writing reports about materials you've read • answering multiple-choice questions on tests • participating in classroom discussions about readings • using more sophisticated vocabulary in your essays • reading quickly enough to do your reading assignments on time • learning important new terms in an area of academic study	• answering multiple-choice "basic comprehension" questions about vocabulary items • answering multiple-choice questions about ideas in passages • choosing vocabulary to write answers to essay questions about a passage • choosing vocabulary for spoken answers to questions about the main ideas in a passage

Vocabulary skills are basic to effective reading and academic success. In your academic classes and on communication-oriented tests like the 2005 TOEFL®, you will make use of vocabulary you have learned in the past. You will also have to figure out the meanings and roles of new vocabulary items (words you do not know) in the passages.

In communication-oriented tests like the 2005 TOEFL®, vocabulary skills are tested entirely in the context of long passages, conversations, and lectures. Unlike earlier versions of the test, the new version does not ask questions about vocabulary in smaller contexts—like individual sentences or even individual paragraphs. It is very important to develop skills for understanding vocabulary in long, multi-paragraph contexts.

In this section, we will review four important vocabulary skills:

- understanding familiar vocabulary in new contexts
- using context to determine the meaning of an unfamiliar vocabulary item
- recognizing definitions in a text
- using your knowledge of word parts

Understanding Familiar Vocabulary in New Contexts

Even some very basic English words, words you have seen often and are very familiar with, mean different things at different times. A reader must recognize which meaning is appropriate in any given context.

For example, consider the word **mark**. It has many different meanings—from a man's name (capitalized), to a written symbol, to the victim of a trick, to many others.

EXERCISE

Read the following passage and answer the question.

The Civil War left a mark on the soul of the nation. It persisted long past the end of Reconstruction, and the Jim Crow South was evidence that the war's wound had scarred over in unnatural ways.

In the passage above, the word mark is closest in meaning to

    a. a written symbol to show the location of a thing

    b. a visible sign that shows where an injury occurred

    c. a target

    d. a grade or evaluation comment

The best answer is **b**, because elements like *wound* and *scar* create a context of injury and the conditions that follow an injury. You can check whether your answer is a good one by trying to replace *mark* with answer **b** in the original. While this creates a rather long and awkward sentence, it works.

Using Context to Determine the Meaning of Unfamiliar Vocabulary

In the previous example, elements of context helped us decide among several meanings of a familiar word, *mark*. Context can also help you figure out the meanings of words you have never seen before or have seen only rarely. Most EAP courses spend a great deal of time on how to determine the meanings of words from context. This is a very valuable reading skill, one that you could practice with every passage in this book. To focus briefly on the technique, let's consider a word that is probably not familiar to most of you, *calcify*.

EXERCISE

Read the following passage and answer the question.

Through the early part of the year, the naturally cautious directors were unusually flexible in their attitude toward expanding the company. They could be talked into it, it seemed, if they heard a good enough argument for growth. By April, however, their natural no-growth attitude had reasserted itself and had calcified. No amount of argument would change it, not with the economy so weak.

In the passage above, the word calcified is closest in meaning to

    a. became less flexible

    b. became more open

    c. became weaker

    d. became easier to understand

The best answer is **a**. This passage describes a contrast in attitudes at two different times—*flexible* at an early point in the year and *calcified* later on—so *calcified* probably has a meaning that contrasts with that of *flexible*. This is an example of how the context provided a clue to the meaning of the word.

Let's look at another example.

EXERCISE

Read the following passage and answer the question.

To conceal his payments to assassins and other distasteful characters, the president drew the necessary cash from a slush fund created by anonymous donors. There were no records of money going into this hidden stash, so there would never be any questions about money going out of it.

In the passage above, the term slush fund is closest in meaning to

    a. an amount of money kept secret from most people

    b. a payment to an assassin or some other criminal

    c. an account with a large, safe public bank

    d. public money, from taxes and other sources, used for paying the normal expenses of running a country

---

The best answer is **a**. Even though *slush fund* is not defined in this passage, you can see from the passage that it has certain features:

- someone can draw cash from it
- it is used in concealing (hiding) payments
- the people who pay into it are anonymous (not wanting their names to be known)
- there are no records of money going into it

Altogether these facts create a sense of something secret, which eliminates choices *c* and *d,* and an amount from which the president can get money, which makes choice *b* unlikely.

Recognizing Definitions in a Text

In many passages, difficult, technical, or unusual words will be defined for you in the passage. To understand the meaning of the word, you must recognize and understand the definition. You may have learned some signals that often show a definition—like the boxed parts in the following examples (terms being defined are in bold type):

    1. parentheses ( ) or brackets [ ]: The workers focused their attention on the **lintel** (the piece of wood that forms the top of a doorframe) and began planning how to replace it.

    2. dashes—: The workers focused their attention on the **lintel** —the piece of wood that forms the top of a doorframe— and began planning how to replace it.

3. *or:* Some ancient builders took inspiration from the **pointed horns,** or cusps, of the crescent moon, so that roofs came to points that served no real structural purpose.

4. *defined as:* The movement of earth's tectonic plates is mimicked by the movements of Ganymede's **lithosphere**, which, in this moon's case, must be defined as the solid ice-and-rock layer at the immediate surface.

There are many other obvious "definition" signals as well *(also known as, which is another way of saying,* etc.), and any of these might prove helpful to you in a reading. Unfortunately, definitions may not always come with such an obvious signal. Sometimes an author defines a term without signaling it. In such cases, you have to look in nearby sentences for information that might constitute a definition. The following exercise offers an example of such a situation.

EXERCISE

Read the following passage and answer the question.

The industry used to lose thousands of ampules a day to damage during shipping. And with the liquid in each ampule worth about $1,200, this was a significant loss. The solution was to employ special sheets of packed foam that enclosed each tiny, liquid-filled glass tube in a cushion of 0.18 cm on each side.

In the passage above, the word ampule is closest in meaning to

    a. liquid inside a tube

    b. damage to a product during shipping

    c. loss of a large amount of money

    d. small glass tube that can be filled with liquid

The best answer is **d.** It's clear from the first two sentences that ampules break and that they hold liquid. Even though there is no explicit definition signal, the author of this passage defines *ampule* with the phrase *glass tube* in the final sentence of the passage.

Using Your Knowledge of Word Parts

Most EAP reading textbooks advise you to study certain word parts—**prefixes, stems,** and **suffixes**—that appear in a large number of English words and have almost the same meaning in each case. Some (with their meanings and examples) appear in the chart.

Prefixes	Stems	Suffixes
in-; "not"; *inflexible*	*flex* or *flect;* "bend" or "bounce"; *reflection*	*-able* or *–ible;* "able to be"; *payable*
pre-; "before"; *preview*	*port;* "carry"; *portable*	*-ous;* "characterized by"; *gracious*
com- or *con-;* "with"; *convert*	*ceed;* "go"; *proceed*	*-tion;* "a condition or process"; *reflection*

The following exercise shows how a knowledge of word parts might help you understand the meaning of an unfamiliar word.

EXERCISE

Read the following passage and answer the question.

The United States has lost the industrial capacity to survive outside a world economy. Not only have we closed our steel industry, but we have decided that virtually all extraction of natural resources, from oil to zinc, should occur overseas.

In the passage above, the term extraction is closest in meaning to

     a. an activity no longer pursued

     b. the process of coming closer to someone

     c. an amount larger than normal

     d. the act of taking something out

The best answer is **d**. You might be able to guess this if you know that the prefix *ex-* often means "out," the stem *tract* often means "pull" or "take," and the suffix *–tion* often turns a word into a noun for a process or condition.

The bad news is that word parts are not always a reliable clue to meaning. For one thing, some parts can have several meanings; the prefix *in-*, for example, sometimes means "not" but sometimes means "in" or "into." For another, English, like any other language, grows and changes. Words that once held very close relationships to the meanings of their word parts no longer do so, and even a native speaker of English has to think very hard to see any connection between the parts and the meaning of a word as a whole. One famous example is the word *homely,* which once (logically) meant "related to the home." Its current meaning is "not very attractive." This modern meaning can be logically connected to the meaning of its parts (a person who is not very attractive may not get invited to many social gatherings, so he or she stays at home a lot), but most native speakers of English probably don't make this connection when they use *homely*.

One piece of advice might be helpful: When trying to decide on the meaning of a word, if you see a familiar word part, try to think of as many English words as possible that have that part. By recalling a large number of similar words, you may get a general idea about the meaning of the difficult word.

EXERCISE

Read the following passage and answer the question.

Workers who have been in the same office for more than 5 years are typically proprietous not only of the space but of the furniture and even the wall color. The company's attempts at minor redecoration are likely to be met with objections and scowls.

In the passage above, the term proprietous is closest in meaning to

      a. full of worry

      b. feeling like an owner

      c. willing to change

      d. reluctant to do different things

The best answer is **b**. You might have been able to guess this if you could think of a number of other words that have the part *prop—property, proprietor, appropriate, expropriate*—and involve the meaning "own." If you can't think of such a list of words, don't worry about it. Not everyone can. In that case, rely on other clues of form and logic to try figuring out the meaning of a difficult vocabulary item.

Practicing with Short Readings

The following section works on some specific vocabulary skills in some very short passage contexts. These are shorter than the book chapters you will read in your academic classes. They are also shorter than most passages on communication-oriented tests like the 2005 TOEFL®, which are at least 600 words long.

After each short passage, circle the letter of the best answer to each question. Check your answers with your teacher or by using the answer key at the back of the book.

EXERCISE 1

The invention of the laser makes for a somewhat murky chapter in technological history. One clear element in it is that the first patent for what we now call a laser was issued (in 1960) to Charles Townes and Arthur Schawlow, who based their patent application on work they had done at Bell Laboratories. Beyond that, things get murkier. Townes and Schawlow had published about the principles of the technology as early as 1958. Gordon Gould claimed to have come up with the idea of a laser (and to have written notes about it) as early as 1957, but he didn't file for a patent until 1959. In any case, Gould gets credit for coining the word *laser* (from "**l**ight **a**mplification by **s**timulated **e**mission of **r**adiation"), and the U.S. Patent

Office eventually granted him a laser-related patent in the late 1970s. A third important character in the story is Theodore Maiman, who, in 1960, built a working optical laser (one involving visible light)—probably the first functional laser.

1. The word murky in the passage is closest in meaning to
   a. exciting
   b. interesting
   c. clear
   d. unclear

2. The word patent in the passage is closest in meaning to
   a. official credit for an invention
   b. a workshop for building sensitive machines
   c. an article in a scientific journal
   d. money that supports research

3. The word optical in the passage is closest in meaning to
   a. complicated
   b. related to seeing
   c. working properly
   d. possible, but not necessary

EXERCISE 2

Since the 19th century, cultural diffusionists have explained shared features among various cultures in terms of a process of contact and borrowing. If two cultures share a distinctive burial style or fishing method, the members of one culture are assumed to have learned it by meeting and observing the members of the other. Diffusionists run the gamut from the extreme to the mild . The former, such as G. Elliot Smith, posit very few centers from which cultural features radiate. In Smith's characterization, there was only one such center—ancient Egypt—for all advanced cultural achievements, such as writing. Less extreme diffusionists include well-known anthropologists of the early to middle 20th century such as Franz Boas and R. H. Lowie. Their approach, while emphasizing the importance of contact among cultures, allowed for individual invention as well. In other words, if two cultures shared a burial style or a peculiar fishing method, one might have borrowed it from the other or each might have come up with the idea on its own. Nor did this mild viewpoint restrict the center of diffusion to one place. Several centers might have functioned simultaneously to spread cultural features, much as a handful of pebbles thrown into a pond will create several ripple patterns radiating from several centers.

1. The word contact in the passage is closest in meaning to
   a. touching
   b. meeting
   c. talking to
   d. borrowing from

2. The word mild in the passage is closest in meaning to
   a. not hot or cold
   b. not weak
   c. not clear
   d. not extreme

3. The word posit in the passage is closest in meaning to
   a. propose
   b. explain
   c. criticize
   d. visit

4. The term allowed for in the passage is closest in meaning to
   a. argued against
   b. showed evidence for
   c. shared information about
   d. were willing to believe in

EXERCISE 3

Our image of physical change as normally incremental and gradual has to be left behind as we consider superconductivity. Superconductivity depends on critical points—of temperature, current density, and magnetic field strength—where sudden changes occur. This became clear long ago, when Heike Kamerlingh Onnes (Nobel laureate in physics, 1913) first achieved virtually zero electrical resistance in a mercury wire cooled to 4.2 K and named the state of the metal "superconductivity." As far as we know, not every material can become superconductive, but any material that can do so has its own Critical Temperature (T_c). For pure metals, this is typically very low, under 20 K. For many newly developed ceramics, T_c is much higher—near or even above 100 K. Critical Current Density (J_c) refers to the fact that, at a given temperature, a material can carry only so much electrical current and stay superconductive. If the current density exceeds J_c, the material will suddenly lose its near-zero resistance and flip to its normal resistive state. Most complex of all is the third factor, Critical Magnetic Field (H_c), which refers to the strength of the magnetic field around the superconductor. Superconductors have a unique ability to prevent an external magnetic field from penetrating the superconductive material—up to H_c. In one kind, called type I or "soft" superconductors, the material reverts to its normal resistive state if the external magnetic field reaches or surpasses H_c.

1. The word gradual in the passage is closest in meaning to
   a. important
   b. happening step-by-step
   c. easy to see
   d. normal

2. The word state in the passage is closest in meaning to
   a. part of a country
   b. comment
   c. group of numbers
   d. condition

3. The word resistive in the passage is closest in meaning to

    a. not conductive

    b. not superconductive

    c. not magnetic

    d. not dense

4. The word surpasses in the passage is closest in meaning to

    a. becomes higher than

    b. becomes lower than

    c. becomes equal to

    d. becomes similar to

EXERCISE 4

Traditionally, bioethics , the study of legal and ethical issues arising in health care, has centered on four essential values: respect for patient autonomy, nonmaleficence, beneficence, and justice. Although some commentators have criticized overreliance on such broad principles for ethical decision-making, others believe that the four principles describe common, core values. Autonomy refers to the patient's self-rule and the opportunity to make meaningful choices; nonmaleficence, to the physician's obligation to do no harm; beneficence, to contributing to patient welfare; and justice, to fairness and equity. These moral principles establish ideals for relationships between physicians and their patients. In addition, emotional responsiveness—the caregiver's feeling response to the patient— enhances the moral quality of the relationship in a way that transcends ethical principles and rules.

Adapted from Michael H. Cohen, *Beyond Complementary Medicine: Legal and Ethical Perspectives on Health Care and Human Evolution* (Ann Arbor: University of Michigan Press, 2001).

1. As used in this passage, the word bioethics refers to

    a. a medical treatment

    b. a legal issue

    c. an area of research

    d. a set of values

2. In this passage, the word principles is closest in meaning to

    a. leaders

    b. basic ideas

    c. choices

    d. doctors

3. In this passage, the word autonomy is closest in meaning to

    a. independence

    b. indecision

    c. information

    d. incapacity

4. In this passage, the word enhances is closest in meaning to

    a. returns

    b. illustrates

    c. decreases

    d. strengthens

EXERCISE 5

By 1960, when Stanley Kramer's *Inherit the Wind* was released, the issues central to the Scopes "Monkey Trial" of 1925 (which the film fictionally portrayed) had become slightly quaint, at least for mainstream U.S. society. The general outlook for real science at school was somewhat brighter in those days (despite all the drills about how to crouch at your desk during a nuclear attack). Kramer could get away with sympathetically portraying evolutionism as progressive and with lampooning Bible-toting creationists. It's an open question whether a film with that point of view—and with such unflattering characterizations of creationists—could long endure in today's film market. It's amazing enough that the basic issue is still with us: Should public schools teach natural selection as scientific fact, or should the Bible's story of creation get equal billing? We've been at this for at least eight decades. We should have nailed it by now, and kids throughout the land should be examining the fossil evidence. What's doubly amazing is that the creationists have grown in strength and number, they dress better, and some

53

of them have unidentifiable accents. Many of them head federal agencies, which in itself erodes the separation of Church and State and helps drive secular humanism to the closet. If an updated *Inherit the Wind* were released today, it might still be nominated for four Academy Awards as the original was in 1960 (left-leaning Hollywood insiders make those nominations), but no teacher in heartland America would risk showing it at the local middle school on film night.

1. In this passage, the word brighter is closest in meaning to
   a. shinier
   b. funnier
   c. more optimistic
   d. more intelligent

2. In this passage, the word lampooning is closest in meaning to
   a. making jokes about
   b. putting into jail
   c. killing with a long stick
   d. paying attention to

3. In this passage, the word nailed is closest in meaning to
   a. connected
   b. decided
   c. discussed
   d. pounded

4. In this passage, the word erodes is closest in meaning to
   a. promotes
   b. eliminates
   c. weakens
   d. results from

EXERCISE 6

Evidence from various sources points to a significant climatic role for solar disturbances, particularly for the absence of any. Much attention has focused on a period from 1645 to 1715, known as the Maunder minimum (named for E. W. Maunder, a late 19th-century astronomer), when sunspot activity was virtually nil. For some time, researchers wondered whether this period of marked inactivity might simply have been a period of poor record-keeping. That issue seems settled, and most historical astronomers accept that reliable observers were watching the sun regularly and that a remarkable paucity of sunspots truly did characterize this long period. The years of the Maunder minimum correspond to tree-ring evidence of higher-than-normal concentrations of carbon 14, which would be consistent with a period of very little solar flaring. Evidence from the late 17th century also reveals a period of colder-than-average global temperatures. This has thrust the issue of solar variability into one of the most intense debates of the 21st century, the contest over the extent and causes of global warming.

1. In this passage, the word climatic is closest in meaning to
   a. leading up to the end
   b. easy to understand
   c. related to weather
   d. able to change the earth

2. In this passage, the word wondered is closest in meaning to
   a. were not sure
   b. had definite proof
   c. were not concerned about
   d. were mistaken about

3. In this passage, the word paucity is closest in meaning to
   a. excess
   b. lack
   c. observation
   d. brightness

4. In this passage, the term be consistent with is closest in meaning to

   a. fit well

   b. cause conflict

   c. build support

   d. be discovered

EXERCISE 7

The battle between Edison and Westinghouse was of a type familiar to modern consumers—a competition between two technical formats. Edison's direct current (DC) squared off against Westinghouse's alternating current (AC), and huge amounts of money were at stake. Victory would depend entirely on the favor of consumers, especially of large institutional customers who would buy in massive volumes. It was a clear precursor of more recent high-stakes competitions for market dominance in cellular phone systems (GSM vs. CDMA), video format (VHS vs. Beta), and, famously, the PC vs. the Mac. Each electrical format had its advantages. Westinghouse's AC could travel much farther without losing intensity. Edison's DC was marginally safer, in that a person receiving a DC shock can more easily let go of an electrified item. Edison tried tirelessly to amplify this minor safety difference with public-relations stunts that were sometimes gruesome, such as electrocuting a horse with 1000 watts of AC. What could have been Edison's biggest advantage—being in the market first—was, in the end, a vulnerability. Edison had invested so much personal money and personal pride in the infrastructure of DC generation that he lost his perspective. The usually practical and farsighted Edison refused to adapt to the obvious. The triumph of DC was virtually assured by the inventiveness of Nicola Tesla, who designed a compact but powerful AC generator that made Edison's massive DC dynamos look dinosaurian. Edison was not often out-invented, but Tesla had done it. Then Westinghouse swept in and beat Edison in his other area of strength, entrepreneurship.

1. In this passage, the word formats is closest in meaning to

   a. inventors

   b. basic systems

   c. design features

   d. stages of development

2. In this passage, the word ⃞marginally⃞ is closest in meaning to

   a. supposedly

   b. certainly

   c. very much

   d. slightly

3. In this passage, the word ⃞electrocuting⃞ is closest in meaning to

   a. cutting with an electrical current

   b. harming with an electrical current

   c. lighting up with an electrical current

   d. replacing with an electrical current

4. In this passage, the word ⃞dinosaurian⃞ is closest in meaning to

   a. too dangerous

   b. too powerful

   c. too large

   d. too expensive

Practicing with Longer Readings

In your academic classes you will read passages much longer than one or two paragraphs. On most of the newer communication-oriented tests like the 2005 TOEFL®, the typical passage is between 600 and 700 words—much longer than the passages on earlier versions of such tests. It's necessary to practice understanding vocabulary in longer passages as well as in shorter readings.

Here are some longer passages, each followed by vocabulary questions. The correct answers to these questions are discussed briefly after each practice reading.

Almost all of the questions are in the same form: "The word ⃞XXXX⃞ in this passage is closest in meaning to." This is followed by four choices. You became familiar with this format in our exercise with short contexts.

In dealing with long contexts, however, some of our vocabulary questions take a slightly different form, asking what the passage **implies** about the meaning of a word. These questions often target words that are difficult to define or restate with a short phrase. This is an important part of working with English vocabulary in your academic classes—where you must do more than simply define words. You have to show a working knowledge of the word.

After the section of practice passages comes a set of four review readings, each followed by a set of vocabulary questions. Test yourself by answering the questions for each passage. Then check your answers by asking your teacher or by looking in the answer key at the back of the book.

Practice Reading 1 (with Answer Analysis)

Adoption touches almost every conceivable aspect of American society and culture. Adoption commands our attention because of the enormous number of people who have a direct, intimate connection to it—some experts put the number as high as six out of every ten Americans. Others estimate that about one million children in the United States live with adoptive parents and that 2 to 4 percent of American families include an adopted child. According to incomplete 1992 estimates, a total of 126,951 domestic adoptions occurred, 53,525 of them (42 percent) kinship or stepparent adoptions. Because of the dearth of healthy U.S. infants for adoption, 18,477 adoptions in 2000 were intercountry adoptions, with slightly more than half of those children coming from Russia and China. In short, adoption is a ubiquitous social institution in American society, creating invisible relationships with biological and adoptive kin that touch far more people than we imagine.

Any social organization that touches so many lives in such a profound way is bound to be complicated. Modern adoption is no exception. That is why it is so important to have a historical perspective on this significant social and legal institution. Newspapers, television news shows, and magazines frequently carry stories about various facets of adoption. Numerous online chat rooms and list-serves focus on issues related to the subject. There is a reason for this prominence of adoption. While raising any family is inherently stressful, adoption is filled with additional tensions that are unique to the adoptive relationship. From the moment they decide they wish to adopt a child, couples begin to confront a series of challenges. First comes the problem of state regulation. A host of state laws govern every aspect of legal adoptions: who may adopt, who may be adopted, the persons who must consent to the adoption, the form the adoption petition must take, the notice of investigation and formal hearing of the adoption *petition*, the effect of the adoption decree, the procedure for appeal, the confidential nature of the hearings and records in adoption proceedings, the issuance of new birth certificates, and adoption subsidy payments. Second, since World War II, the entire edifice of modern adoption has been enveloped in secrecy. Records of adoption proceedings are confidential, closed both to the public and to all

petition: legal request

the parties involved in the adoption: birth parents, adoptees, and adoptive parents. Third, in a nation that sanctifies blood kinship, adoptive families and adoptees are stigmatized because of their lack of biological relationship.

With the onset of World War II, a revolution began in the world of adoption that only a historical perspective can explain. A few examples will illustrate this point. In reaction to the stigmatization, rationalization, and secrecy associated with adoption, the adoptee search movement emerged and began to demand the opening of adoption records. Opposing these adoptees, some birth mothers argued that they were promised secrecy when they relinquished their children for adoption and that abrogating that promise constituted an invasion of privacy. Since World War II, intercountry adoptions have increased tremendously, but critics have denounced such adoptions as a shameful admission of a nation's inability to care for its own people, exploitative of its poorest class, destructive of children's cultural and ethnic heritage, and riven by baby-selling scandals. Since the mid-nineteenth century, formal adoption—the legal termination of the birth parents' (traditionally defined as a heterosexual couple) parental rights and the taking into the home of a child—has been the way Americans have created substitute families. But nontraditional families are becoming more common. Thirty percent of adoptive parents are single mothers, and gay and lesbian couples are increasingly winning the legal right to become adoptive parents. And as an outgrowth of in vitro fertilization technology, researchers have developed "embryo adoption," where an infertile couple can adopt a donated frozen embryo, bringing into question the very meaning of the institution of adoption. The embryo is implanted into the uterus of the adopting mother, who then gestates and gives birth to the baby. Embryo adoption obviates the need for legal adoption because many state laws maintain that a woman who gives birth to a child is the biological parent. The growth of assisted reproductive technologies, along with almost every aspect of modern adoption—whether the state's intervention into the family or removal of children from their country of origin—raises profound emotional and ethical considerations that only the history of adoption can begin to illuminate.

Adapted from E. Wayne Carp, ed., "Introduction: A Historical Overview of American Adoption" in *Adoption in America: Historical Perspectives* (Ann Arbor: University of Michigan Press, 2002).

QUESTIONS ABOUT PRACTICE READING 1

1. The word intimate in this passage is closest in meaning to

    a. weak

    b. sexual

    c. beneficial

    d. close

2. The word dearth in this passage is closest in meaning to

    a. excess

    b. loss

    c. lack

    d. affection

3. The word intercountry in this passage is closest in meaning to

    a. inside the U.S.

    b. outside the cities

    c. controlled by the government

    d. involving several nations

4. The word ubiquitous in this passage is closest in meaning to

    a. declining

    b. dangerous

    c. widespread

    d. foreign

5. The word confront in this passage is closest in meaning to

    a. spend money on

    b. decide about

    c. encounter

    d. overcome

6. The word host in this passage is closest in meaning to

    a. a person who has invited others to an event

    b. a large group of individual items, appearing together

    c. a religious point of view

    d. a strong flow of water through a narrow tube

7. The term enveloped in in this passage is closest in meaning to

    a. stopped by

    b. made easier by

    c. made up of

    d. surrounded by

8. The word onset in this passage is closest in meaning to

    a. end

    b. beginning

    c. disaster

    d. winning

9. The word abrogating in this passage is closest in meaning to

    a. breaking

    b. keeping

    c. making

    d. changing

10. The word termination in this passage is closest in meaning to

    a. end

    b. beginning

    c. name

    d. insect

11. The reading implies that an embryo is a kind of

    a. adoption

    b. living thing

    c. chemical

    d. organization

12. The word obviates in this passage is closest in meaning to

    a. points out

    b. uses drugs in

    c. strengthens

    d. avoids

DISCUSSION OF PRACTICE READING 1

Question /Item	Answer	Explanation
1. **intimate**	d	The statistics that follow show large numbers involved—people who have close relationships with adoption.
2. **dearth**	c	The following facts show people going overseas to find babies, indicating not enough (a lack of) adoptable babies in the U.S.
3. **intercountry**	d	The context involves the United States, Russia, and China. Also, word parts could be a clue: *inter-* ("between") and *country* ("nation").
4. **ubiquitous**	c	The phrase *in short* indicates a summary of previous information—which was about large numbers of people being involved through-out America. *Widespread* means "found in many places" and fits this idea.
5. **confront**	c	The listed challenges that follow don't mention money *(a)*, or people winning over the challenge *(d)*. Nor do the listed challenges involve decisions by the couple (they are governmental or social). Only *encounter* ("face" or "come up against") fits the facts.
6. **host**	b	Clearly a large group of challenges follows. Guests are not involved, nor is religion. A narrow tube that carries water is a *hose*, not a *host*.
7. **enveloped in**	d	You might be familiar with an envelope as the thing that goes around (surrounds) a letter.
8. **onset**	b	The word parts *on-* and *set* might give you the idea of a beginning. Later, the passage talks about conditions after the war, so there is some reason to think the onset would be earlier than that.
9. **abrogating**	a	If you know English expressions related to promises, you'll know that breaking a promise means "not doing what you promised to do." This matches the situation exactly. Choice *d (changing)* is not very good, because we don't see a new kind of promise re-placing the old.
10. **termination**	a	Word parts can help here. *Termin-* means "stop." Think of a bus terminal (where many buses stop). Choice *d (name)* doesn't fit the context.
11. **embryo**	b	Notice that the reading says an embryo can be "adopted," can be "donated," and can be "implanted in the uterus of the mother, who then gestates and gives birth to the baby." This points to choice **b.**
12. **obviates**	d	You have to make a logical connection between this word and the "because" clause after it. We know that in an embryo adop-tion, the "adopting" mother gives birth to the baby. If state laws then call her the "biological parent," there is no need for her to legally adopt the child. This offers a way of getting around the need for adoption.

Practice Reading 2 (with Answer Analysis)

Although it is tempting today to consider the Michigan that became a territory in 1805 an unaltered Eden, it had in fact been home to generations of people since the end of the last glaciation approximately 10,000 years ago. Although their impact on the land was far less dramatic than anything seen in the last two centuries, Native Americans had indeed affected the face of the state in both subtle and significant ways. By one informal estimate, up to one-third of the landscape of Michigan showed the effects of Native American populations.

There was obvious evidence of the hand of humans. Near present-day Kalamazoo, Gordon noted ground that "looked like an old corn field which has been turned into a common, with regular rows of the usual width crossing the land, transversely." He also reported conversations about "the settlement of this Country by a civilized race before the Indians," linked to signs that the appealing oak openings of southern Michigan had once been cultivated. The civilization that produced these traces and their purpose—whether agricultural or spiritual or both—have never been fully described.

Numerous mounds and earthworks dotted the southern reaches of the state, some appearing to represent burial grounds, others perhaps having religious significance or representing defense against attack. One of the most striking was the great mound not far upstream the Rouge River from the Detroit River, at Del Rey. Originally 700 to 800 feet long, 400 feet wide, and over 40 feet high, the mound contained "an immense number of skeletons," according to Bela Hubbard, who participated in the early government land surveys and later became a noted naturalist and writer. He ascribed the *remains* to the Hurons and other Algonquin tribes. Like most other such features, it was stripped and looted over the years and even by the 1830s was barely half of its original height. It no longer exists.

remains: parts of a dead body that have not yet decomposed

One of the most significant yet least noted Native American influences on the natural resources of the state was the use of fire as a management tool. Parklike oak lands covered much of the southern three tiers of Michigan counties. Early settlers found them tempting because unlike thickly wooded lands, which required considerable effort to clear, the oak openings could be quickly put under the plow, yielding good crops almost immediately. In many cases, the settlers may have been enjoying the results of Native American land practices. Indians used fire to maintain trails and forest openings, clear fields for domesticated crops, herd animals toward a harvesting zone, and fertilize cropped land and encourage wild food plants. In addition to creating the oak openings, fire may well have maintained the jack pine plains of central lower Michigan. Native American agricultural practices are also thought to have converted beech-maple forests in the northernmost extremity of the Lower Peninsula to pine-oak by the time of European settlement.

First contact between Europeans and Native Americans had also significantly altered the face of Michigan by the early nineteenth century. The fur trade, conducted principally by French and English firms for approximately 200 years in the Great Lakes region, had significantly depleted the beaver population of Michigan. This, in turn, altered the region's hydrology.

Adapted from Dave Dempsey, *Ruin and Recovery: Michigan's Rise as a Conservation Leader* (Ann Arbor: University of Michigan Press, 2002), 13–14.

QUESTIONS ABOUT PRACTICE READING 2

1. The word dramatic in this passage is closest in meaning to
    a. shocking
    b. entertaining
    c. noticeable
    d. beneficial

2. The word landscape in this passage is closest in meaning to
    a. population
    b. territory
    c. natural resource
    d. shoreline

3. The word hand in this passage is closest in meaning to
    a. part of a game
    b. part of the body
    c. damage
    d. influence

4. The word traces in this passage is closest in meaning to

    a. signs

    b. messages

    c. roads

    d. openings

5. The word dotted in this passage is closest in meaning to

    a. ruined the beauty of

    b. marked the border of

    c. improved the soil of

    d. appeared at various places within

6. The word striking in this passage is closest in meaning to

    a. impassible

    b. impressive

    c. unlikely

    d. ancient

7. The word ascribed in this passage implies something is

    a. gave credit for

    b. gave blame for

    c. wrote letters about

    d. made carvings of

8. The word tempting in this passage implies something is

    a. immoral

    b. time-consuming

    c. attractive

    d. fertile

9. The word clear in this passage is closest in meaning to

    a. discover

    b. purchase

    c. remove trees from

    d. plant crops in

10. The word converted in this passage is closest in meaning to

    a. transported

    b. transformed

    c. shared

    d. turned over

11. The word conducted in this passage is closest in meaning to

    a. operated

    b. dominated

    c. explained

    d. invented

12. The word depleted in this passage is closest in meaning to

    a. eliminated

    b. reduced

    c. increased

    d. sickened

DISCUSSION OF PRACTICE READING 2

Question/Item	Answer	Explanation
1. **dramatic**	c	The passage contrasts *dramatic* with *subtle* ("hard to notice"). Also, if you know that a drama is a kind of play, you might reason that something dramatic is easily seen. If you made this connection, you would have to use the context as a clue *not* to choose *b*.
2. **landscape**	b	The idea of changes to an area of land is carried through several sentences in this paragraph. Landscape is parallel to land in Sentence 2 and to "face of the state" in Sentence 3.
3. **hand**	d	This familiar word is used in an unusual meaning. By looking at the context, you can eliminate the most common meaning ("body part"). Of the remaining choices, *influence* most closely relates to the details about how humans have changed the land.
4. **traces**	a	The phrase *these traces* refers to the previous sentence, which mentions *signs*.

Question /Item	Answer	Explanation
5. **dotted**	d	If you are familiar with the word *dot,* you can get an image of points appearing at different places. Also, the context shows that this sentence is meant only to introduce the existence of the mounds and earthworks. Choices *a, b,* and *c* present ideas that are not supported in the rest of the paragraph, so they are unlikely meanings.
6. **striking**	b	The details that follow are about its large size and the large number of skeletons inside. These features cause it to impress people who see or hear about it—make them think it is great and unusual.
7. **ascribed**	a	This is a difficult item, because the context is not very strong. Choices *a* and *b* both fit the context. However, the idea of blame (choice *b*) would require some evidence that the mounds were wrong or harmful in some way. The passage doesn't contain any sense of "wrongness." Notice that, in this case, word parts could mislead you. The word part *scribe* often refers to writing, but not here. The modern meaning of *ascribe* does not imply any writing.
8. **tempting**	c	The rest of the sentence tells why people would want to go to these places, so *attractive* ("desirable") is the best choice.
9. **clear**	c	Choice **c** names the most likely effect of fire on fields.
10. **converted**	b	Word parts (*con-* meaning "with" and *vert-* meaning "turn") could help you. Also, the phrase "to pine-oak" later in the sentence indicates a change. *Maple, beech, pine,* and *oak* are all names of kinds of trees.
11. **conducted**	a	Choices *a* and *b* both seem logically possible, but *dominated* does not fit well with the adverb *principally.*
12. **depleted**	b	Word parts could help you. The prefix *de-* means "away" or "not," and *-plete* means "full"; think of the word *complete.* Choice *a* is not a good fit, because beavers still live in such areas. Even if you didn't know that, you could reject choice *a* because it doesn't go well with the adverb *significantly.*

Review: Vocabulary

The following section contains three long passages for practice. Each passage is followed by some vocabulary questions similar to those you might be asked in an English for Academic Purposes class or on a communication-oriented test like the 2005 TOEFL®. (Content-oriented questions were practiced in the previous part of this section.)

This section of practice passages does not include any writing or speaking questions. Such questions are practiced in the Writing and Speaking parts of this book and in the Practice Test.

Vocabulary Review Passage 1

(1)   Herbal medicine is perhaps the fastest growing category of complementary and alternative medicine. Most patients do not tell their physicians about use of dietary supplements, and relatively few physicians presently inquire about such use or are versed in herbal medicine. A few herbs have become more popular and/or proved more effective than their synthetic counterparts, while others have raised concerns about potential adverse herb-drug interactions.

(2)   Regulation of dietary supplements presents perhaps the greatest area of regulatory controversy in complementary and alternative medicine regulation today. Ongoing efforts by one agency of the federal government, the Food and Drug Administration (FDA), to increase enforcement efforts have generated intense debates among lawmakers, consumers, providers, and supplement manufacturers.

(3)   In addition, the complementary and alternative medicine practices involving dietary supplements illustrate the clash in paradigms alluded to earlier: while herbal medicine is being widely researched and efforts are being made to understand herbs from a strictly pharmacological perspective, many complementary and alternative medicine practitioners regard herbs as sacred, having properties beyond those conferred by their chemistry. In Native American traditions, for example, the relationship between humans and herbs involves profound relationship exchange; in traditional oriental medicine, herbs are chosen to influence *chi*, the Chinese notion of vital energy, rather than produce specific pharmacological responses. Even researchers recognize that many herbs, particularly in Chinese and Tibetan medicine, have multiple active ingredients that may have a *synergistic* effect on the body. And some herbal formulas have effects that are not understood—for example, research has shown *that* but not *why* St. John's wort elevates mood. Whether herbs have a biofield effect—for example, the consciousness of the herb (such as a property relating to happiness) interacting with the consciousness of the human being—has not been extensively considered.

synergistic: acting together in a way that increases the power of the components

(4)   The starting point for current debate regarding regulation of dietary supplements in the United States is the federal Dietary Supplements Health and Education Act (DSHEA), enacted in 1994. One of the major justifications

the statute provides for its enactment is the need to "protect the right of access of consumers to safe dietary supplements . . . in order to promote wellness." This justification is amplified in the report of the Senate Committee on Labor and Human Resources on the DSHEA. The committee specifically found that the FDA had "pursued a regulatory agenda which discourages . . . citizens seeking to improve their health through dietary supplementation" and that "[i]n fact, the FDA has had a long history of bias against dietary supplements . . . [and] pursued a heavy-handed enforcement agenda against dietary supplements for over 30 years."

(5)   In light of these findings and comments, the DSHEA has had enormous popular appeal yet has generated controversy among regulatory authorities. Since the statute's enactment, various regulatory proposals have circulated to further restrict consumer access to dietary supplements. Rather than devoting detailed analysis to one or more such specific proposals, I will address a broader and more pervasive question—namely, ideally, how should the government regulate dietary supplements? In setting controls on the dietary supplement market, should regulation tip toward restriction or freedom? How do underlying beliefs about consumer health and intelligence shape regulatory values, policies, and rules? In what ways do the paradigmatic differences between conventional medicine, on the one hand, and complementary and alternative medicine, on the other, suggest the way that underlying belief systems ultimately influence the regulatory stance and resulting legal rules?

Adapted from Michael H. Cohen, *Beyond Complementary Medicine: Legal and Ethical Perspectives on Health Care and Human Evolution* (Ann Arbor: University of Michigan Press, 2001).

1. The word alternative in this passage is closest in meaning to

   a. unusual

   b. ineffective

   c. natural

   d. scientific

2. The word adverse in this passage is closest in meaning to

    a. harmful

    b. unknown

    c. well-publicized

    d. beneficial

3. The word generated in this passage is closest in meaning to

    a. turned

    b. stopped

    c. evaluated

    d. caused

4. The term alluded to in this passage is closest in meaning to

    a. defined

    b. joked about

    c. mentioned

    d. sent to

5. The word pharmacological in this passage is closest in meaning to

    a. chemical

    b. spiritual

    c. dietary

    d. strict

6. The word notion in this passage is closest in meaning to

    a. cream

    b. idea

    c. dream

    d. country

7. The word multiple in this passage is closest in meaning to

    a. foreign

    b. helpful

    c. increased

    d. several

8. The word property in this passage is closest in meaning to

   a. land

   b. possession

   c. plant

   d. aspect

9. The word justifications in this passage is closest in meaning to

   a. alignments

   b. supporters

   c. reasons

   d. simplifications

10. The word regulatory in this passage is closest in meaning to

    a. normal

    b. straight

    c. controlling

    d. official

11. The word restrict in this passage is closest in meaning to

    a. limit

    b. promote

    c. report

    d. end

12. The word tip in this passage is closest in meaning to

    a. turn over

    b. lean

    c. advise

    d. sharpen

13. The word conventional in this passage is closest in meaning to

    a. usual

    b. strange

    c. effective

    d. useless

Vocabulary Review Passage 2

(1) In 1947, two years after the bombs were dropped, the Atomic Bomb Casualty Commission (ABCC) was established by the U.S. National Academy of Sciences to study their health effects on the survivors. In 1975, funding was partially shifted to the government of Japan and the ABCC was given a new name, the Radiation Effects Research Foundation. (It was agreed by both Japanese and Americans that the words "atomic bomb" should be removed from the name.)

(2) The actual studies did not begin until 1950, five years after the bombs were dropped , when Japan took a national census. Citizens were asked where they had been on the fateful days of August 6, 1945, and August 9, 1945, and a survivor population of 195,000 was identified. Over the next ten years, about half of the survivors were interviewed and asked where they were standing in relation to the blasts and whether they'd experienced symptoms associated with radiation exposure—whether they'd suffered bleeding, coughing up blood, blood in the stool, purpura spots (vivid, purple spots in the skin that are evidence of bleeding), patches of spontaneous bruising, acute lesions of lips and tongue, hair loss. On the basis of the symptoms they described and their distance from the explosions, the *dose* they'd received was estimated. Dose estimates ranged from low to over four hundred rads, with every possible gradation in between, though estimates were approximate, taken on trust and memory, and dose reconstruction was crude. The radiation the bombs gave off was calculated on the basis of tests conducted in the Nevada desert. The blasts had created a kind of human laboratory for studying the effects of radiation. The survivors became the largest population of humans exposed to radiation for whom estimates of doses are available. One Japanese radiation expert noted that he had been able to experiment only on rabbits, while the Americans had conducted a human experiment.

dose: amount taken in

(3) No medical study ever has had such resources lavished on it and so many scientists involved. It had—and still has—staffs of hundreds, scientists from all over the world; it has state-of-the-art equipment, computers, and data-gathering and analyzing facilities. Since the enterprise is so large and lavishly funded, and since in epidemiology, the larger the sample, the greater the statistical accuracy—or so it is believed—there has been a tendency to accept these studies without question. The ABCC/RERF has produced "pages and pages, volumes and volumes of official reports, unofficial reports and what have you," as Alice says.

(4)   There are many powerful committees concerned with radiation protection, and they all accept the calculations of the Radiation Effects Research Foundation (RERF). The International Commission on Radiation Protection (ICRP), the United Nations Scientific Committee on the Effects of Atomic Radiation (UNSCEAR), the International Atomic Energy Agency (IAEA) all agree that RERF estimates are applicable to all situations involving radiation risks, including nuclear work and medical x-rays. In addition to the international committees are the national committees—the National Radiation Protection Board (NRPB) in England and the Biological Effects of Ionizing Radiation Committee, a special committee of the National Academy of Sciences (NAS), in the United States. The national committees are free to modify the recommendations of the international committees, but in practice they do not—they take the word of the International Commission on Radiation Protection and the ICRP takes the word of the Radiation Effects Research Foundation. The ICRP's 1990 report, ICRP 60, is based on RERF data.

(5)   The U.S. committee on Biological Effects of Ionizing Radiation (BEIR) is the most prestigious of the national committees. It has produced several reports, numbered in sequence, BEIR I, BEIR II, and so on. The 1990 report, BEIR V, is commonly regarded as the gold standard for radiogenic risk estimates and the most comprehensive overview of the health effects of radiation. It too is based on RERF data.

(6)   The RERF assumes a linearity of dose-response relationships: you can move down a line from high to low dose and can figure out, according to a principle of linear extrapolation, radiation risk at low dose. BEIR V and ICRP 60 proclaim that if the dose is small and is accumulated over time (as it is in the case of nuclear workers), cancer risk will be less than that predicted by linear extrapolation. It has been assumed that if the dose is low enough, risk will disappear entirely; this implies there is a safe level of radiation, a threshold beneath which radiation presents no danger (though this position is being modified, as we'll see).

(7)   When the ABCC began its study in 1950, it concluded that the population had returned to normal; the RERF concurred. According to their calculations, the death rate from all causes except cancer had returned to normal.

Adapted from Gayle Greene, *The Woman Who Knew Too Much: Alice Stewart and the Secrets of Radiation* (Ann Arbor: University of Michigan Press, 2001), 131–32.

1. In this passage, the word dropped is closest in meaning to

    a. rejected

    b. decreased

    c. caused to stop

    d. caused to fall

2. In this passage, the word blasts is closest in meaning to

    a. criticisms

    b. celebrations

    c. bombs

    d. explosions

3. In this passage, the word lesions is closest in meaning to

    a. cuts

    b. studies

    c. vacations

    d. photographs

4. In this passage, the word gradation is closest in meaning to

    a. injury

    b. level

    c. test

    d. thanks

5. In this passage, the word laboratory is closest in meaning to

    a. place for manufacturing

    b. place for washing

    c. place for experimenting

    d. place for medical treatment

6. In this passage, the term state-of-the-art is closest in meaning to

   a. up-to-date

   b. government-funded

   c. creative

   d. conditional

7. In this passage, the word lavishly is closest in meaning to

   a. in large amounts

   b. from time to time

   c. with great difficulty

   d. in a clean way

8. In this passage, the word accept is closest in meaning to

   a. exclude

   b. include

   c. believe

   d. receive

9. In this passage, the word modify is closest in meaning to

   a. reject

   b. read

   c. discuss

   d. change

10. In this passage, the word linearity is closest in meaning to

    a. flexibility

    b. steadiness

    c. increase

    d. suddenness

11. In this passage, the word accumulated is closest in meaning to

    a. reduced

    b. responsive

    c. noticed

    d. built up

12. In this passage, the word threshold is closest in meaning to

    a. body

    b. shelter

    c. point

    d. grasp

Vocabulary Review Passage 3

(1)   Since the 19th century, cultural diffusionists have explained shared features among various cultures in terms of a process of contact and borrowing. If two cultures share a distinctive burial style or fishing method, the members of one culture are assumed to have learned it by meeting and observing the members of the other. This process of adopting another culture's traits is known as acculturation. It stands in contrast to invention, which is the process of coming up with a cultural practice independently.

(2)   The basic practices of most human societies were established long before recorded history, so their origins remain a matter of speculation. Archaeology and physical anthropology can go only so far in producing indisputable physical evidence of the pedigree of a cultural trait. It is well-known, for example, that the sweet potato is native to South America yet cultivated in Southeast Asia. The route it traveled and the nature of its passage must be inferred from tenuous evidence, which is necessarily interpreted in the light of prevailing theory. Diffusionism offers one interpretation of the evidence and has always had its advocates, but it hardly prevails. Indeed, much of the anthropological community rejects diffusionist explanations as pseudo-science.

(3)   Diffusionists run the gamut from the extreme to the mild. The former, such as G. Elliot Smith, posit very few centers from which cultural features radiate. In Smith's characterization, there was only one such center—ancient Egypt—for all advanced cultural achievements, such as writing. Less extreme diffusionists include well-known anthropologists of the early to middle 20th century such as Franz Boas and R. H. Lowie. Their approach, while emphasizing the importance of contact among cultures, allowed for individual invention as well. In other words, if two cultures shared a burial style or a peculiar fishing method, one might have borrowed it from the other or each

might have come up with the idea on its own. Nor did this mild viewpoint restrict the center of diffusion to one place. Several centers might have functioned simultaneously to spread cultural features, much as a handful of pebbles thrown into a pond will generate several ripple patterns from several centers.

(4) Laypersons are perhaps most familiar with diffusionist thought through the well-documented adventures of Thor Heyerdahl, whose non-academic approach and unconventional theories appealed somewhat less to anthropologists than to the general public. Cultural similarities between the Americas and the islands of Polynesia had intrigued Heyerdahl ever since, as young *newlyweds,* he and his wife Liv had gone to live in the hills above a village on the Marquesan island of Fatu-Hiva. Similarities among Polynesian statues and artifacts of both South America and British Columbia had planted in Heyerdahl the idea of some prehistoric contact. This idea was not unique to Heyerdahl. Many anthropologists have long been willing to believe in pre-Columbian journeys from Polynesia to America—and then even back again. Heyerdahl made his mark by going further than anyone else to demonstrate that the direction of this diffusion was from the opposite direction: east to west, from the Americas to the islands. In 1947, his *Kon-Tiki,* a balsa-log raft constructed in a traditional style, successfully rode the Humboldt Current from Peru to Polynesia. Heyerdahl's film account of the voyage would eventually win him an Academy Award (Best Documentary, 1951), but his achievement was hardly applauded among mainstream anthropologists. The prevailing view was that Heyerdahl had shown only what might have occasionally happened to a few severely off-course sailors, not any pattern of ongoing contact.

newlyweds: people who were recently married

(5) The *Kon-Tiki* expedition, as well as several later voyages by Heyerdahl using early shipcraft, sounds a theme common among the most controversial diffusionist claims: sea contact among currently disparate cultures. Recent controversies have centered on pre-Columbian contact between the coasts of Europe and North America. That Norse sailors crossed to present-day Canada in early times is now well accepted. That they actually influenced any of the cultures of North America is not. Yet the debate continues over certain runic carvings (those using an ancient Scandinavian writing system) found at points as far inland as Minnesota and Kentucky. This encourages

those diffusionists who credit the Vikings with doing more than landing at L'Anse aux Meadows in about 1000 C.E., staying for three years, and either dying or going home. Similar claims have been made for other Europeans, including the Welsh. At the same time, the anthropological establishment is reluctant to give credence to such claims, not just because they sound fanciful but also because their European focus is presumed to lack respect for the cultural inventiveness of Native Americans.

1. In this passage, the word acculturation is closest in meaning to
    a. giving out a cultural trait
    b. taking on a cultural trait
    c. observing a cultural trait
    d. originating a cultural trait

2. In this passage, the word speculation is closest in meaning to
    a. seeing
    b. recording
    c. borrowing
    d. guessing

3. In this passage, the word pedigree is closest in meaning to
    a. nature
    b. ancestry
    c. animal
    d. location

4. In this passage, the word tenuous is closest in meaning to
    a. weak
    b. obvious
    c. old
    d. disputed

5. In this passage, the word prevails is closest in meaning to

    a. exists

    b. explains

    c. interprets

    d. dominates

6. In this passage, the term run the gamut is closest in meaning to

    a. change

    b. escape

    c. range

    d. operate

7. In this passage, the word shared is closest in meaning to

    a. gave to each other

    b. confided in each other

    c. possessed together

    d. learned about

8. In this passage, the word laypersons is closest in meaning to

    a. nonspecialists

    b. anthropologists

    c. academics

    d. diffusionists

9. In this passage, the word intrigued is closest in meaning to

    a. gone inside

    b. made secret plans

    c. interested

    d. worried

10. In this passage, the word applauded is closest in meaning to

    a. praised

    b. mentioned

    c. criticized

    d. clapped

11. In this passage, the word disparate is closest in meaning to

    a. coastal

    b. frustrated

    c. advanced

    d. different

12. In this passage, the word credence is closest in meaning to

    a. expression

    b. challenge

    c. belief

    d. attention

PART 2

Listening

Four General Test-Taking Strategies for the Listening Section

A few general listening strategies will improve your performance on the listening section of the 2005 TOEFL®.

1. Commit your attention to the audio. Listen with focus to the speakers, and engage yourself in the content of the talk. Do not let your mind wander.

2. Take notes. Write as much as you can while listening.

3. Envision the speakers. Make them real people in an actual setting you can see in your mind. Some communicative tests contain visual prompts. These can help you envision the speakers and scene. On the 2005 TOEFL®, a photo of the setting is displayed on the screen as you listen.

4. Focus on words that you can understand. Do not obsess over words that you don't know.

Listening in English is the best way to become a better listener and to prepare for the listening sections of communication-oriented tests like the 2005 TOEFL®. By practicing listening, you can increase your speed of comprehension and familiarize yourself with spoken English. Listening regularly to English can help make English more a part of your daily life. In particular, listening to academic-style lectures and discussions can help you build your academic listening skills.

Building Skills: Listening for Main Ideas

Basic Skills	Some Related Academic Tasks	Related Tasks on Tests like the 2005 TOEFL®
1. **Identifying the main idea of a talk or conversation** 2. **Notetaking** 3. **Indentifying speaker's purpose or attitude**	• learning more efficiently • writing a well-focused summary • answering multiple-choice questions on tests about main ideas • taking notes during a class lecture • identifying the purpose of lectures • participating in class discussions	• answering multiple-choice questions about main ideas • answering questions about speaker's purpose or attitude

On academic listening tasks and on communication-oriented tests like the 2005 TOEFL®, you will be heavily tested on your global comprehension of a passage. In other words, many test questions will ask you to identify the main ideas of a passage. Many standard listening passages have one topic that is then divided into three or four main ideas. Questions about main ideas commonly take the following forms:

Example Main Idea Questions

What are the people mainly discussing?

What is the topic of the lecture?

What are the three main ideas in the presentation?

What are the main points in the talk?

How to Find Main Ideas

Identifying the main idea of a listening passage is similar to identifying the main idea of a reading passage, which you learned in Part 1. If you have not studied the concept of identifying main ideas in Part 1: Reading in this book, you should do so before you continue. In brief, every passage has one main topic. The topic can be stated in one sentence. The topic is usually presented in three or four main ideas.

To identify main ideas, follow these steps:

1. Pay special attention to the beginning of the talk. The main idea is usually mentioned near the start of a talk. It may be mentioned in the first lines of the talk, but it also might follow some opening comments.

2. Listen for words that are repeated throughout the talk. These may give a clue to the main idea.

3. When you hear a supporting detail, ask, "What point does this detail support?" Details include facts, figures, examples, and specific instances that support the main idea. For example, to make the main point that basketball players are tall, you might mention the detail that a certain player is seven feet tall.

4. Listen for phrases that set up the main idea:

   - *The point is . . . .*
   - *Today I'm going to talk about . . . .*
   - *When you talk about global warming, people usually think . . . .*

5. Take notes about the talk. Write down each main idea. Do not rely on your memory to hold onto the talk.

6. Pay attention to summarizing comments at the end of the talk. The main idea is often restated at the end of talk.

Practice 1 (with Answer Analysis)
Lecture: Economic Conditions

Listen to part of an economics lecture originally given by Clair Brown, Professor of Economics at the University of California, Berkeley. Answer the questions that follow by circling the best response. Press Play.

1. What is the main topic of the talk?

    a. aircraft manufacturing

    b. employment

    c. national financial situation

    d. personal savings

2. What is the state of the U.S. economy?

    a. It's in a recession.

    b. It's unclear, but growth is slow.

    c. Indicators consistently show strength.

    d. It's strong with some signs of turning.

3. How does the professor organize the information in this part of her lecture?

    a. She relays events in the order that they occurred.

    b. She states the main idea then supports it with details.

    c. She states several details that lead her to conclude with her main idea.

    d. She restates the main idea in several different ways.

ANSWER ANALYSIS

Now look at the correct answers and the discussions that follow.

1. The main topic of the talk is economic conditions, **c.** The other three answer options refer to details in the talk. The talk mentions the aircraft sector, unemployment and jobs, and personal savings, but only as support for the main idea.

2. The U.S. economy is in a period of slow growth, but it can't yet be called a recession, so the answer is **b.** The first sentence of the lecture says this using different words. *(We are not sure if the U.S. economy is in a recession because there are mixed indicators.)* The other answer options use vocabulary that commonly refers to the economy: *recession, indicators, strength, signs of turning.*

3. This lecture is organized in a classic fashion, making **b** the correct answer. Note how the lecturer stated the main idea and then supported it with details. Answers *a* and *c* are possible organizational structures for a talk on the economy, but they are not used here. Answer *d* describes a lecture that would not be very interesting or convincing. In fact, few trained speakers would repeatedly state their main idea.

Identifying the Main Idea

EXERCISE 1

Listen to the talk on economic indicators again. As you listen, read the beginning few words from each sentence of the talk (page 84) that follow. Next to each sentence, write a number from 0 to 5 to indicate how this sentence relates to the main idea of the passage. Note that some sentences connect to the main idea in two or more ways. Use the numbers 0 through 5 to identify the sentence. You may start and stop the audio freely. (Answers may vary. Sample answers are in the answer key.) Press Play.

0 = Sentence does not specifically support the main idea.
1 = Sentence states the main idea in the opening of the talk.
2 = Sentence repeats words from the main idea.
3 = Detail in sentence supports main idea.
4 = Speaker draws focus to main idea.
5 = Speaker restates the main idea near end of talk.

_____ "We are not sure . . . ."

_____ "The unemployment rate . . . ."

_____ "Unfortunately this is not sustainable . . . ."

_____ "Personal consumption climbed . . . ."

_____ "However, people were . . . ."

_____ "The U.S. has the lowest . . . ."

_____ "Factory orders rose . . . ."

_____ "Productivity in the second quarter . . . ."

_____ "Ideally, productivity should grow . . . ."

_____ "Still, productivity grew . . . ."

_____ "These are mixed signs . . . ."

_____ "In any case, we are in . . . ."

EXERCISE 2

The organization of this talk on the state of the economy is typical. The professor states the main idea, gives supporting details, and concludes by restating the main idea. Based on this information, where would you expect to hear the main idea in the talk? Check your answer in the answer key.

    a. at the beginning and end of the talk

    b. after some opening comments

    c. in the middle of the talk

    d. just before the conclusion of the talk

EXERCISE 3

Read the transcript of the economics lecture you just heard. Underline the main idea. It is stated twice.

We are not sure if the U.S. economy is in a recession because there are mixed indicators. The unemployment rate fell from 5.9% to 5.7% from July to August, which is good news. Unfortunately this is not sustainable job growth because the new jobs were mostly the result of a one-time increase in government jobs. Personal consumption climbed 1% in July, which is good because it comprises two-thirds of GDP. However, people were spending more and the savings rate dropped to 3.4%, as personal income remained unchanged. The U.S. has the lowest savings rate of any developed economy.

Factory orders rose 4.7% in July after falling 2.5% in June, though most of these orders were in the aircraft sector. Productivity in the second quarter grew at an annual rate of 1.5%, which is very low. Ideally, productivity should grow at 2% to 3%, so we experience growth in per capita income. Still, productivity grew at 4.8% for the year that ended in June, which is very good news. These are mixed signs about the economy, so we cannot tell if we are in a recession right now. In any case, we are in a period of slow growth.

Check your answers in the answer key.

Practice 2
Conversation: Two Students

People do not usually formally state the topic of a conversation. Instead, their topic and their main points may appear gradually, in bits and pieces. Or, their comments may give clues to the topic, which may never be explicitly stated. When listening to a conversation, you must pull together many details of the conversation to summarize the point.

Listen to the following conversation between two university students. Answer the questions that follow by circling the best response. Pause the audio after the lecture and before your hear "Question 4." When you are ready to answer Question 4, press Play. You will have to restart the audio for Question 4. Check your answers in the answer key. Press Play.

1. What is the main topic of the talk?
    a. library rooms
    b. note-taking skills
    c. a lecture
    d. a homework assignment

2. How do the students feel about the lecture?
    a. It was hard to follow because there was so much information.
    b. It was confusing because some of the facts and tables contradicted others.
    c. It didn't relate clearly to the reading or handouts.
    d. It was so boring that they had a hard time staying awake.

3. What do they plan to do?

    a. look for good books on the topic

    b. meet with the professor to ask for clarification

    c. work together on their homework

    d. review the information and share their notes

4. Listen again to part of the talk. Then answer the question.

    What does the man mean when he says, "We had to make it up somewhere"?

    a. Ultimately they had to take the test.

    b. They had to cover extra material from the missed days.

    c. They were bound to find gaps in their information.

    d. Research was necessary to fill in the blanks.

Organization and Note-Taking

In an academic setting, most students take notes. It is a fundamental academic skill. Additionally, many modern communication-oriented tests like the 2005 TOEFL® also allow note-taking. Taking notes is one of the most important skills for listening to long passages because it can significantly increase your chance of answering questions correctly. No one is expected to listen to long talks or speeches and remember everything; taking notes allows a listener to write down what is important and what he or she wants to remember.

> **Benefits of Note-Taking**
> - Provides a written record of what you heard
> - Focuses your attention
> - Forces you to link ideas
> - Organizes information
> - Offers opportunity for study and review
> - Reveals gaps in the lecture or in your understanding
> - Helps you ask relevant questions
> - Increases your score on tests

Taking notes is a complex skill. It's an art, not a science. Two people listening to the same lecture may take very different notes. They may vary both in content and in style.

Note-takers must choose what to include and what not to include. They must decide, with very little planning, how to organize the notes.

Good note-takers must recognize what is important in a lecture. They must recognize how information is related. They can summarize what they've heard quickly and write about it concisely.

Still, there is no such thing as "perfect notes." Because of their nature, notes are frequently incomplete or messy. It is normal to add quick words in the margin, or to draw arrows between thoughts to show an important connection. Some note-takers add their own questions or comments in the margin.

Like any skill, taking good notes requires practice. The more you work on it, the better you will be. As well, you can actively learn new note-taking skills, including those that are taught in this part of the book. In addition to the practice offered in this textbook, you may practice taking notes in classes, while listening to news on the radio or TV, and while listening to any planned presentation.

Note Style

Good notes show both the ideas in a lecture and the relationship of those ideas to each other. One common way to take notes is by using **indentations.** In this method, the note-taker aligns general points with the left-hand margin. Under each general point, the note-taker indents the specific points and supporting information. Under each specific point, the note-taker further indents specific examples. In formal note-taking, an outline may include structural cues such as I, A, 1, 2, a, b, as in the following model:

I. The first general point

    A. A specific point that supports the general point

    B. Another specific point that supports the general point

        1. A detail about the specific point (a number, for example)

        2. Another detail about the specific point (a story, for example)

II. The second general point

While taking notes for the 2005 TOEFL®, you may not have much time to take formally organized notes. Still, even scattered notes can be helpful if they reflect the connection between the ideas in the lecture.

Time Effectiveness

Do not worry about spelling, punctuation, or grammar in your notes. Efficiency is the key. You may even take some notes in your native language, if that is faster for you.

EXERCISE 4
LECTURE: GATHERING INFORMATION

Listen to part of a psychology lecture that was originally given by Clark McKown, Ph.D., a faculty fellow in the Department of Psychology at the University of California, Berkeley. Complete the notes below so that you will be able to answer the questions that follow. For this exercise, you may listen to the lecture as many times as you want to in order to understand enough to complete the notes. Press Play.

Topic: Types of Data

I. Clinical Interview (bipolar video)

    A. Unstruct.

        1. skill

        2. ++ Many sides of person

        3. -- _____

    B. Structured

        1. better inter-rater rel.

        2. _____

II. Psychological Testing

    A. Personality Inventory: MMPI

        1. 400 questions

        2. empirical

dep, mania   3. 9 scales rel. to DSM

        4. ↑ score, ↑ trait

    B. _____

        1. ++ = diagnose learning disorders

    C. _____

        Ex. Rorschach: neutral stim. shows unconscious thought

        Ex. TAT picture stories

        1. Neg points

            -- ?? Really show unconscious?

            -- _____

III. _____

    A. Observe

    B. Make Inferences

    C. Third-party reports

        1. esp. children/classroom

IV. Biological Measures

    A. Neuroimaging

    B. _____

        —Sample behavior shows brain function

        —Before/after measurement

Answer the following questions about the lecture. Use your notes as needed.

1. What is the main topic of the lecture?

    a. types of data

    b. reliability

    c. biology

    d. brain damage

2. Each box contains examples of a certain type of data. Write the letter of each type of data in the space where it belongs. Use each letter only once.

    a. clinical interviews

    b. psychological testing

    c. behavioral measures

    d. biological measures

Structured discussion Unstructured consultation

Personality inventories Projectives

Neuroimaging techniques Neuropsychological tests

Observation Third-party reports

3. What type of tests would be useful in diagnosing learning disorders?

    a. intelligence tests, such as IQ tests

    b. observation of a child in a classroom

    c. structured interviews

    d. neuroimaging techniques

4. What is a projective?

    a. a study in which a researcher observes a subject doing a project

    b. an image that is manipulated or created by a subject

    c. a test based on a subject's verbal response to a visual stimulus such as a picture

    d. a type of hypnosis that reveals unconscious fantasies

You answered four questions about the lecture. For how many questions did you look at your notes? _____

Check your answers in the answer key.

Practice 3
Lecture: Gender

Listen to part of a biology lecture originally given by Toby Bradshaw, Professor of Biology at the University of Washington. Take notes. Answer the questions that follow by circling the best response. Press Play.

1. What is the main topic of this talk?
   a. genes
   b. sexuality
   c. chromosomes
   d. sex determination

2. What determines gender in crocodilians?
   a. environment
   b. diet
   c. chromosomes
   d. soil composition

3. What three types of sex determination are discussed?

    a. chromosomal, dietary, and WZ

    b. hormonal, seasonal, and temperature-based

    c. lunar, cyclical, and solar

    d. XY, environmental, and WZ

4. How does the professor organize the information in this lecture segment?

    a. He states the topic, gives examples, then he repeats the main idea.

    b. He gives examples and then asks students to draw a conclusion.

    c. He talks about various theories and then states his own opinion.

    d. He states a thesis and then discusses the merits of research on the thesis.

Check your answers in the answer key.

Building Skills: Listening for Details

Basic Skill	Some Related Academic Tasks	Related Tasks on Tests like the 2005 TOEFL®
Identifying the details of a talk or conversation	• learning efficiently • supporting a main idea with details • answering multiple-choice questions on tests • taking notes during a class lecture • weighing the value of evidence • participating in class discussions	• answering multiple-choice questions about details • writing about what you've heard • speaking about what you've heard

In homework, on academic tests, and on communication-oriented tests like the 2005 TOEFL®, your ability to identify details is a common activity. Detail questions often begin with question words: *who, what, when, where, why, how, which,* or *whose.* The following are typical detail questions.

Example Questions about Details

Who supported this theory?

What happened after the money was lost?

When did this discovery take place?

Where was this disease first identified?

Why did the strikers protest?

How did the community react to the election?

How to Listen for Details

You have already studied the concept of main ideas. Listening passages on academic tests usually have one topic. This topic is presented in a few main ideas. These main ideas, in turn, are supported by details. Details often include facts, figures, statistics, and anecdotes.

Identifying the details of a listening passage is a similar task to understanding content in a reading passage. If you have not studied the section about understanding content in Part 1: Reading in this book, you should do so before you continue.

One of the most important ways to grasp and remember details from a lecture is to take notes. When you write down ideas, you have a visual representation of the relationship of the ideas. This record is crucial to your answering many detail questions correctly.

To identify details, follow these steps:

1. Identify the topic and the main ideas of the talk. The relevant details are usually given after each main idea is stated. The details strengthen the main ideas.

2. Listen for statements that answer information questions containing *who, what, when, where, why, how, which,* or *whose.*

3. Listen for key phrases that introduce a detail:
   - *For example, ...*
   - *To show you what I mean, ...*
   - *I want to point out a few things, ...*

4. Anticipate the information that you will hear.

5. Take notes about the talk. Write down one or two key words that identify each detail. Do not rely on memory to hold onto details.

6. Listen for the meaning of each detail. Engage yourself mentally in the content of the talk. This will help you take better notes and remember information.

Practice 1 (with Answer Analysis)
Lecture: Mental Illness

Listen to part of a psychology lecture originally given by Clark McKown, Ph.D., a faculty fellow in the Department of Psychology at the University of California, Berkeley. While you listen, complete the notes below. The first general point and its supporting details have been done for you. To help you follow the main points, they have been numbered in this outline. However, if you would like to take notes in addition to those for which space is provided, you are encouraged to do so. For the purposes of this practice, you may start and stop the audio freely. Then, answer the questions that follow by circling the best response(s). (Note the use of abbreviations in these notes. You will study abbreviations later in this chapter.) Press Play.

Topic: DSM-IV

1. DSM-IV = categorical: do/don't

   Dprsn, schiz.—unvsl. flngs.

   Diag. crit. defs. illness

   Gradations

   ♀ in bed = depressed

   ♀ w/Normal life = depressed

2. Mental ill. has stigma

_____

_____

Balance harm vs. benefits of treatment

3. _____

   <u>Indvdl. disorders</u>

   <u>Disorders that occur together</u>

4. <u>Culture-Bound Syndromes</u>

   _____

   <u>Not in DSM-IV</u>

   <u>Latin Amer.</u>

   _____

5. <u>DSM-IV: ++</u>

   _____

   _____

   _____

1. What is the risk of labeling somebody with a mental disorder?

   a. The person may begin to act out new symptoms.

   b. Somebody with one disorder may self-diagnose a second, accompanying disorder.

   c. Professionals may stop searching for a diagnosis that would be more accurate.

   d. Society's judgment of mental illness may be harmful to the patient.

2. According to the lecture, which of the following is true of the DSM-IV taxonomy? (Choose two answers.)

   a. It categorically identifies whether a person has a mental illness.

   b. It allows users to self-diagnose by answering specific questions.

   c. It defines mental weakness as personal weakness.

   d. It relies on diagnostic criteria.

3. Which of the following are mentioned in the lecture as being true of the disorder called "nervios"?

   a. It has been identified in Latin America.

   b. The symptoms include crying and shaking.

   c. The DSM-IV covers it comprehensively.

   d. It is more common among men.

4. What is the lecturer's attitude toward the DSM-IV?

   a. It is the most comprehensive taxonomy available.

   b. It helps us discuss and research mental illness.

   c. Its weaknesses make it a dangerous tool.

   d. Its axes and limiting criteria make it very complex.

Compare your note-taking to the notes in the answer key. Check your multiple choice answers in the answer analysis that follows.

ANSWER ANALYSIS

1. The second main point in the lecture addresses mental illness. The lecturer says, "The act of labeling somebody with a mental disorder can harm someone." The correct response is **d**. Choices *a* and *c* might seem like realistic responses, but they aren't mentioned in this lecture. Choice *b* refers to the co-occurrence of certain illnesses that is mentioned in the lecture, but mental illness is not specified.

2. Question 2 is a good example of a question with two answers. For this question, you must choose two responses. The first main point in this lecture addresses the fact that the DSM-IV is a categorical taxonomy. The two correct responses to this question are **a** and **d**. Choice *b* is not a reasonable option because the lecturer mentions nothing about self-diagnosis. Choice *c* refers to the identification of mental weakness as personal weakness, but the DSM-IV does not make this judgment.

3. The answer is **a**. The lecture doesn't talk about the symptoms of nervios, so *b* is not correct. The lecturer argues that the DSM-IV may not cover nervios comprehensively enough, so *c* is not true. There is no mention of nervios occurring more commonly among men, so *d* is also incorrect.

4. The lecturer's attitude toward the DSM-IV is summarized in the final paragraph: "The DSM-IV has weaknesses, but there are advantages of a taxonomy. With a taxonomy, we can speak the same language when talking about mental illness. This allows us to build a science of mental illness and psychotherapy. It allows us to do research and clinical intervention." The correct response is **b**. Choices *a, c,* and *d* repeat words from the lecture, but none states an opinion stated by the lecturer.

Anticipating Information

Anticipating the information that you will hear can help you understand and retain information. Predicting the contents of a talk can help you to stay engaged in the topic.

To practice predicting information in a presentation, ask yourself *who, what, when, where, why, how, which,* or *whose.* These questions describe virtually every type of information that you will hear.

EXERCISE 1
CONVERSATION: A PROFESSOR AND A STUDENT

You will listen to a conversation between a professor and a student. They are discussing the student's grade in class. For the purpose of this exercise, you will not listen to the whole conversation from start to finish. Rather, you will listen to short segments. After each short segment, try to predict what you will hear next. You will need to start and pause the audio seven times for this exercise. (Pause the audio when the narrator says stop, in this exercise.)

<u>*Remember:*</u> *This is a skill-building exercise. It is designed to help you anticipate information. In academic and communicative testing situations, it is unlikely that you will see questions asking you to predict upcoming information. The questions in this exercise do not necessarily have correct or incorrect responses. Rather, the purpose of this exercise is to help you practice the skill of anticipation.*

Press Play.

1. What information do you predict will come next?

     a. the spelling of "Zodorsky"

     b. the purpose of the student's visit

     c. how the student came to school

     d. the student will name his major

Restart the audio to answer the second question.

2. What topic do you think the student will talk about next?

     a. his final test score

     b. his plans to take poli sci 102

     c. his distress about the textbook

     d. his feelings about his grade

Restart the audio to answer the third question.

3. What information do you predict will come next?

     a. the weight of note-taking in one's grade

     b. the importance of the mid-term paper

     c. the professor's opinion of the syllabus

     d. the reason that attendance isn't graded

Restart the audio to answer the fourth question.

4. What information do you predict will come next?

    a. a question about the grading policy

    b. a complaint about the computer software

    c. an explanation of the missing homework

    d. a comment about the quantity of homework assignments

Restart the audio to answer the fifth question.

5. What information do you predict will come next?

    a. an excuse for the poor mid-term grade

    b. an excuse for the whole second part of the quarter

    c. an explanation for the grade increase

    d. a defense for the poorly written paper

Restart the audio to answer the sixth question.

6. What information do you predict will come next?

    a. a description of the extra credit work

    b. an explanation of the student's choice of majors

    c. thanks for taking the time to discuss

    d. the name of the student's teaching assistant

Restart the audio to answer the seventh question.

7. What information do you predict will come next?

    a. a complaint from the professor about the disorganized notebook

    b. a request from the student for time to organize the papers

    c. a phone call to Coleman

    d. a question about the records

Restart the audio to hear the end of the dialogue.

To check your answers, listen to the whole dialogue again. It is recorded without interruption. Then, see the suggested answers in the answer key. Press Play.

Organizational Signals

When you are listening to a prepared speech, you may hear specific words that give information about the organization of the information. Let's call these **signal words.** These words help you understand the relationship of ideas in the speech to the main point. They can also help you predict what kind of information will follow.

Signal words show different types of information. For example, one typical type of signal word shows the order of presentation: *first, second, next, last.* Other words may introduce an idea that repeats or summarizes previous ideas.

Let's look at some common signal words in spoken English. Add some more that you know.

Words that Show Order	Words that Show Repetition or Summary	Words that Show a Relationship between Ideas	Words that Introduce a Detail or Example
First, second, third	*As I said,*	*In the same way,*	*For example,*
Next, last	*We already looked at*	*By contrast,*	*For instance,*
In addition,		*To make this even clearer,*	*To show you what I mean, let's talk about*
	So, we've talked about	*As a result/consequence,*	
	In summary,	*Including*	

EXERCISE 2
LECTURE: POVERTY

Listen to part of a lecture originally given by Dr. Jerry W. Sanders, lecturer in the Department of Peace and Conflict Studies at the University of California, Berkeley. Listen for the signal words in

his lecture. As you hear each one, check it off. You may listen more than once if necessary. Press Play.

_____ *including*

_____ *as a result of*

_____ *a classic example*

_____ *as a result of*

_____ *on this point*

_____ *for instance*

_____ *this is the point that*

_____ *also*

_____ *as a result of*

_____ *that kind of question*

Remember that speech is not always as predictable as we may hope. A lecturer may begin speaking from highly structured notes, but he or she may later leave the notes and begin speaking freely.

For this reason, a lecture does not always follow the same tight organization usually found in formal writing. For example, you may hear a first point clearly and a third point clearly, but the speaker may forget to mention the second point sufficiently. This should not stress you. Gaps in a lecture will naturally lead to gaps in your knowledge and your notes. (In real-life listening, such gaps are frequently the basis for questions to the speaker.)

<u>Remember:</u> If a speaker omits information about a topic, you won't be tested on that information.

For more practice with signal words, listen to other lectures on the accompanying audio CDs, or listen to presentations on the radio or television. Write down the key signal words that you hear.

Practice 2
Lecture: Poverty

Listen again to Dr. Sanders' lecture on poverty and violence. Take notes. Answer the questions that follow by circling the best response(s). (You will listen to the same track on the audio.) Press Play.

1. What is the main idea of this lecture?

   a. A recent forum, "We the People," set up a rubric for peace.

   b. The definition of *violence* should include structural violence where people are harmed and killed unintentionally.

   c. The International Monetary Fund's standards for creditworthiness are stringent.

   d. There is inequity in distribution of the world's resources.

2. How does the professor explain "structural violence"? (Choose two answers.)

   a. He defines it and gives examples.

   b. He brainstorms possible meanings.

   c. He compares it to other forms of violence.

   d. He explains its chronological development throughout recent history.

3. Why does the speaker mention the International Monetary Fund?

   a. as an example of a democratizing, international organization

   b. because the IMF hosted the "We the People's Forum"

   c. because IMF policies lead to structural violence

   d. as an example of an organization with good documentation

4. What prompted Ghandi's pronouncement that "poverty is the most deadly form of violence"?

   a. Guns in inner-city slums cause violence.

   b. Poverty and violence are intertwined.

   c. Poverty causes war.

   d. More people die from hunger than from war.

5. According to the lecture, what causes the death of one child every four minutes?

   a. wars, both civil and international

   b. malnutrition and lack of healthcare

   c. accidents, including land mines

   d. domestic violence

Check your answers in the answer key.

Abbreviations and Symbols in Note-Taking

Taking notes effectively requires speed. You must write quickly. You will not have time to write down every word. To save time, you should use abbreviations and symbols when taking notes.

Symbols

Some symbols are used commonly in English. You may create your own symbols as well. Remember, you are the only person who needs to be able to understand your symbols. You take notes for yourself, not for others.

Symbol	Meaning
&	and
@	at
=	is
≠	is not
<	is less than
>	is greater than
∴	therefore
+	a benefit
−	a drawback
♂	man
♀	woman
↑	increase
↓	decrease
!!	surprising news
$$	money

Abbreviations

An abbreviation is a shortened form of a word. Abbreviations often include the first few letters of a word. Or, they may include the consonants in a word, leaving out the vowels. Some abbreviations are standardized—almost everybody understands them and uses them in the same way. Other abbreviations may be created by just one person for personal use.

Abbreviation	Meaning
gov.	government
int'l.	international
prob	problem
pres	president
bio.	biography
MD	medical doctor
TV	television
U.	university
w/	with

EXERCISE 3

Review the lecture notes on pages 90, 91, and 97. Circle the notes that are abbreviations or symbols. Next to each abbreviation or symbol, write out the actual word(s). Check your answers in answer key.

EXERCISE 4
LIST COMMON WORDS AND PHRASES

Listen to the common words and phrases. Write each in an abbreviated form. You will have only a couple of seconds to abbreviate. Press Play.

1. _____
2. _____
3. _____
4. _____
5. _____
6. _____
7. _____
8. _____
9. _____
10. _____

11. _____
12. _____
13. _____
14. _____
15. _____
16. _____
17. _____
18. _____
19. _____
20. _____

Answers will vary. To check your work, read through your list of abbreviations. Next to each abbreviation, write out the full word or phrase that is abbreviated. Then listen to the exercise again. Check the full word and phrase list on page 291.

Practice 3
Lecture: Modern Social Change

Listen to part of a lecture that was originally given by Dr. Jerry W. Sanders, lecturer in the Department of Peace and Conflict Studies at the University of California, Berkeley. While you listen, take notes about the lecture. Use abbreviations and symbols for maximum efficiency. Answer the questions that follow by circling the best response(s). Press Play.

1. What point does the lecturer make about the book *Turbulence and World Politics?*

   a. The growth of multiple perspectives is bound to increase conflict.

   b. Technology has decreased the need for geographic travel.

   c. Human beings have evolved more slowly than other species.

   d. Recent technological achievements have been rapid.

2. What areas of human interconnectedness does the professor mention? (two answers)

   a. technology

   b. culture

   c. religion

   d. genetics

3. What examples does the professor use to explain finance scapes? (two answers)

   a. international crime finances

   b. money sent back to Mexico by Mexican citizens

   c. campaign moneys used to sway political outcomes

   d. tourist dollars spent overseas

4. Complete the table according to information in the lecture by matching the examples with the correct **scape.** Two of the examples will not be used.

Ethnoscape	Finance Scape	Conflict Scape
•	•	•
•	•	•

a. Verbal "wars" through the media

b. People move from country of work to country of birth

c. Commodity speculation

d. People engage in politics from far away

e. Interracial marriage

f. "They" appear to be a threat to "us"

g. Money sent to country of origin

h. Interdependent risk factors lead to common fate

5. According to the professor, how is culture changing?

   a. Cultures and traditions are being diluted by tourism.

   b. Cultural identification is less strongly rooted in geography.

   c. Culture is inextricably tied to land.

   d. The Internet is creating one, global culture.

Check your answers in the answer key.

Building Skills: Pragmatic Understanding

Basic Skill	Some Related Academic Tasks	Related Tasks on Tests like the 2005 TOEFL®
Identifying the underlying meaning of a sentence, or the speaker's attitude or purpose.	• identifying the function of communication • understanding a speaker's purpose • following the flow of conversations • answering multiple-choice questions on tests • taking notes during a lecture • participating in class discussions • learning efficiently • understanding a point of view • identifying speaker bias • distinguishing fact from fiction • participating in class discussions	• answering multiple-choice questions about meaning or purpose • writing about the speaker's purpose • speaking about what you've heard

Pragmatic understanding refers to an understanding of how the speaker feels: What are the speakers' positions and motives? With pragmatic understanding, you need to see how specific comments contribute to the general topic. In other words, you need to be able to *read between the lines*. Pragmatic understanding is a more advanced listening skill than the basic comprehension skills practiced earlier in this chapter.

Some questions about pragmatic understanding may be based on a specific, short segment of a talk. In such cases, listeners usually have more than one opportunity to listen to the relevant segment of the lecture before they must answer any questions.

Example Questions about Pragmatic Understanding

What does the professor imply when he says this: "It doesn't take a rocket scientist."

What does the man want to know when he asks why the woman paid so much?

Why does the student repeat the course name?

What is the professor's opinion of this research?

What is the student's attitude toward his classmates?

How does the counselor feel about the team's progress?

How to Listen for Pragmatic Understanding

To identify pragmatic understanding, follow these steps:

1. Grasp the main idea and supporting details.

2. Listen for meaning, rather than for individual words.

3. Listen to the wording and tone of each utterance. Try to identify the speaker's intention.

4. Pay attention to the context of the utterance. Listen to the phrases and ideas that immediately surround the comment in question.

5. Identify views or beliefs that the speaker implies.

6. Ignore words that you don't know. Focus on words that you do understand, and let the flow of the topic guide your understanding.

Practice 1

Listen again to Dr. Jerry W. Sanders' lecture about "scapes." Listen from start to finish. Then listen to the following questions and repeated segments from the lecture. Answer the questions by circling the best response. Press Play.

1. Listen again to a part of the lecture. Then answer the question.
   What does the professor mean when he says "no one knows how many miles"?
   (Choose two answers.)

   a. Some routes are longer than others.

   b. The map doesn't list mileage.

   c. People don't care how many miles it is.

   d. Time is more important than distance.

2. Listen again to a part of the lecture. Then answer the question.
   What does the professor mean when he says this: "Some people see technology and see a smiley face."

   a. Some people laugh about the complications that technology introduces.

   b. Some people like technology.

   c. Some people can easily see more than one perspective.

   d. Some people can identify the good in an evil situation.

3. Listen again to a part of the lecture. Then answer the question.
   Why does the professor ask "What does 'us and them' really mean anymore?"

   a. He feels that the grammar check in some word processing programs is causing pronoun usage to shift.

   b. He wants a student to list the major enemies of the U.S.

   c. He believes that interracial marriages have diluted ethnic divisions.

   d. He thinks that traditional boundaries between people are deteriorating.

4. Listen again to a part of the lecture. Then answer the question.
   What does the professor want to know when he asks, "Who are these people?"

   a. the names of these people

   b. the mental state of these people

   c. an explanation for these people

   d. the authority of these people

Check your answers in the answer key.

Reading between the Lines

When we listen to someone speak, we listen for the actual meaning of the words. We do not usually analyze their grammar, their idioms, or their choice of words. Instead, we try to grasp their ideas.

Likewise, when a speaker speaks, he or she is trying to relate specific ideas. A speaker does not usually analyze his or her grammar, idioms, or choice of words. Instead, the speaker tries to convey a concept. A speaker may use idioms, similes, questions, short phrases, disjointed words, or even fabricated words, to express a thought.

In addition to the words that a speaker chooses, the speaker may use intonation, variation in speed, facial expressions, or gestures to express an idea. Meaning also rests heavily on context.

A successful listener can follow the chain of thinking. A successful thinker is rarely surprised by what a speaker says because each utterance should follow logically from previous comments. Both speaker and listener rely heavily on context to define the meaning of words.

EXERCISE 1

The following exercise is based on several possible meanings behind the question, Who are these people? *Taken literally, this expression means, simply, that the speaker wonders who the people are. However, taken in context, the speaker may be asking about the speakers' self image, their origins, their authority, or about something else.*

Read the following possible meanings, a *through* d, *for the expression* Who are these people? *Then listen to four short passages. Each passage contains the expression,* Who are these people? *but each passage uses this expression in a different context. For each passage, determine the underlying meaning of this phrase. Choose one answer,* a, b, c, *or* d, *to identify the speaker's real meaning. Check your answers in the answer analysis section following the questions. Press Play.*

   a. How can we account for these people?

   b. How can these people be so bold?

   c. What are the geographic or genetic origins of these people?

   d. What contractual authority do these people carry?

1. What does the speaker mean when she says, "Who are these people"? _____
2. What does the speaker mean when she says, "Who are these people"? _____
3. What does the speaker mean when she says, "Who are these people"? _____
4. What does the speaker mean when she says, "Who are these people"? _____

ANSWER ANALYSIS

1. The speaker is clearly a professor who can't account for the number of students on the class roster. The correct response is **a.**

2. The speakers are amazed by the forward approach of the evangelists on their campus. The correct response is **b. D** may also be a correct response.

3. The lecturer is speaking about the anthropological origins of a specific group of people. The correct response is **c.**

4. The speakers wonder about the rights of the dormitory inspectors. The correct response is **d.**

Practice 2
Lecture: Genes

Listen to part of a psychology lecture originally given by Amori Yee Mikami, lecturer in the Department of Psychology at University of California, Berkeley. <u>Pause</u> *the audio after the lecture. Then answer the questions by circling the best response. Answer Questions 1 and 2. Restart the audio to answer Questions 3, 4, and 5. Press Play.*

1. What is the main topic of the talk?

    a. twins

    b. heritability

    c. genetic mutation

    d. heredity

2. How do researchers study heritability?

    a. They examine details about one person.

    b. They look at details of blood relatives, especially twins.

    c. They do a broad survey of the whole population.

    d. They take blood samples from specific groups.

3. Restart the audio. Listen again to the statement made by the professor. Then answer the question: Why does the professor tell the students that they do not have to memorize the graph?

    a. The graph is on the website.

    b. The main idea is more important than the details.

    c. The concept is poorly presented in this graph.

    d. The numbers will be given on the quiz.

4. Restart the audio. Listen again to a part of the lecture. Then answer the question: What does the professor imply when she says that "this is one of researchers' favorite things to do"?

    a. These studies enable researchers to refute some findings.

    b. Researchers in Minnesota share the same hobby.

    c. Researchers prefer to study children.

    d. Twins separated at birth give researchers compelling data.

5. Restart the audio. Listen again to a part of the lecture. Then answer the question: What does the professor imply when she says, "Now are you convinced? No, why?"

    a. She thinks that the students are convinced.

    b. She thinks that the students don't understand the concept.

    c. She thinks that the data is not sufficiently convincing.

    d. She thinks that the data sounds falsified.

Check your answers in the answer key.

Listening for Attitude

When you listen for attitude, focus on words and phrases that show a judgment. These words may directly express a personal stance: *like, dislike, love, disgust.* These words may introduce a personal opinion: *in my opinion, the way I see it.*

EXERCISE 2

CONVERSATION: TWO STUDENTS

Listen to a conversation of about four minutes between two college students. Listen for words that express a judgment or stance. Write them down when you hear them. The first few are done for you. For this practice, you may listen more than once. Press Play.

1. _I think_ _____   11. _____

2. _You're right_ _____   12. _____

3. _practical_ _____   13. _____

4. _Like_ _____   14. _____

5. _____   15. _____

6. _____   16. _____

7. _____   17. _____

8. _____   18. _____

9. _____   19. _____

10. _____   20. _____

Compare your answers with those of a classmate. Discuss your choices. Check your answers in the answer key.

Practice 3 (with Answer Analysis)
Conversation: Two Students

Listen again to a part of the conversation. Take notes. Answer the questions that follow. Press Play. Restart the audio to answer Question 6 (it is a new track on the CD).

1. What is the main topic of the conversation?

   a. sports

   b. food

   c. American images of Japan

   d. a new club

2. How do the speakers feel about a cooking club?

   a. Many students would be interested.

   b. It's too expensive.

   c. Wine would be prohibited on campus.

   d. The club wouldn't be able to find basic ingredients.

3. What does the woman think about flower arranging?

   a. It's a great Japanese art.

   b. Few students have heard of it.

   c. It's uninteresting.

   d. It would only appeal to women.

4. What is the man's attitude toward a kendo club?

   a. Students could be easily excited about it.

   b. The uniforms are hard to find in Oklahoma.

   c. Few students would join a kendo club.

   d. He won't support it.

5. How does the female student feel about their final decision? (Choose two answers.)

   a. She is confident that kendo will be a success.

   b. She thinks they should continue their effort to gauge student interest.

   c. She doubts that Student Activities will help fund it.

   d. She doesn't want responsibility for the final decision.

6. Start the audio. Listen again to a part of the conversation. Then answer the question: What does the woman imply when she says, "Even my roommate has heard of kendo"?

   a. Her roommate doesn't know much about sports.

   b. Her roommate is athletic.

   c. Her roommate reads a lot and knows a lot about Asia.

   d. Even though her roommate is American, she still knows about kendo.

ANSWER ANALYSIS

1. The students are discussing a new club for their university, so the correct response is **d.** Choices *a, b,* and *c,* sports, food, and American images of Japan, are mentioned as minor points in the talk, but none is the main topic.

2. The speakers worry that they wouldn't be able to find Japanese food ingredients where they live. The correct response is **d.** Choices *a* and *b* seem reasonable. "Wine," *c,* repeats in this answer's choice and in the talk.

3. The woman thinks that flower arranging is slow and boring. The answer is **c.** Choice *a,* flower arranging is a great Japanese art, is not an opinion of the woman. Choices *b* and *d* are logical and possibly true, but the woman mentions neither of these options.

4. The correct response is **c.** The man thinks that few Americans even know about kendo. Student excitement, *a*, is the opposite of the man's expectation. Choice *b* is a reasonable expectation, but it isn't mentioned in the talk. With choice *d*, the man will support kendo, if that's what the woman wants.

5. The answers are **b** and **d.** Her last line is "No, no, I don't want this whole decision on my shoulders. I mean, I'm guessing folks will be interested. But maybe we should ask around some more. Just to see." In *a*, early in the talk, the woman sounds excited, but later she reveals that she isn't confident about the success of kendo. In *c*, the man, not the woman, is worried about funding from Student Activities.

6. The correct answer is **d.** The speakers says "even my roommate" to imply that she would not normally expect her roommate to know about kendo. In other words, even though her roommate is American, she has heard of kendo. Answering this question correctly requires that you listen for meaning behind the actual words. This is an important and difficult listening skill.

Identifying Purpose

Most speeches have a purpose. The purpose may be to inform, to persuade, to insult, or to direct listeners. The goal of any communication is its *purpose*. When we talk about purpose, we are looking specifically at the speaker's intended result.

Remember, the speaker not only chooses words. The speaker uses intonation, emphasis, repetition, facial expressions, and so on, to express purpose.

EXERCISE 3

The following exercise is based on several possible purposes behind the sentence, "the weekend reading includes a photocopied handout." Taken literally, this expression means, simply, that the reading includes a handout. However, in context, the comment may have various underlying purposes, such as reminding listeners, encouraging action, or even complaining.

Read the following possible purposes, a through d, for using the expression, The weekend reading includes a photocopied handout. Then listen to the four short passages. Each passage contains the expression, but each passage uses this expression for a different purpose. For each passage, determine the speaker's purpose for saying this phrase. Choose one answer, a, b, c, or d, to identify the function of the comment. Press Play.

a. To inform listeners of their homework assignment.

b. To inspire listeners to do the reading.

c. To complain about the quantity of reading.

d. To ask for more information about the handout.

1. What does the speaker mean when she says, "The weekend reading includes a photo-copied handout"? _____

2. What does the speaker mean when she says, "The weekend reading includes a photo-copied handout"? _____

3. What does the speaker mean when she says, "The weekend reading includes a photo-copied handout"? _____

4. What does the speaker mean when she says, "The weekend reading includes a photo-copied handout"? _____

Check your answers in the answer key.

Practice 4
Lecture: Politics and Resources

Listen to part of a lecture given originally by Dr. Jerry W. Sanders, lecturer in the Department of Peace and Conflict Studies, University of California, Berkeley. Take notes. Pause the audio after the lecture. Answer the questions that follow by circling the best response(s). Restart the audio to answer Questions 5 and 6. Press Play.

1. What is the topic of the lecture?

    a. Morgenthal's text, *Politics of All Nations*

    b. the Palestinian/Israeli conflict

    c. distribution of oranges and orange products

    d. resources and conflict

2. What is the traditional way of dealing with conflict?

    a. dialogue

    b. struggle

    c. denial

    d. deceit

3. What does the lecturer imply about Morgenthal's text, *Politics of All Nations*?

    a. It supports his point about power and fighting.

    b. Its basic tenets don't match the theory of Realism.

    c. It proposes a superior model for conflict resolution through dialogue.

    d. It overestimates the authority of the United Nations.

4. Why does the lecturer mention the United Nations?

    a. as an example of an anarchical organization

    b. to give Morgenthal's book validity

    c. because the U.N. has dealt with food-distribution

    d. to relate the orange analogy to real-world situations

5. Restart the audio. Listen again to a part of the lecture. Then answer this question: What is the lecturer's purpose in asking, "Are we sure we have the right issue?"

    a. to warn students about the danger of making assumptions

    b. to remind students that there's more at stake than hunger

    c. to encourage students to think more deeply about the issue

    d. to help students see that hunger is the core issue

6. Restart the audio. Listen again to a part of the lecture. Then answer the question: Why does the lecturer mention "the testosterone-filled generation coming up"?

    a. to remind students that conflict is not quickly resolved

    b. to imply that youth create the greatest challenge to negotiators

    c. to prove that conflict is ultimately hormonal and therefore inevitable

    d. to show that even a poor compromise can have lasting value

Check your answers in the answer key.

PART 3

Writing

Four General Test-Taking Strategies for the Independent Writing Section

A few general test-taking strategies will help improve your performance on the writing section of the 2005 TOEFL®.

1. Take a few minutes to plan your essay before you begin to write.

2. Answer the question that is asked.

3. Do not attempt to write out an answer in your native language and translate it.

4. Try to leave a few minutes to read over your writing when you are finished.

5. Take notes during the reading and lecture. This will help you summarize. Try to take notes in English.

6. As you read the passage, try to predict what related topics the lecture might be about.

7. Try to balance information from the reading and the lecture in your writing. Do not rely too heavily on either one.

In this section, you will learn how to do the types of tasks that may be required of you on a multi-skills test like the 2005 TOEFL®: *writing a timed essay, and writing about a reading and a lecture.*

There are many ways English teachers and professors in academic classes use writing to assess what you know. An essay written in a short amount of time, for example, can show a teacher in a biology class that you know the process of photosynthesis. It can also show your English teacher that you have mastered sentence, paragraph, and essay structure in English. In this part you will study the process of writing an organized, well-supported, timed essay.

Another important academic task is synthesizing information that you have read or heard in a lecture and putting that information into your own words. This task involves many of the skills that you have already worked on in the reading and listening sections of this book, such as *identifying the main idea* and *supporting details in a reading or lecture.* These writing skills are crucial to success on academic tests and in your academic coursework.

The best way to improve your writing is to write a lot! Even if no one ever reads the writing that you do, practicing writing in English will improve your fluency and increase your confidence—two crucial aspects of test-taking. After you have completed the activities in this section, you can further practice writing by keeping a journal of your thoughts, feelings, or experiences. Summarizing readings and lectures in English will improve your writing skills and your ability to retain new information. Whenever you summarize, you are practicing the skills necessary to be successful on a multi-skills test.

Building Skills: The Independent Writing Task

Basic Skill	Some Related Academic Tasks	Related Tasks on Tests like the 2005 TOEFL®
Timed writing	• responding to a writing prompt • taking essay tests • organizing academic essays • writing thesis statements	• independent writing task

One task in the writing section of the TOEFL® Test is the independent writing task. For this task you will write a timed essay in response to a prompt that asks about your opinion or preference. You will have scrap paper in order to make notes in preparation for writing, but you will have to type your essay into a computer.

Doing "timed writing," as it is often called, is usually painful and scary for students, especially when they are writing in another language. But by working on the individual skills it takes to accomplish the task, you can improve your timed writing ability.

A sample essay in response to a typical test question follows. In the following sections, you will learn about each step in the writing process that produced this final product.

Respecting community health

In the last fifty years or so, smoking in the U.S. has gone from being part of the glamorous Hollywood image of movie stars to an evil habit destined to destroy the health of everyone. While the image shift has been a public relations change more than any change in smoking itself, medical research has proven that smoking and even second-hand smoke can cause lung cancer, emphysema, and other breathing disorders that can be fatal. With this recent medical knowledge have come laws that regulate when and where a person has the right to smoke, along with much public debate about the rights of smokers versus the rights of nonsmokers. I believe that smoking should not be allowed in public places because the rights of a community to be healthy outweigh the rights of an individual to smoke.

It is well known by now that second-hand smoke damages health. When in a restaurant or other public place, smokers and non-smokers, which may include children and the elderly, must share the same air in the enclosed space. Although there may be a smoking section in the restaurant, smoke cannot easily be contained in that one area. Non-smoking customers as well as employees are exposed to this smoke that puts their health at risk.

In addition to the damage caused by second-hand smoke, smoking in public places perpetuates the smoking habit. For example, as school children walk by a public park, they may see adults smoking and learn that it is an acceptable adult behavior, increasing their chance of becoming smokers themselves. In this way, public smoking may serve to advertise for the tobacco companies. Because smoking is expensive and bad for health, this perpetuation of smoking as an acceptable habit harms the community as a whole.

Finally, public spaces are meant for everyone. The nature of public spaces is that they be for the community. One could argue that by banning smoking in those places one is excluding smokers from the community. However, public spaces free of smoke perpetuate the health of a community and respect the rights of non-smoking members to control the air that they breathe. By not allowing smoking in public places, the rights of the community to health and happiness are better respected.

Understanding the Question Type

Many timed writing prompts will ask you to express your opinion or preference. On the 2005 TOEFL®, question types are limited to this format. There are many different ways that a prompt can ask for your opinion or preference about something. Some are listed in the chart below.

Opinion	Preference
Do you think that smoking should be allowed in public places? Why?	Would you prefer to have a roommate who smokes or doesn't smoke? Why or why not?
Agree or disagree with this statement: Smoking should be allowed in public places.	Agree or disagree with this statement: I prefer to live with someone who does not smoke.
Should smoking be allowed in public places? Why or why not?	Does your roommate have a right to smoke even if it bothers you?

No matter how the question is asked, your essay needs to:

- state your opinion or preference
- support your opinion or preference with reasons and examples

The more clearly and completely you accomplish these two tasks, the higher your score will be.

Generating Ideas

The first step in writing an independent essay is to generate ideas to write about. Of course, you can generate ideas by simply thinking before you write, but even experienced writers whose first language is English benefit from writing a few ideas down on paper. This will help you to choose an effective, logical organization for the information in your essay, which will increase your score.

Brainstorming

One way of getting ideas into writing is called **brainstorming**. Brainstorming usually means writing a list of words, phrases, or sentences without stopping or worrying about whether the ideas are good or not. During a timed essay, you might spend three to five minutes brainstorming.

For example, if the topic was "Do you think that smoking should be allowed in public places? Why?" a brainstorm might look like this:

> No!!
> Second-hand smoke
> Right to clean air, control surroundings
> Smoke dirty
> Expensive
> Smoke hard to contain
> Damage to children's health, older people
> Public places = clean for everyone
> Bad example for children
> Advertises for tobacco companies

This brainstorm is in the form of a list. You might use indentation to show the relationship between main and supporting ideas, which may save you time later.

You might also try using a spider or cluster diagram (sometimes also referred to as a mind map) to do your brainstorm; it depends on which style works the best for you. In this type of brainstorming, you are showing relationships between ideas, which can save you time in the future.

For example, a cluster diagram for the smoking question might look like this:

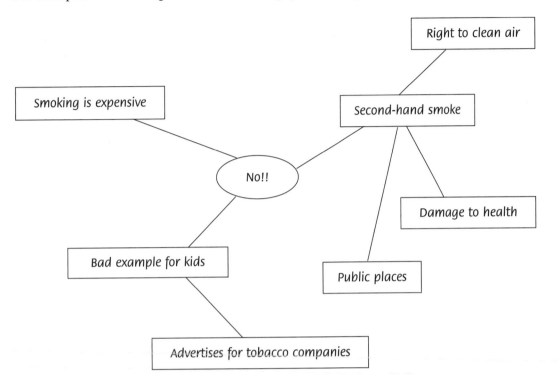

EXERCISE 1

Read the prompts below. Set your watch for five minutes, and brainstorm ideas for each one on a piece of paper.

Prompt 1: Do you think it is better for international students studying abroad to go to a large university or a small university? Why?

Prompt 2: Agree or disagree with this statement: You parents are your best teachers.

Prompt 3: Would you prefer to travel the world for four years for free or to go to college for free?

Organizing Your Ideas

Organizing your ideas according to North American academic writing style will make your essay easy for the raters to read. A well-organized essay will probably get a higher score than a poorly organized essay. You should probably spend up to five minutes organizing your ideas.

As a general rule with a timed academic-style essay, you should:

- state your thesis or main idea in the first paragraph or introduction
- support this thesis with two or three body paragraphs, each of which would have a main idea and supporting ideas or examples
- end your essay with a conclusion

This style may be familiar to you if you have studied "the five-paragraph essay." Your essay does not need to have exactly five paragraphs. Of course, writing styles vary, and good writers can write effectively both within and outside of this basic outline. However, for the purposes of time and rapid improvement, you might want to follow this traditional organization style.

Your essay should *not* be one paragraph! Even if your introduction and conclusion are one sentence each, having multiple paragraphs shows that you understand accepted North American academic rhetorical style. This is important for your academic work and on the 2005 TOEFL®.

Choosing and Grouping the Best Ideas

The first step in organizing your ideas is simply to look at your brainstorm and choose the best ideas. Remember that you want to have about three body paragraphs. You can work with your brainstorm to cross out some ideas and group other ideas together, as in the following list.

> No!!
> Second-hand smoke *
> Right to clean air, control surroundings ✓
> Smoke dirty ✓
> ~~Expensive~~
> Smoke hard to contain *
> Damage to children's health, older people *
> Public places = clean for everyone ✓
> Bad example for children ■
> Advertises for tobacco companies ■

There, the writer crossed out the idea that smoking is expensive because this idea does not have anything to do with the main idea. (Remember, the main idea is that people should not be allowed to smoke in public places.)

Second, the writer grouped together similar ideas. All the ideas that are marked with a star (*) are about second-hand smoke. All the ideas that are marked with a check (✓) are about the rights of people when they are in public places. All the ideas that are about setting a bad example are marked with a square (■).

EXERCISE 2

Look at the brainstormed lists that follow. Cross out the ideas that do not belong. Group together ideas that are related. Then, check your answers in the answer key.

Prompt 1: Would you prefer to live in the country or the city? Why?

> I prefer the city
> There are lots of things to do

Museums, restaurants, shopping

Don't need a car

Good public transportation

Cultural centers are in city

My work is in art, there's more access to art in the city

Energy from people

More job opportunities

Easy to travel to and from, lots of flights

Easy to meet people because there are so many

Job and social life is close to apartment

Prompt 2: *Agree or disagree:* For learning English, it is better to live in a small town than in a big city.

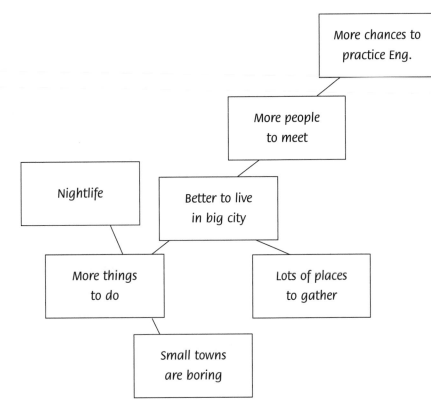

On your own: *Look at the brainstormed lists that you wrote in Exercise 1. Cross out the ideas that do not belong. Group together ideas that are related.*

Informal Outlining

After you have brainstormed, chosen your best ideas, and grouped your ideas together, you may choose to make an outline in order to show the relationships between ideas and the order that you will write them. Some writers may be able to skip this step and go directly to writing, but it is a good idea to practice this skill to be sure that your writing has a plan.

In your writing class, you may have learned how to make a formal outline. For the purposes of a timed essay, you should not worry about outlining in a formal style. You simply want to write a plan for your essay that will illustrate the relationships among your ideas and get you ready to write.

Returning to the original brainstorm about smoking, we see that an informal outline might look like this:

> Smoking should <u>not</u> be allowed in public places.
>
> >Paragraph/Topic: Second-hand smoke damages health
> >
> > >—children's health, older people
> > >
> > >—smoke cannot be contained in a smoking section
> >
> >Paragraph/Topic: The rights of people in public places
> >
> > >—People have a right to clean air, control of their surroundings
> > >
> > >—Smoking is dirty, smells bad
> > >
> > >—Public places should be clean for everyone

Here the writer used simple indenting, rather than formal outlining techniques, to quickly make a plan for the essay.

EXERCISE 3

Using the modified brainstormed lists from Exercise 2, write an informal outline for each one.

On your own: *Write informal outlines for the prompts that you brainstormed in Exercise 1.*

Stating Your Opinion Clearly

In order to make your opinion clear, you need *a clear thesis* and *clear topic sentences*.

Thesis Statements

In North American academic writing style, your main idea is usually stated in one or two sentences near the beginning of your paper. In a timed multi-paragraph writing assignment, the thesis statement is often in the first paragraph.

Your thesis statement needs to:

1. be specific
2. state your opinion or preference
3. appear clearly in your introduction
4. be the main idea of the whole essay

Examples of thesis statements that are **not** specific:

Smoking is bad.

I think there are many reasons we should and should not ban smoking in public places.

In the first example, the grader or reader of the essay may be able to infer that the writer wants to ban smoking in public places, but this opinion is not stated clearly. In the second thesis statement, the opinion of the writer is not known since both sides of the argument are stated.

Examples of a **specific** thesis statement:

Smoking should not be allowed in public places because the rights of a community to be healthy outweigh the rights of an individual to smoke.

EXERCISE 4

For each group of thesis statements that follow the sample typical writing prompts, choose the one that you think is the most specific. Be ready to explain why you think it is the best.

Prompt 1: Should physical exercise be a required part of every school day? Why or why not?

   a. Physical exercise should be a required part of every school day.

   b. Physical exercise is important for children.

   c. Physical exercise should be a required part of every school day because children naturally need to move their bodies, it establishes a good pattern of exercise that can carry on into adulthood, and it develops teamwork.

Prompt 2: Agree or disagree with the following statement: Not everything that is learned is contained in books.

   a. Not everything that is learned is contained in books because my family has an oral history that is important.

   b. It has been said that "not everything that is learned is contained in books." This view is supported by the rich oral traditions of cultures and the knowledge about how to be in the world that we get from our families, which is rarely written down.

   c. I agree with the statement that not everything is learned through books.

How to Write a Fast Thesis Statement

One fast way to write a specific thesis statement is to turn the **question prompt** into your **thesis statement**. For example, if you are given the prompt

Do you think that smoking should be allowed in public places? Why?

simply turn the question into a statement:

I think that smoking should be allowed in public places because _____.

EXERCISE 5

Read these prompts. Now turn them into thesis statements.

Prompt 1: When you have a problem, do you think that it is better to ask your family members or your friends for advice? Why?

Prompt 2: Watching television has become an everyday activity for many people in the world, sometimes replacing activities such as sports and visiting with friends. Do you think that television watching has a good or bad effect on society? Why?

Prompt 3: Agree or disagree with the following statement: It is important to maintain the traditions of your culture. Give reasons and examples to support your opinion.

Prompt 4: Because of the Internet, international travel, and other new technologies, countries all over the world have more contact with each other than ever before. Do you think that your country has become more similar to other countries in the world? Give reasons and examples to support your opinion.

Prompt 5: Do you think that it is better to have friends who are a lot like you or who are different from you?

Strong Topic Sentences

In the same way that an essay has a thesis statement, each paragraph has a topic sentence that states the topic, or main idea, of the paragraph. A strong independent task essay has topic sentences that clearly reinforce and support your opinion.

Working with the same prompt about smoking, here are some examples of topic sentences for a paragraph in the body of the essay.

Strong: *Smoking should not be allowed in public places because non-smokers are forced to inhale harmful second-hand smoke.*

Less strong: *Smoking in public places causes second-hand smoke.*

Weak: *Many people smoke in public places.*

The first topic sentence is strong because it supports the main idea. It states *why* smoking should not be allowed in public places. It gives a concrete reason, which can then be further explained with examples. The second topic sentence simply states a fact, not an opinion. Although this fact relates to the general topic of the essay, it doesn't add any support. The final topic sentence makes a general statement that does not relate strongly to the main idea.

EXERCISE 6

Look at the topic sentences written in response to the prompts. Choose the best topic sentences, and be ready to explain why you think they are the best.

Prompt 1: Many people move away from their families and hometowns because they can find better work in another city. Do you think it is better to live near your family, but have a not-so-great job, or to live away from your family, but have a better job?

Possible topic sentences:

    a. One reason that it is better to live near your family is that your family can support you as you raise your own children.

    b. Your parents can help you raise your children.

    c. Children need grandparents, especially children who misbehave.

Prompt 2: At a university, students like to study in different places. Some like to study in the library. Others prefer a coffee shop, while still others like to study in their rooms. Where do you prefer to study and why?

Possible topic sentences:

    a. The library is the best place to study, and Americans can easily see their tax dollars at work when they go to a public library.

    b. Studying at the library is the best option because I have access to any other resources that I might need while studying.

    c. It's better to study in the library because you can easily find what you need.

On your own: *Write your own topic sentences for each of these prompts.*

Supporting Your Point

After you have written a topic sentence, your next task is to support your topic sentence with reasons and examples. Your support is like the frame of a house: without it, the roof will fall down. In other words, if you do not support your ideas well, your entire argument will be unconvincing. Remember that the focus of the questions on many tests, and especially on communicative tests like the 2005 TOEFL®, is your opinion or preference. Reasons and examples will help to make your opinion clear and convincing.

Choosing Examples

During a timed-writing essay that asks for your opinion or preference, you will rely on your experiences, beliefs, and general knowledge to find examples to support your point. On the 2005 TOEFL®, you are not expected to supply facts or statistics. If you have not experienced something directly, it is okay to use the experiences of friends, family members, or public figures.

For example, in the first body paragraph of the model essay about smoking in public places (page 120), the writer uses commonly known facts to support her point, such as "it is well known that second-hand smoke damages health." In the next paragraph, the author uses her beliefs and assumptions about how smoking influences children to support her point.

Developing Your Supporting Ideas

A strong essay will have well-developed ideas. This means that your ideas are fully explained with reasons and examples. Many students make the mistake of assuming that the reader can follow the writer's ideas to their logical conclusions. They assume they do not need to write out all the reasons for their point or explain how the ideas relate to their main idea. However, in North American academic style, the burden is on the writer to provide reasons and to explain how supporting ideas relate to the main idea. On a test, full development shows that you have enough facility in English to explain your ideas completely. One way to improve your development is through using questions.

USING QUESTIONS FOR DEVELOPMENT

When trying to develop a paragraph, ask yourself these questions (don't *write* these questions, just ask them to yourself):

- What do I mean by that?
- What is an example of what I just wrote?
- So what? Who cares?
- Why is that important?
- What is the result of what I just wrote?
- What larger issue does this connect to?

Example:

Do you think that English is the most important language in the world? Why or why not? Use specific reasons and examples to support your opinion.

> *Topic sentence (opinion): English is not the most important language in the world because so many people know English.*

What do I mean by that?

> *The most important languages in the world, and the ones that we should be focusing our attention on, are languages that are dying.*

What is an example of what I just wrote?

> *For example, Navajo is a Native American language that is dying as Navajo children learn English in order to be successful in the larger U.S. economy and culture.*

So what? Who cares?

> *As a result, many Navajo children lose their Navajo, causing the language to die slowly.*

Why is that important?

> *When a language dies, so do cultural stories, history, and heritage.*

What is the result of what I just wrote?

> *When we lose a language, we lose a piece of history.*

What larger issue does this connect to?

> *This is why the real important languages are those that are dying everyday. When a language is lost, we lose something as humans that we can never get back, and we damage the human race because of it.*

Complete paragraph:

English is not the most important language in the world because so many people know English. The most important languages in the world, and the ones that we should be focusing our attention on, are languages that are dying. For example, Navajo is a Native American language that is dying as Navajo children learn English in order to be successful in the larger U.S. economy and culture. As a result, many Navajo children lose their Navajo, causing the language to die slowly. When a language dies, so do cultural stories, history, and heritage. When we lose a language, we lose a piece of history. This is why the real important languages are those that are dying everyday. When a language is lost, we lose something as humans that we can never get back, and we damage the human race because of it.

Now, of course, you do not have enough time to do this on paper during the writing exam. The idea is to ask yourself these questions mentally so that your writing reflects your fully developed thoughts.

EXERCISE 7

Read the topic sentence. Then read the list of supporting sentences that follow it. Use the list of development questions to number the sentences in the order that they should appear in the paragraph. Hint: *You should also look at other clues, such as pronoun references, to make your choices.*

Prompt: Do you agree or disagree with the following statement? Students can teach teachers. Use specific reasons and examples to support your point.

Topic sentence:

Teachers can learn from students because students bring a fresh perspective to the topics that are being taught.

_____ For example, a student may interpret a piece of literature in a completely new way that is informed by the perspective of his or her generation.

_____ A richer learning environment means that more learning will take place, and in a more satisfying way.

_____ Some teachers have been working with the same subject for so long that they have already formed opinions about it that are not easily altered.

_____ This creates a community of scholarship that is more like the ideal of most educational institutions.

_____ Realizing this makes for a much richer learning and teaching environment.

_____ The result is that teachers and students operate in a reciprocal relationship with each other, giving and taking and learning together.

_____ The teacher may have never formed that interpretation without the help of the student.

132

Follow-up questions:

1. In what ways does the author create a *logical progression* of ideas? What signals this progression?

2. What other ways can you think of to show a logical progression of ideas?

Answers to these questions are not given in the answer key. Before the exam, you can practice with them in order to make development come more naturally while you are writing.

EXERCISE 8

Choose any of the outlines you wrote from other exercises in the Writing section. Choose one part of the outline that could become a paragraph. Write a topic sentence (see page 131), and then practice developing your paragraph using the questions in this section.

Topic sentence:_____

What do I mean by that?

_____

_____

What is an example of what I just wrote?

_____

_____

So what? Who cares?

_____

_____

Why is that important?

_____

_____

What is the result of what I just wrote?

_____

_____

What larger issue does this connect to?

_____

_____

Connecting to a Larger Issue

By connecting the ideas in your timed writing to a larger issue, you can increase your content score on a timed writing exam. Connecting to a larger issue makes your writing more complex and interesting.

A *larger issue* is a theoretical or cultural belief or topic that takes the given prompt and broadens it. For example, if you are writing about this prompt:

> *Some people think that children should take physical education classes at school,*
> *while others believe that school time should be devoted only to academic classes.*
> *Which do you believe and why?*

you might connect your answer to the *larger issue* about the purpose of education (to train you for a job, to make sure you get into college, or to make you a well-rounded person, for example).

EXERCISE 9

Match each prompt on the left with the issue that it most closely relates to on the right. Write the letter of the issue in the blank.

Prompt

_____ 1. Agree or disagree with the following statement: The childhood years are the most important years of one's life.

_____ 2. Do you prefer to live with a roommate or alone during your university studies?

_____ 3. Would you prefer to go to a university that is in a big city or a small town?

_____ 4. Do you agree or disagree with the following statement? Every citizen is responsible for the actions of his or her government.

_____ 5. What is the most important quality to have as a student?

Issue

a. Receptiveness to the ideas and ways of other people

b. Cultural differences in rural and populated areas

c. Cultural beliefs about aging

d. Values about what makes a person intelligent

e. The power of an individual to shape the future of a society

On your own: *Brainstorm other issues that these prompts might connect to.*

See the sample essay and the discussion that follows.

Prompt:

Do you think that English is the most important language in the world? Why or why not? Use specific reasons and examples to support your opinion.

Dying Languages

Many people consider English to be the most important language in the world because of the number of people who speak English and the economic and political power of the U.S., which uses English. These factors have made English the new "international language" of business and world politics. However, I don't agree that English is the most important language in the world. Every language is important because it represents a part of humanity, of the collective knowledge of humans. Like art and music, language represents a culture and experience unique to the people who speak it. That's why the most important languages in the world are dying languages.

English is not the most important language in the world because so many people know English. The most important languages in the world, and the ones that we should be focusing our attention on, are languages that are dying. For example, Navajo is a Native American language that is dying as Navajo children learn English in order to be successful in the larger U.S. economy and culture. As a result, many Navajo children lose their Navajo, causing the language to slowly die. When a language dies, so do cultural stories, history, and heritage. When we lose a language, we lose a piece of history. This is why the real important languages are those that are dying everyday. When a language is lost, we lose something as humans that we can never get back, and we damage the human race because of it.

In conclusion, every language is important. All languages offer a window into the lives, beliefs, and experiences of the people who speak them. Language is not just a tool for communication, but a way in which we as human beings express ourselves to each other. This expression goes beyond simple utilitarian communication and reveals something about the human experience. The astounding fact that the human brain, which is much the same across all human beings, can come up with so many different and equally workable, complex language systems is reason enough that we need to preserve all the languages we can. Preserving dying languages is a way of preserving our humanity, and that's why English is not the most important language in the world, but rather those languages which we might soon lose forever are the most important.

EXERCISE 10

Answer these questions based on the sample essay on dying languages.

1. What is the larger issue that the writer is connecting her ideas to?

   _____

   _____

   _____

   _____

2. In what part of the essay did the author connect to the larger issue (introduction, body, conclusion, etc.)? Circle the sentences that connect the topic of the essay to the larger issue.

   _____

   _____

   _____

   _____

Formatting

Formatting seems like a small issue, but for readers of English essays, format is more important than you might think. Remember these formatting rules.

- **Indent the first line of every paragraph.** When writing by hand, indent about half an inch (two centimeters). When using a computer, use the tab key [tab] on your keyboard to indent.

    Indenting shows your readers—the people evaluating your essay—that you understand what a paragraph is. If a reader does not see an indentation, he or she wonders whether you are starting a new paragraph. *You never want your reader to wonder or be confused.* In North American academic writing style, the burden is on you to be clear—not on the reader to figure out what you mean.

    In addition, indenting shows your readers that you know the accepted conventions for writing a paragraph in English.

A paragraph with a proper indentation is shown here.

<u>Note:</u> In business style, it is sometimes acceptable to simply skip a line to indicate that you are starting a new paragraph. This is <u>not</u> acceptable <u>academic</u> style, and so you should not use this type of formatting on a test.

It is well known by now that second-hand smoke damages health. When in a restaurant or other public place, smokers and non-smokers, which may include children and the elderly, must share the same air in the enclosed space. Although there may be a smoking section in the restaurant, smoke cannot easily be contained in that one area. Non-smoking customers as well as employees are exposed to this smoke, which puts their health at risk.

- **Do <u>not</u> start each sentence on a new line.** Like indenting, the connection of sentences is an accepted writing convention in English. Starting each sentence on a new line immediately alerts the evaluators of your essay that you have not yet mastered simple formatting conventions—and this makes your score go down.

  Writers in English use paragraph formatting to show the relationship between ideas. Using paragraph formatting shows that a group of sentences relates to the same idea, and thus belongs together. It also proves to your readers that you know this and have carefully organized your essay so that each paragraph talks about one main point. This increases your score in organization.

EXERCISE 11

The following paragraph has some formatting problems. Answer the questions below.

In addition to the damage caused by second-hand smoke, smoking in public places perpetuates the smoking habit.

For example, as school children walk by a public park, they may see adults smoking and learn that it is an acceptable adult behavior, increasing their chance of becoming smokers themselves.

In this way, public smoking may serve to advertise for the tobacco companies. Because smoking is expensive and bad for health, this perpetuation of smoking as an acceptable habit harms the community as a whole.

1. What is wrong with this paragraph's formatting?
2. How might the formatting of the paragraph be confusing to the reader?

- **Give your essay a title**. Put this title in the center of the first line on your paper. Again, this may seem like a small point, but giving your essay a title helps your readers know your main idea and a little about what to expect from your essay. And, of course, it shows that *you have a main idea* and *you can identify it*.

  Your title should be specific to your main idea. For example, if the question is "Should smoking be allowed in public places? Why or why not?" your title should not be "Smoking" or "Smoking in Public Places." A better choice might be "The Harms of Smoking in Public Places" or "Smoking in Public Places Is a Right."

Practicing on Your Own

Studying for a timed independent writing exam is very different from studying for a math or biology exam because you cannot memorize information in order to do better on the exam. Instead, you must practice writing the way you might practice a musical instrument so that when the time comes to perform, you do so naturally. Here is some more advice about ways to practice on your own.

1. *Brainstorm proactively.* Set a timer and try to keep your brainstorming to three minutes.

2. *Practice changing the prompt into thesis statements and topic sentences.*

3. *Practice outlining.* Choose a prompt. Set your timer for five minutes, and take the whole five minutes to write an outline for that prompt. If you have time left over, develop your outline more.

4. *Give yourself 30 minutes to write an essay.* After you are finished, evaluate your essay (see page 140). If you have a study partner, you can both take the practice test and then evaluate each other's writing.

5. *After taking a practice test, look at one body paragraph closely and look for ways to improve it.* This will give you an idea of common mistakes that you make. Could you add more examples? What grammar did you change? Are you using word forms correctly? Work to improve on those things the next time.

6. *Keep a journal in English.* Everyday, choose one writing prompt, and write about it for 15 minutes. Don't worry about organization or grammar while writing in the journal. Just let your ideas flow. This will improve your fluency and confidence in writing in English.

Practice: Independent Writing Test

To give yourself this test, you will need a timer or clock, several sheets of paper, and a pen or pencil. If you are doing this practice test on your own, be sure to stop after 30 minutes. You need to practice under an actual time limit. When you are finished with the test, read through your answer, and compare it to the sample essays in this part of the book (Writing).

Prompt:

You will have thirty (30) minutes to plan, organize, and write a response to the following prompt. Use specific reasons and examples to support your answer. Write your essay on the paper provided.

Agree or disagree with the following statement: Parents are the best teachers.

Sample Responses to the Practice Writing

How You Will Be Graded

On communicative tests like the 2005 TOEFL® and on most timed essay tests, raters are looking for good content (ideas), organization, development, and language use (grammar and vocabulary). This type of grading is called "holistic" because it attempts to give a number that represents the level of the essay as a whole. In other words, an essay with weak content and strong language use may score similarly to an essay with strong content and weak language. Although you probably cannot accurately rate your own essay, you will gain a better understanding of what raters expect and can compare your practice essay to the sample essays to get an approximation of your score.

The following sample essays were all written by university students who are non-native speakers of English. The responses all address the prompt. Comments about how the essays would score on a test are given. By reviewing these samples and their comments, you should be able to better understand what qualities the raters are looking for in your independent-task essay.

Four responses to the prompt are provided. They are ranked in order from high to low scores. A score of 5 or 4 would be *high,* a 3 is *medium,* and a 2 or 1 is *low.* Re-read the prompt, and then study the sample responses and discussions that follow.

Grading Criteria

A review of the 2005 TOEFL® Test scoring criteria for the independent writing task shows that raters highly value:

- logical content with well-connected ideas
- a clear thesis statement
- sufficient development of each supporting point
- a wide range of vocabulary used correctly
- grammatically correct sentences using a variety of sentence types

Essays with the following features will receive lower scores:

- overly simplified vocabulary or insufficient control over vocabulary use
- overly simplified or inappropriate transitions
- logical disconnects in supporting argument
- insufficient development
- unclear or weak thesis statement

Sample Responses

SAMPLE RESPONSE 1: 5 (high)

There is a principal reason for agreeing with the statement that parents make the best teachers and this is the fact that children are closer to parents than to any other people.

Since a child is born, actually we could say even before birth, he/she is permanently communicating with his parents. The baby and the child receive most stimulus from the family environment and particularly from the persons of the father and the mother. They learn to smile in a certain way by mimicking their parents and like this all other behaviors including speaking, eating and walking. Is not it many times funny to see how a three-year-old resembles the walk of his father beyond the anatomic constitution? Taken as the child grow, the influence continue in different ways. Particularly in the grasping of values, opinions, and likes that are developed through the daily living in this community that is the family.

Notice the sophisticated vocabulary use in this paragraph with words like "stimulus," "mimicking," and "grasping."

Even though she may make some errors (see line 6), they do not detract from her overall performance.

> Notice this sophisticated transition that doesn't rely on a transition word, but rather on a reference to the ideas in the previous paragraph.

There are other reasons to argue against the arguement. We can say that parents do not make the best teachers for instance, when they are distant and don't give enough attention to their children. This may seem difficult to believe, how can a mother be distant? The point is that this absenteeism can be felt in different aspects since the parents' job is a quite comprehensive one. So we could all recognize, up to a more or less degree in different individuals' experiences, things that we definitely better learned from other people. These might have been lucking in our parents' example or we might just have decided to go other way.

However, for better or worse, our parents' teaching is the most influencing in most thing we learn in our lives.

Comments: A few key things that raise this essay's score. First, this writer has control over sophisticated vocabulary. In addition, she uses this vocabulary in highly embedded sentence structures, and she does this correctly. These two factors immediately impress the reader. The writer also takes a rhetorically interesting turn here. Though her first paragraph lays out her reasons for agreeing with the statements, she also makes a nod to the opposite perspective in her second body paragraph, and she does this well. Though there are certainly some imperfections in the writing, she presents herself as a strong, confident writer of English.

> **Embedded Sentence Structures**
>
> Embedded sentence structures are sentences that are made up of more than one clause. They may include relative clauses, adjective clauses, and other types of dependent clauses. Embedded sentence structures are usually the mark of advanced writing ability in English.
>
> Example: *"The point is **that** this absenteeism can be felt in different aspects **since** the parents' job is a quite comprehensive one."*
>
> *That* and *since* both introduce dependent clauses. Here the writer uses them smoothly and correctly.

SAMPLE RESPONSE 2: 4 (high)

When I think about the relationship between parents and their children, I can say that parents are the first teachers of their children. Therefore, I agree with the idea of parents are the best teachers. I have several reason that support my opinion, such as parents are the first people who their children meet them, children spend most of their time with their parents, and children usually watch their parents carefully while they grow up.

> In line 2 he relies on the idea that first = best.

> Notice the correct grammar in the thesis statement (lines 1 and 2).

> See the note on page 142 about transitions.

First, parents are the people who their children see them first when they are born. In other words, when a child is born at a hospital, this child see the parents' faces. Eventually, they get along and have a lot of time together. Ever since a child is born, he or she starts to look at the parents and see who they are. This child eventually acts like the parents. For example, the child learns how to smile, how to make a noise, and finally how to talk with some simple words. In brief, parents are very important to have for children because they learn where they are and who they are.

Second, children spend most of their time with their parents because they live with their family together. Children always try to learn something from the parents because they get their first education in the family. They learn how to make friends, how to be polite in society and everything like that. Simply, children learn things that they can only learn them from their parents.

Third, if there is a child in a family, parents should be very careful because children usually watch their family perfectly. They ask everything that is not familiar to them or that doesn't make any sense to them. For example, when a child see his or her parents argue with each other, this child might think a lot of things, such as why they argue, they have to be polite each.

> Beware of the common error (in line 11): many students use the adverb "perfectly" when they really mean "completely," "closely," "fully," or even "in an organized way."

Finally, I believe that parents are the first and very important teachers. Parents give the children an education which can't be learned in any place.

Comments: Overall, a strong essay. The author has very few grammatical errors. His vocabulary is not particularly sophisticated, but what is here is used correctly. He also has good organization and development.

> **Transitions**
>
> Avoid this common pitfall: using overly simple or inappropriate transitions. In this essay, the author uses the words *first, second, third* to mark the transitions between paragraphs. However, there is no inherent ordered or enumerated relationship between these ideas. The purpose of transitions is to show the logical relationship between ideas. Save transitions like *first, second, third* for essays that explain a process or the steps taken to do something. Instead, opt for transitions like the one in the first sample essay, "There are other reasons . . . ." This transition makes a reference to the previous paragraph's ideas and then connects these ideas to those in the new paragraph.

SAMPLE RESPONSE 3: 3 (medium)

In general, I can agree with the statement that is "Parents make the best teachers." In this case, the problem is the definition of "teachers" at least for me, but I'd like to think the definition as "People who teach something to someone." I think parents could be one of our best teachers because of bellow reasons.

First, parents have to teach everything by themselves until their children enter kindergraden or elementary school. Nobody can teach children until the time except for parents, and parents' education is very important because the education could make children's value.

> See the note above about transitions.

> The statements in the second paragraph are too absolute. Be careful of words like *all, nothing, none, never.*

Second, parents can teach something that is not teached in school. Children learn these things from parents even though they are a student. For example, how to talk with our grandfather and grandmother, how to call our friend, how to use chopsticks (especially in Asian countries) and so on. They are very important for living in society, so we have to learn them.

Third, parents have a lot of time with their children. It is clear that they have more time with their children than teachers who are in school. So parent could have lots of impact to their children. It means parents influence to children whether they want to do this or not.

By the above three reasons, I agree with the statement. Parents have many opportunities to teach something to children, and they have much more impact than teachers who are in school. So parents could be one of the best teachers, and parents must be one of the best teachers in the world.

> **Not an idiomatic transition.**

Comments: The author makes some good points here, but in general they are not well supported or developed. For example, in the third paragraph the author makes the point that parents teach us things that we don't learn in school. The support that follows, however, is simply a list of examples, rather than an explanation of the examples and how they might contribute to "living in society," which he writes in the last sentence of that paragraph. Here more explanation and more precise vocabulary are needed (such as saying that our parents teach us the social skills that we need to function as part of our culture, rather than "they are important for living in society"). Overall, the grammar, despite several errors, does not keep us from understanding it. Still, there is little sophistication or complexity in the writing.

SAMPLE RESPONSE 4: 2 (low)

In my point of view, I do agree with that parents make the best teachers. Everybody has parents. They teach us many things, I agree with the following reason.

> **Try to avoid huge generalizations such as the one in line 2. They have little meaning.**

> **Be careful to write a grammatical thesis when responding to an agree/disagree question (line 2).**

Firstly, They are the first teachers for everybody. They teach us such as they teach us how to speak, how to walk even how to ride. Nobody cannot learn how to walk by themselves, they have to have someone to teach them which is their parents. They make us alive because if they do not teach us, how can I be like this, having friends or even good opportunity to study.

Secondly, They also teach us about the moral, and how to treat with the other in the good way. For example, they teach us how to say, "Hello." It shows that you are friendly, but if we see our friends on the street, we did not say anything. He/she will think that your parents did not teach you to say, "Hi" to people.

Thirdly, when we have a problem, we can ask the teacher. My point is we can also ask the parents. Even though they do not know about the answer which is about math or science, but they can answer how to find the answer such as they can tell me how to read the book or how to find the answer in the book, because they have more experience than us. They know how to figure out when it has problem.

Everybody has parents. They teach us many things after when we was born, until they die. Moreover, they can figure out the problem that we cannot, so I agree with this statement: parents make the best teachers.

In lines 11 and 12, the writer does respond grammatically to agree/disagree prompt.

Comments: Although it seems that this author has good ideas, she does not quite have the language to express them clearly. For example, in the third paragraph, she talks about how parents teach us morals. However, her support for this point is about saying "Hello" when you meet someone. How does this teach morals? It is a bit of a stretch to see the connection. Similarly, in the second paragraph the author jumps from a point about how parents teach us to walk to a point about being a good student. These logical jumps make the reader work hard, and they imply that the author does not have the language skills to make the connections herself. This is also seen in the relatively simple vocabulary and its incorrect use.

The Grammar of Agreeing and Disagreeing

A common way of eliciting an opinion in academic contexts is asking a student to agree or disagree with a statement. Because of this common question type, you should master how to use the verbs *agree/disagree* grammatically in context.

There are essentially three ways to use these verbs:

I agree with + [noun phrase]

Example: I agree with the statement.

I agree + [*that*-clause]

Example: I agree that parents make the best teachers.

I agree with the statement: [complete sentence]

Example: I agree with the statement: Parents make the best teachers.

Building Skills: The Integrated Writing Task

Basic Skill	Some Related Academic Tasks	Related Tasks on Tests like the 2005 TOEFL®
Summarizing	• writing reports about materials you have read • writing essays using readings as support • answering multiple-choice questions about a reading or lecture on tests • participating in classroom discussions about readings or lectures • writing an abstract or a summary to show you understand a reading • taking notes	• composing "prose summaries" of a lecture or passage • writing an essay about the ideas in a passage • writing an essay about the ideas in a lecture

This section will help you to prepare for the integrated writing task on the 2005 TOEFL®. In this task, you will read a short passage, hear a short lecture, and then write a response to a prompt that asks you to combine information from what you have read and heard. Your response is intended to be a summary and synthesis of the information in the reading and the lecture. You will need to balance this information, and avoid relying too heavily on information from one or the other.

The skills needed to complete an integrated writing task are very similar to the ones you learned about in previous parts of this book. Here you will work on writing those main and supporting ideas *in your own words*. This involves selecting information to include in your writing, and writing that information in your own words.

Selecting Information

As previously mentioned, the prompts for this type of test item will ask you to summarize, or reproduce in your own words, information that you have read and heard. For example, the prompt might be:

> *Based on the reading and the lecture, explain how _____ differs*
>
> *from _____.*

This prompt is asking you to write about the major differences between two things. To respond to test items of this kind, you will first need to identify the main idea and select relevant information from the passage. You also need to know how to leave out unimportant information. Part of this is accomplished when you take notes about the reading or lecture.

You will not see the prompt until after you have finished reading and listening, so taking notes about the important ideas also helps you to anticipate the prompt. Prompts for these test items ask you to summarize in some way, so you should take notes with this aim in your mind.

You need to be able to organize the information that you selected from the passage. To do this, you need to determine whether to follow the same organization as the original passage or to develop your own organization. This may include synthesizing or condensing information from the passage. That means you need to put ideas together that might not have appeared together in the original passage, or combine important points.

Paraphrasing

You need to be able to *paraphrase* information from the reading or listening passage. **Paraphrasing** means writing the same information but in your own words. On the 2005 TOEFL®, you will not get a high score if you copy directly from the text. It is important that you understand what paraphrasing is.

Learning how to paraphrase is a very important academic task. The purpose of paraphrasing on a test is to show that (a) you comprehend (understand) the material, and (b) you have the language ability to write about it in new ways. When you simply copy from the text in response to a question, you may be demonstrating your *comprehension* of the question and the text, but you are not showing your *language ability*. An answer that does not demonstrate language ability will receive a low score on the 2005 TOEFL®.

Good paraphrases demonstrate your language ability if they:

1. use a **different grammar** or sentence structure from the original

2. are often **shorter than the original** because they leave out details and statistics

3. are **simpler than the original**, so it is important to use the words you know, even if you think your vocabulary or grammar is too simple

To use your own words, it helps **not to look** at the original text. This is easy when you are paraphrasing ideas from a listening passage, since you cannot see the text. The best way to paraphrase is to read or listen to the original passage, understand it, and then write the same ideas using your own words without looking at the original.

Read the original passage, the paraphrase, and the explanation. (This passage comes from the reading section, pages 5–6.)

Original:

Liberals (as distinct from socialists or communists) believe that the free market and private ownership of property are beneficial to society. They diverge from conservatives on the issue of how much trust to put in unfettered capitalism. In the liberal view, government must regulate capitalist enterprise to keep the moneyed forces of society from exploiting labor unfairly and from appropriating too many resources unto themselves.

Paraphrase:

Both liberals and conservatives think that free market capitalism is good for society, but liberals do not trust unregulated capitalism and therefore want government regulation so that the rich do not get too rich.

Here are some steps the author took in paraphrasing the original.
- Read and understood the passage.
- Isolated any vocabulary that she did not know or was unsure of, for example, *unfettered capitalism* and *moneyed forces*. As was taught/reviewed in Part 1: Reading, from context you can guess that *unfettered* means *unregulated,* since when you read the following sentence it says "in the liberal view, government must regulate capitalist enterprise." To show the test-raters that you understand this complex vocabulary, *do not* use the word *unfettered* in your paraphrase; use the synonym *unregulated* or another synonym that you know.
- Showed understanding of advanced usage patterns. You can guess that *moneyed forces* are forces with money, just like "armed warriors" would mean "warriors with arms." Replacing this with a synonym, the simple word *rich,* tells the rater a lot about your language ability.
- Expressed the main idea in a paraphrase that is (1) shorter than the original, (2) grammatically different from the original, (3) in her own words, and (4) simpler than the original.

EXERCISE 1

Read the following passages from Part 1: Reading, in this book. Then read the paraphrases, and answer the questions that follow.

> Through the early part of the year, even the most cautious directors were flexible in their attitude toward expanding the company. They could be talked into it, it seemed, if they heard a good enough argument for growth. By April, however, their attitude had calcified and settled into a firm no-growth position. No amount of argument would change it, not with the economy as weak as it had become.

Paraphrase 1: The directors were flexible in their attitude toward expanding the company but by April their attitude had calcified and settled into a no-growth position.

Paraphrase 2: During the first few months of the year, even the very cautious directors were bendable in their ideas about enlarging the company. Somebody was able to talk them into it, if they had a good argument. But by April, their position had stuck into a strong anti-growth position. No arguing could alter it, not with an economy that was not strong.

Paraphrase 3: The attitudes of the directors changed over the course of the year. In the beginning their minds might be easily changed, but because of a weak economy later in the year they would not change their minds.

    a. Which paraphrase(s) are shorter than the original?

    ———————

    b. Which paraphrase(s) are simpler than the original?

    ———————

    c. Which paraphrase(s) use different grammatical structures than the original?

    ———————

    d. Which paraphrase(s) use different vocabulary?

    ———————

    e. Which paraphrase do you think is best and why?

    ———————

EXERCISE 2

Choose the best paraphrase for each passage.

1. Our image of physical change as normally incremental and gradual has to be left behind as we consider superconductivity. Superconductivity is all about critical points—of temperature, current density, and magnetic field strength—where sudden changes occur.

   a. Superconductivity is concerned with sudden, rather than gradual, changes in temperature, density, and magnetic field strength.

   b. We normally think of change as gradual, but superconductivity looks at sudden changes.

   c. Our idea of physical change as usually incremental and gradual must be left behind when we talk about superconductivity, which is about sudden changes.

2. The cat's dominance over mice can be presented both negatively, as when Tarquin hears Lucrece's prayers like a cat dallying with the mouse panting under his paw (*The Rape of Lucrece*), or positively, as when Westmoreland in *Henry V* compares England to a cat preventing Scottish mice from plundering England.

   a. The cat's dominance over mice can be presented in both a negative and a positive light.

   b. *The Rape of Lucrece* shows cats in a negative way, as hunters, while *Henry V* shows cats in a positive way.

   c. In works of literature, the cat's relationship to mice has been portrayed positively and negatively.

3. Evidence from various sources points to a significant climatic role for solar disturbances, particularly for the absence of any.

   a. The absence of solar disturbances most likely has an important effect on changes in climate, according to a variety of sources of evidence.

   b. Evidence shows a significant role for sun disturbances.

   c. Evidence from many sources points to an important role in climate change for solar disturbances or their absences.

4. Traditionally, bioethics, the study of legal and ethical issues arising in health care, has centered on four essential values.

    a. Four essential values define the field of bioethics.

    b. Bioethics is the study of the legal and ethical issues related to health care.

    c. Based on four key values, the field of bioethics is concerned with the legal and ethical issues related to health care.

5. By 1960, when Stanley Kramer's *Inherit the Wind* was released, the issues central to the Scopes "Monkey Trial" of 1925 (which the film fictionally portrayed) had become slightly quaint, at least for mainstream U.S. society.

    a. The Scopes "Monkey Trial" of 1925 was out of fashion by the time Stanley Kramer's *Inherit the Wind* was released in 1960.

    b. For mainstream U.S. society, the controversy surrounding the Scopes "Monkey Trial" of 1925, which was portrayed in the movie *Inherit the Wind*, was silly and old-fashioned by the film's release in 1960.

    c. By 1960, which was the time when Stanley Kramer's *Inherit the Wind* was released, the problems of the Scopes "Monkey Trial" of 1925 (which is what the film was about) were no longer important for mainstream U.S. society.

EXERCISE 3

Now practice paraphrasing by reading the passages and paraphrasing them. (All passages are taken from the Building Skills: Vocabulary section in Part 1: Reading in this book. You may want to review this section before you paraphrase.)

Passage 1: The Civil War left a mark on the soul of the nation. It persisted long past the end of Reconstruction, and the Jim Crow South was evidence that the war's wound had scarred over in unnatural ways.

Your paraphrase:

Passage 2: To conceal his payments to assassins and other distasteful characters, the president drew the necessary cash from a slush fund created by anonymous donors. There were no records of money going into this hidden stash, so there would never be any questions about money going out of it.

Your paraphrase:

Passage 3: The industry used to lose thousands of ampules a day to damage during shipping. And with the liquid in each ampule worth about $1,200, this was a significant loss. The solution was to employ special sheets of packed foam that enclosed each tiny, liquid-filled glass tube in a cushion of 0.18 cm on each side.

Your paraphrase:

Passage 4: The United States has lost the industrial capacity to survive outside a world economy. Not only have we closed our steel industry, but we have decided that virtually all extraction of natural resources, from oil to zinc, should occur overseas.

Your paraphrase:

Passage 5: Workers who have been in the same office for more than five years are typically proprietous not only of the space but of the furniture and even the wall color. The company's attempts at minor redecoration are likely to be met with objections and scowls.

Your paraphrase:

Indicating the Source of an Idea

Whenever you use another person's ideas in your own writing, you **must** make it clear to your reader where certain information comes from. In North American academic style, this is key to showing that you understand the difference between your ideas and those that come from someone else, and that you have the writing skills to show your understanding.

Obviously, on a test you cannot write a bibliography or use a documentation system like MLA style. You simply do not have time. However, when you write about the ideas from the reading or lecture, you should use phrases for attributing ideas to another source.

According to the author/lecturer . . . .

In the reading, the author states that . . . .

In the author's/lecturer's opinion, ...

According to the theory in the reading/lecture . . . .

Here is how you might use these phrases in a short paragraph paraphrasing this passage.

Original passage:

Liberals (as distinct from socialists or communists) believe that the free market and private ownership of property are beneficial to society. They diverge from conservatives on the issue of how much trust to put in unfettered capitalism. In the liberal view, government must regulate capitalist enterprise to keep the moneyed forces of society from exploiting labor unfairly and from appropriating too many resources unto themselves. Government has a duty to oversee banking, the credit system, and the mechanisms for trading securities. The liberal believes in the great game of capitalist production but sees government as a sort of referee who must constantly cite the most powerful players in the game—the biggest and richest industries—for violating the rules.

Paraphrase:

According to the author, both liberals and conservatives think that free market capitalism is good for society, but liberals do not trust unregulated capitalism and therefore want government regulation so that the rich do not get too rich. The author states that liberals believe in capitalist production, but that they also believe that the government must always punish those who break the rules or act unfairly.

Checking Your Writing

You will want to review what you wrote to make sure that it is the best that it can be. When you review your work, you will want to check for these things:

✓ that you balance information from the reading and the lecture

✓ that the information in your writing accurately reflects the information in the reading and the lecture

✓ that your writing contains facts and inferences from the reading and lecture and <u>not</u> your own opinion

✓ that the language is different from the language in the reading and the lecture (that you used your own words)

✓ that you have cited your source(s)

You should ideally leave about five minutes to check over your work. However, you may only be able to leave two or three minutes. The important thing is to try to leave time to read your writing at least once when you have finished.

Writing in Response to a Reading

On the 2005 TOEFL®, the integrated writing task will require you to both listen *and* read before you write. For practice, we will first break the task into two parts: writing in response to a reading and then writing in response to a lecture.

Read this passage and answer the question that follows.

Hormone Production

Endocrine disorders (malfunctions of the human hormone-producing mechanisms) can have serious consequences. Hormones are crucial physical messengers, regulating and coordinating such functions as digestion and the balance of serum minerals. Severe shortages of hormones can mean a virtual shutdown of essential bodily processes. Endocrine disorders are routinely treated by administering hormones obtained from sources outside the body of the person suffering the disorder. The supply of such chemicals in nature, however, is far short of that needed in modern medicine. Since hormones are proteins, they are perfect candidates for production by genetically engineered bacteria. This production represents one of the most useful and widespread applications of rDNA (recombinant DNA) technology.

More than 5 million people worldwide take the hormone *insulin* each day to control some form of diabetes. Most of the insulin sold comes from cow or pig pancreases collected at abattoirs as a byproduct of meat production. While insulin from these sources is generally safe, it has slight structural differences from the human form. Rather than slipping comfortably past the immune defenses of the recipient, these insulin molecules are easily recognized as outsiders. Consequently, a few people taking bovine or porcine insulin develop allergic reactions as their immune systems reject the foreign intrusion. This problem is avoided by substituting human insulin, which, to be available in significant quantities, must be manufactured by genetically altered bacteria.

Insulin was the first therapeutic rDNA product approved by the FDA for sale in the United States. It went on the market in 1982 under the brand name Humulin. The development work had been done by the pioneering biotech firm Genentech; Eli Lilly and Company produced and marketed Humulin.

The biotechnology used in making insulin is more complicated than that used in making human growth hormone. The insulin molecule is made up of two polypeptide chains (linked strings of amino acids), which join to make the active form of insulin. In the production of genetically engineered insulin, the DNA that codes for the A chain is introduced into one batch of *E. coli* bacteria and the DNA for the B chain into a different one. The bacterial cells are induced to make the two chains, which are then collected, mixed, and chemically treated to make them link. The resulting insulin molecules are identical to those secreted by the human pancreas.

Human growth hormone (hGH) was another early target of rDNA approaches to hormone deficiency. HGH controls the growth of bones and regulates weight gain. In some children, the pituitary gland fails to produce enough hGH for normal development, and this is evidenced by markedly short stature (perhaps only 60%–70% of normal height for a given age) and other growth deficiencies. The condition can be ameliorated, but only if hormone supplementation takes place during the growth years of childhood. Beyond this critical period, many bones (such as the femur) lose their ability to elongate.

Early in the development of hGH therapy, the only sources of the hormone were the pituitary glands of human cadavers. Suppliers and marketers worried that drawing a chemical from the glands of the dead might eventually create a public relations problem. But a more serious problem was that the source was not prolific enough. First of all, the number of cadavers from which the pituitary gland could be harvested was very limited and not easily increased (within the bounds of the law). Secondly, each cadaver yielded a very small amount of the hormone—only about 4 mg, whereas one week's treatment for an individual deficient in hGH requires about 7 mg. No successful animal sources were found. Clearly, new sources were needed.

The supply of human growth hormone is maintained by applying rDNA techniques and achieving high-volume synthesis. A gene for hGH production is spliced into *E. coli,* which are cultured and exploited in very large amounts. A 500-liter tank of bacterial culture can produce as much hGH as could have been derived from 35,000 cadavers. Growth hormone produced by this technique was approved for human use in 1985 and is now commonplace.

Adapted from Cynthia S. Gross, *The New Biotechnology: Putting Microbes to Work* (Minneapolis: Lerner, 1988).

WRITING TASK

You will have thirty (30) minutes to answer the prompt below.

Based on the passage, explain how hormones produced by rDNA techniques are used in the treatment of endocrine disorders.

Understanding the Prompt

First, you must understand the prompt. To start, focus on the question words *explain how.* The test writers want you to *explain the ways in which* hormones produced by rDNA techniques are used.

Next, it might help to take out some of the technical vocabulary. Substituting other words, the prompt could read:

According to the reading, explain how hormones are used to treat diseases.

Stripping the prompt down to its bare parts will help you focus on what the prompt is asking you to do.

Selecting Ideas

Second, you must be able to identify the main ideas and supporting details in the passage. In Part 1: Reading, you already discussed this. You need those same identification skills to compose your essay.

You already know that this passage has a thesis statement, which is "Hormones produced by rDNA techniques are critical tools in the treatment of endocrine disorders." This is clearly laid out in the first paragraph of the passage, which serves as an introduction.

Next, you must identify the supporting details in the passage. This passage uses two examples to support the main idea: insulin and human growth hormone. To answer the question, you need to understand that hormones produced by rDNA techniques have been used to recreate both insulin and human growth hormone and are then used to treat endocrine disorders. You will definitely want to include an explanation of these two examples in your essay.

What about other information in the passage? Details like, "A single cadaver can yield only about half of the hGH needed by one person for a week's treatment" are <u>not</u> important to the main idea of the passage and are also <u>not</u> necessary to answer the prompt. This type of information is too detailed. In general, you should stay away from statistics in your essay.

Organizing

Now that you understand the prompt and have selected important ideas to include, you must organize those ideas. Just as you should include an introduction, body, and conclusion when you are writing your own opinion essay, you should follow that same basic organization here. Here's one way to approach the organization of your response:

- *Introduction:* Explain the need for producing hormones artificially and the general uses of these hormones (to treat endocrine diseases).
- *Body:* Explain how rDNA techniques are used in the two main cases from the passage: insulin and human growth hormone.
- *Conclusion:* Reinforce, restate main ideas.

You may chose to organize your essay another way; there exist many acceptable ways of organizing.

Paraphrasing

As you write, you will still be able to see the reading passage. Beware of copying sentences directly from the text. Be sure to paraphrase!

SAMPLE RESPONSE

When someone has an endocrine disorder, they need more hormone than their bodies can produce. This poses a problem for medical science: how to get enough hormone to treat people with these disorders. Until recently, getting enough of the hormone was impossible because it had to come from natural sources, like using hormones from animals or from dead people. But with the advent of rDNA technology, it is now possible to make a sufficient amount of hormones to treat endocrine disorders in humans.

There are two major diseases whose sufferers benefit from this technology: diabetes and human growth hormone deficiency. People who suffer from diabetes used to rely solely on insulin that came from the pancreases of slaughtered pigs and cows. However, some people were allergic to this insulin since it came from a non-human source. Using rDNA techniques, scientists can now make human insulin by manufacturing genetically modified bacteria.

Similarly, treatment for human growth deficiency has been improved by rDNA techniques. Previous, Human Growth Hormone, which regulates the growth of bones and weight gain, could only be harvested from the pituitary glands of dead humans. This, of course, produced only a limited supply. Now liters upon liters of HGH can be produced using gene techniques, far more than ever before.

Without the scientific advancements in rDNA technology, many people would go untreated for diseases such as diabetes and human growth hormone deficiency. Thanks to these scientific advancements, many people can get the treatment they need.

Practicing Writing in Response to a Reading

To give yourself this test, you will need a timer or clock, several sheets of paper, and a pen or pencil. If you are doing this practice test on your own, be sure to stop after 20 minutes. You need to practice under an actual time limit. When you are finished with the test, read through your answer, and compare it to the sample essays in the previous section.

You will have ten (10) minutes to read the following passage. You may take notes while you read. After you have read the passage, you will be asked to respond to a writing prompt. You will not be able to re-read the passage while you are writing.

READING

When President Bill Clinton's approval ratings plummeted in 1994, the cartoonist Herblock drew him staring in shock at his cat, Socks, who was resolutely walking out of the White House with his possessions in a bundle on his shoulder. This image would have been inconceivable a century ago. It is based on the assumption that a cat can be a valued friend, who can be counted on to provide solace during affliction.

Four centuries ago, few people could have conceived of a cat as a friend at all. Common English-language expressions from long ago make clear that our ancestors viewed the cat as a hunter of rodents and did not approve of its methods. Instead of forthrightly chasing down its prey, like a dog, a cat lies in wait, stalks, and pounces on its unsuspecting victim; instead of immediately killing its prey and wolfing it down, it may prefer to defer eating and play with its catch. Accordingly, *catty* means slyly spiteful, and *feline* connotes stealth. To *play cat and mouse with* is to toy heartlessly with a victim in one's power, and the children's game *puss in the corner* involves surrounding and teasing one of the players by offering and withdrawing opportunities to escape.

Only in recent times, as we have come increasingly to like and value cats, has the English language begun to reflect any appreciation of the animal's beauty, coordination, poise, and style. Although a woman would still object to being called a *cat*, she may like to be praised for feline grace and seductiveness. The great baseball player Johnny Mize, a large but well-coordinated man, was called "the big Georgia cat"; and "Harry the Cat Brecheen" was a particularly lithe and graceful pitcher.

In the 1930s, African-Americans began to describe a smart man who appreciates swing or jazz music as a *cat* or *hepcat*. This sense has been extended to refer to any streetwise, self-assured, stylishly dressed man-about-town—one who has the cool sophistication suggested by the cat's poise and elegant detachment, along with the defiance of mainstream social conventions suggested by its refusal to conform. A *cat* may also be a member of the avant-garde that defies traditional artistic conventions.

Finally, a whole family of expressions reflects a general perception of the cat as fortunate and superior: if something is really special, it is described as *the cat's whiskers, the cat's meow,* or *the cat's pajamas. Fat cats* enjoy luxury and special privileges, and *the cat that swallowed the canary* is a proverbial example of triumphant satisfaction. One who sits *in the catbird seat* is in an enviable or controlling position.

Adapted from K. Rogers, *The Cat and the Human Imagination: Feline Images from Bart to Garfield* (Ann Arbor: University of Michigan Press, 1998).

WRITING TASK

You will have thirty (30) minutes to respond to the prompt below.

In your own words, explain how changing attitudes toward cats have affected the English language in the last 100 years.

SAMPLE RESPONSES

Before reading the authentic student sample responses and the discussions that follow, let us first see what this prompt is asking you to do and how you might go about doing it. Remember that on an integrated writing task on the 2005 TOEFL®, you will only see the prompt after you have read the article. Because you don't know what the prompt will be, your notes have to capture all the main ideas and important support.

In this particular reading, there are some important things to note. As you read the sample responses, you should look for how each writer deals with these issues.

- The main idea of this passage is about how changing attitudes toward cats affected the English language.

- By reading the first phrase of each paragraph, you can see that the passage talks about changes *over time.*

- The anecdote about Bill Clinton's cat is used only as a way to introduce the topic and get the reader's attention. It is *not,* therefore, a key supporting idea.

In addition, you should note some things about the prompt before you read the samples below.

- The prompt asks for a summary of the main idea of the passage. If you had successfully identified the main idea of the passage, you would know this.

- You must use your own words.

Finally, you should think about these questions before reading the responses below. These questions will help you to put yourself into the minds of the writers.

- How should I organize my response?

- What key examples should I include?

- What grammatical structures will I need in order to write my answer?

Grading Criteria

A review of the 2005 TOEFL® Test scoring criteria for the integrated writing task shows that raters will highly value:

- clear statement of the main idea

- ability to express ideas in your own words

- logical organization of content

- ability to choose and use appropriate examples or supporting details from the passage

- ability to combine ideas from the reading and lecture into a coherent whole

- correct use of vocabulary, though surface errors are tolerated

- use of embedding and other sophisticated grammatical structures, though some errors are tolerated

Essays with the following features will receive lower scores:

- lack of control over necessary grammatical structures

- lack of control over necessary vocabulary use

- unruly organization of content

- too much emphasis on information from reading only or lecture only

- misreading of the original passage that leads to writing non-relevant or misinterpreted support and examples

- misunderstanding of the prompt

Now read the following responses and their comments. They are ranked in order from high to low.

Sample Responses

SAMPLE RESPONSE 1: 5 (high)

You will notice that the writer makes a few errors, such as the error of word form in line 3. However, these surface errors do not detract from the meaning.

If you think about it, you may realize how our domestic feline animals enrich our English language. There are several commonly used references to cats in our colloquial (for example "to play cat and mouse") and more literary idiomatic use like "the cat's whiskers."

Main idea is clearly stated in lines 2–4.

These several expressions are grounded on different perceptions about cats, which evolution can be traced back in different time periods.

A century ago, the cat was, in its mainstream interpretation, just 'a rodents' hunter, which peculiar toy with its victim brought up the mentioned popular expression referring to power abuse.

This paragraph begins with a very complex and native-like sentence!

In the 1930s, as jazz made its appearance as a clever and sophisticated new rythem, men in jazz circles were called of "cats" for their resemblances with the animal's poise and detachment. Another attribute of a cat to be used for characterizing people was the lack of compliance to conformity.

A different aception used in the language, refers to a general perception of superiority and the satisfaction that comes from it as denoted in "the cat that swallowed the canary."

Finally, one of later use, refers to a friends relation between cats and human beings as reflected in "the cat taking his owner's burdens."

Comments: The first and perhaps most striking thing about this essay is the sophisticated use of vocabulary. Keep in mind, however, that using vocabulary *correctly* is most important, and the writer here does that as well. It is clear from this essay that the writer understands the main idea of the passage and is able to express that idea in her own words. The writer chose to follow the same organization in her essay as the organization of the original passage. That is fine, especially since the prompt asks you to discuss the change over time. Thus, she organizes the essay chronologically. Finally, the writer uses many sophisticated grammar structures, proving her mastery of the language.

SAMPLE RESPONSE 2: 4 (high)

Good statement of the main idea!

In English language, the meaning of the word of "cat" has been changed from negative meanings to positive meanings.

Long time ago, people perceived cats are just an unhonest animal because they seem to be selfish. So, in English language, people usually used the word of "cat" as negative meaning.

The writer uses transitions in the third paragraph that signal time, just like in the original passage, but he is careful to use his own words and not the same exact words as appear in the original.

As time goes on, image has changed. For example, people became to think about animals beauty, then people recognized cat's beauty. So people thought about "cat" more positively, and the word has been used in positive meanings. For example, African-Americans have used the word for good jazz music players.

If the writer could have added an example in the second paragraph, as he did in the third paragraph, it would have made his essay even stronger.

Lately, people are thinking about cats as our friend. People use the word positively even in family scene. So meaning of the word has absorutely been changed.

As I mentioned above, the word's meaning has been affected by people's thinking in English language. Firstly, people thought cats are just hunter and an unhonest animal. However, the image has changed positively, and people think cats are a good animal now. The changing has influenced to English language directly. It means the word's meaning has changed from negative to positive.

Comments: From reading this essay it is easy to tell that the writer understood the main idea in the passage. Also, he is able to use his own words to express this idea, even though there are surface errors in plurals, word forms, tense, and aspect. The writer chooses a chronological organization, which is clear and appropriate.

Grammar note: To write about opinions, a writer needs to use several verbs that introduce opinion. For example, the writer might want to say, "In the past, people thought cats were devious hunters." Here, the word *thought* is used to express people's former opinions about cats. Other verbs of opinion include *believe, perceive, consider, think of, regard,* and *look on.* Proper use of these verbs is desirable, yet many of the responses, including the one above, misuse them.

SAMPLE RESPONSE 3: 3 (medium)

The first sentence tells the main idea, but it simply restates the prompt.

The above article talks about the changing attitudes toward cats which have affected the English Language in the last 100 years. So how did they affected English language, I will provide four reasons.

The thesis mentions 4 reasons (line 3), but the prompt did not ask for reasons.

First, four centuries ago, people did not concern a cat as a friend. They thought cats were hunters of rodents and didn't like them because cats always lied in wait, stalk, and played their catches, so many English words toward cats meant bad things or sly human beings.

The comments in paragraph 3 about women bear no resemblance to the original text, an indication that the writer has misread the passage.

Secondly, with the developing of culture, in recent times, more and more people like cats and value them increasingly, especially, many famous women are called cat's whisker or cat's something else. Hence, In English Language, it mean beautiful, or famous women when the phrase include cat.

Thirdly, In 1930, African-American looked cats as smart man, thought they were streetwise. Consequently, a cat symbols a member of avant-gard or smart person in English language.

In line 12 the writer needs to use a verb of opinion, but does not do so successfully.

Finally, now general perception of the cat is that they are looked as human's valued friends and as fortune, superor especially after Clinton's rating approval. Therefore, in English Language, cat will mean special and anjoy luxury special privileges. For example, someone who is in catbird seats means he or she is in an eviable condition.

In paragraph 6 the writer uses this common transition incorrectly.

In a conclusion, From above, you can understand how changing attitudes toward cats have affected the English Language in the last 100 years from involved ways to valued ways.

Comments: In this essay, the main idea and some key supporting ideas are discernable, but the writer struggles to express the ideas clearly and in her own words. Also, you can tell that there are some things that she did not understand from the reading. For example, she says, "Finally, now general perception of the cat is that they are looked as human's valued friends and as fortune, superor especially after Clinton's rating approval." Here she clearly states her final idea, that cats are now seen as valued friends, but she misreads the anecdote about Clinton, saying that his approval rating has somehow caused the status of cats to go up. The many surface grammatical errors also lower the score. The writer has trouble with marking tense and with word forms. At some points, the wording is too clearly borrowed from the original and then misused, such as *avant-gard* for *avant-garde* and *eviable* for *enviable*. Perhaps she wrote those words in her notes or remembered them, but because they were not her own words, she couldn't use them properly. The organization, again, is basically chronological. However, the writer presents the chronology as a list, as indicated by the *first, second, third,* transition words. This does not work as organizational structure for this prompt. Finally, the writer misuses verbs of opinion. For example, she uses *concern* instead of *consider* in the second paragraph and *looked* rather than *looked on* in the fourth and fifth paragraph.

SAMPLE RESPONSE 4: 2 (low)

In line 8 there's a hint of the connection between people's attitudes and language about cats, but it is not sufficiently developed.

The Clinton anecdote in lines 3 and 4 is misused here. It does not have relevance to the prompt, and it is misread.

The cat is an animal which looks clean, be careful and smart. We have had cats for long time ago. They always be people friends, but in recent years, the cats have affected the English language, For example Bill Clinton, the President of USA in 1994, had one cat. He like cat a lot. He said that the cat could be a valued friend, who could be counted on.

In recent years, African-American people, they would give the name to the people who appreciated swing or jazz music as a cat or hepcat. That showed the way of people when they thought about cat. It was clever, smart, good at, self-confidence or stylish.

The third paragraph shows no connection to changing ideas about cats.

The last sentence does not make sense and is not relevant.

We can call a women who is pretty a cat, The cat was compared with the women because they had something same such as the women was beauty the cat was beauty too. Coordination, poise, and style of women that reflect value of cat too.

When we think of cats they look clever, smart and clean. They were compared to the person who clever, smart and clean, In our society, we have a lot of people who look like cats.

Comments: Here the writer seems to have been able to grasp the main idea of the passage about the relationship between cats and language, but is unable to express this idea well or to provide sufficient support. The prompt and the passage emphasize the change of both the attitude toward cats and the English language *over time,* but the writer fails to be able to capture this aspect. The organization of the essay is very loose, simply stating the main idea at the beginning and following with two paragraphs of examples, with no indication of chronology or even an alternative logical structure. Again, the two examples about the African-American usage of *cat* and calling a woman a cat are relevant, but the writer fails to include other important supporting examples or to put these examples in relation to time order or a change in attitudes toward the cat. The writer relies on simple vocabulary and sentence structure, which is relatively free of major errors.

SAMPLE RESPONSE 5: 2 (low)

Cats are known as good friends these days. People like having cats in their family because cats seem very kind, cute and hot-blooded animals to their owners. People even give names to their cats to show the characteristics of the cats. For example, a cat can be named "sleepy" if she or he loves sleeping. A cat can also be named "muscle" if he or she looks like very strong. When I finally think about the relationship between cats and people, I can notice that cats have affected people's life and the language that they use.

> The examples in lines 4 and 5 about naming are the first clues that the writer is headed in the wrong direction!

First of all, according to the article that I read before starting this essay, cats were known with totally different characteristics by people long time ago. For example, the ancestors viewed that cats were hunters. In fact, a very few people would think that cats are good friends at that time. Because of this different idea, people and cats didn't get along with each other, so they didn't affect each other at all.

> In the second paragraph he writes about changing attitudes toward cats, but not about the relationship of this to language.

Ever since cats and people have started to get along with each other and learn the attitudes toward each other, they started to think that people and cats actually can be good friends. Eventually, the number of people who own a cat has increased, and cats have become a member of the people's families.

In addition to having closer relationship between cats and people, cats have started to affect the English language that people all use to communicate in the country. People have started to use cats in their drawings or paintings in the newspapers. They have showed the cats as good and understandable friends. On other words, English has started to relact the beauty and style of the cats.

> In the first sentence of this paragraph he almost gets the relationship to language here, but not quite.

People have gotten some special names from cats. For example, a famous baseball player got the name, "big Georgia cat" which gave this player the meaning of being a perfect player or smart player.

Moreover, families have started to believe that cats bring them luck because they are fortunate and superiors. If something is very special in a family, the people called like "cat's pajama's" or "meow" in order to show their feelings to these special events.

> In paragraphs 5 and 6, the writer pulls out these examples from the passage but does not relate them to the idea of *changing* attitudes.

Comments: The writer here certainly can write a lot and with relatively few grammatical or vocabulary errors. However, the main problem here is that he misreads the prompt. Instead of writing a *summary* of the passage, he writes a *reaction* to the passage. As a reaction, it is very good, and it is impressive that he was able to write so much in such little time. However, it does not address the prompt, which will lower the score. Remember that two skills are being tested here: reading and writing. The writing skills of this student are clearly good, but because he misreads the prompt, we cannot easily determine anything about his reading skills. We also know nothing about his summary writing skills from his response.

Writing in Response to a Lecture

Now you will practice writing in response to a lecture. Most of the skills that you already know will apply, with a few small differences. First, of course, reading and listening are different. You cannot see a lecture, so you will have to rely on your own notes and your memory in order to get the main ideas. In some ways this is more difficult, but for paraphrasing it is actually better for you not to be able to see the text that you are paraphrasing—it forces you to use your own words. Also, if you have worked on and developed your skills for listening to a lecture (see Part 2: Listening), you already can identify main ideas and supporting ideas as you listen.

Note-Taking

To help you write your response to a lecture, you should take notes on the lecture that you hear. If you have not already, read the note-taking hints in Part 2: Listening in this book (page 88). You should especially focus on the note-taking section.

🎧 Lecture: Poverty

Listen again to part of Dr. Jerry W. Sanders' lecture on poverty from Part 2: Listening in this book. Then follow the three basic steps to construct your response to the prompt. Press Play.

> **WRITING TASK**
> You will have ten (10) minutes to write a response to the following prompt.
>   Explain how structural violence is different from direct violence. Include examples of structural violence and how it works.

Understanding the Prompting

First, you must understand the prompt. Remember that you are not able to see the prompt before hearing the lecture. As you listened to the lecture, you should have been able to understand that the professor was talking about *structural violence* and how it is different from *direct violence*. He clearly lays out this point when he states, "Structural violence is the unintended consequences or by-products of institutional activities. The goal of this kind of violence is not to kill, harm, or maim people but, nevertheless, people are harmed as a result of these practices."

Knowing this, the prompt should come as no surprise to you. You should expect a prompt that will ask you to summarize the information in this lecture, and that is what this prompt does. This lecture gives a definition of structural violence and then some examples of it. The prompt asks you to define structural violence and give examples. In essence, it is asking you to summarize the lecture.

Organizing

Since the lecture is basically organized as a definition followed by examples, it is certainly appropriate to organize your response with the same structure. Because you only have ten minutes to respond, you will likely only be able to write one paragraph, which is fine. This task lends itself very well to a typical academic-style paragraph format, namely, stating the main idea in the topic sentence and then giving examples in the supporting sentences.

SAMPLE RESPONSE

Structural violence is violence that results from some institution or policy. It is different from direct violence in that it is not a result of war or violent crime, but nevertheless it causes death and suffering just the same. An example of structural violence is the policy of the International Monetary Fund that insists on certain things from a country before that country can receive loans. These things include decreased public spending and increased privatization. As a result of this policy, more people are impoverished, which is itself a kind of violence. In fact, poverty is another example of structural violence. Preventable deaths from malnutrition or lack of access to health care are evidence of structural violence. When the people in one country have a very short average life span, say, 30 years, while those in another country have a much longer life span, say 80 years, this is a result of structural violence.

Because of the very short amount of time given for your response, you will probably only have one or two minutes to review your writing. However, as you do so, ask yourself these questions:

- Did the information in your writing accurately reflect the information in the lecture?
- Did your writing contain facts and inferences from the text and <u>not</u> your own opinion?
- Is the language different from the language in the lecture (you used your own words)?
- Did you cite your source?

Practicing Writing in Response to a Lecture
Lecture: Genes

Now practice writing in response to a lecture on your own.

Listen to part of a lecture from a biology class. You may take notes as you listen, but you will not be able to hear any part of the lecture again. Press Play.

> ### WRITING TASK
> You will have ten (10) minutes to write a response to the following prompt.
>
> In your own words, write a paragraph briefly explaining the lecture's main points about family and twin studies.

SAMPLE RESPONSES

Before reading the sample responses and the discussions that follow, let us first see what this prompt is asking you to do and how you might go about doing it. Remember that during an integrated writing task on the 2005 TOEFL®, you will only see the prompt after you have heard the lecture. Because of this, as you are listening you cannot focus on a certain idea in your note-taking and comprehension, as you might if you knew the prompt. Instead, you must use the skills that you built in the listening section of this book and identify main ideas and important supporting ideas. If you are a good note-taker, you will be able to write these ideas down in your notes so that you have the basic content of what you heard as you respond to the prompt.

In this particular lecture, there are some important things to note. As you read the sample responses, you should look for how each writer deals with these issues.

- This lecture is simply explaining the academic area called "twin and family studies." It also talks about the kinds of research people in that academic discipline do.
- The basic organization of this lecture is an explanation of what twin and family studies are, followed by supporting examples of studies conducted and major research questions that inform this area of study.
- This lecture does contain some important but unfamiliar vocabulary, such as *monozygotic twins*. However, all of the vocabulary is defined within the passage.

In addition, you should note some things about the prompt before you read the samples below.

- The prompt asks for a summary of the main idea of the passage.
- You must use your own words.

Finally, you should think about these questions before reading the responses below. These questions will help you to put yourself into the minds of the writers.

- How should I organize my response?
- What key examples should I include?

Now read the following responses and their comments.

Sample Responses

SAMPLE RESPONSE 1: 5 (high)

> The writer uses her own words well in lines 1 and 2 and shows her true understanding of the lecture.

So-called 'family and twin studies' mainly address the question of whether more related individuals present more related behavior patterns. 'More related' can be genetically or environmentally. For genetical relationships, twins, preferable monozygotic (i.e. identical) twins are studied. As a study shows, monozygotic twins separated at birth show very similar behavior patterns as adults. For environmental closeness, scientists look at adoptive children and how they resemble their adoptive and their biological parents. Scientists observe different traits and how they seem to be more genetically or more environmentally influenced as the children have more similarities with their adoptive or their biological parents.

> Small errors in word form such as those in lines 2 and 3 do not detract from the overall meaning.

> Similarly, the unidiomatic transition that begins the third sentence is also unimportant when compared to the excellent content here.

Comments: This writer shows her understanding of the lecture through clear explanation of the content in her own words. This writer has an excellent command of the content and of the structures she is choosing. Some mistakes in word form and unidiomatic transitions do not reduce the score.

SAMPLE RESPONSE 2: 3 (medium)

Clear main idea stated in lines 1 and 2.

The lecture basically talks about the types of twins and their similar actions between each other. There are two kinds of twins. One is named identical twins, and the other one is monodentical twins. The lecture gives the specific examples to explain how these two types are different from each other. According to the lecture, identical twins are more similar and closer to each other than the other type of twins are. I can see the differences between two types of twins from the research in the lecture. The researcher seperated two identical twins and put them into two different family and life styles. They eventually noticed that these twins exactly like to do same things, such as go to same shoping stores or eating same food.

This use of "monodentical" in line 3 instead of "identical" shows that the writer is attempting to incorporate new vocabulary that he has decoded through recognition of word parts.

Comments: This response is rated medium because the writer is able to communicate the main ideas and important supporting details of the lecture generally well. However, he does not go into as much detail as the high-rated response. He gives a general description of family and twin studies in the first section, but does not explain its goals or main areas of research. He focuses on different types of twins, rather than on twins separated at birth or adopted into different homes. In this way, he slightly misses the point. He does very well with vocabulary and grammar.

Writing in Response to a Reading and Lecture

The integrated writing task on the 2005 TOEFL® will ask you to read a short passage and listen to a short lecture about the same subject, and then write about the ideas in both the reading and the lecture. For this task you will need the skills that you worked on in the previous two sections, plus the skill of synthesizing information. It is important to remember that this kind of task can easily show an area that is weak for you: If you can read well but your listening is not as good, you might write an essay that leans too heavily on the reading, or vice versa.

Practice 1: Adipose Tissue

You will have five minutes to read the following passage. You may take notes while you read. After you have read the passage, you will hear a short lecture, during which you may also take notes. Finally, you will write a short summary of the main ideas you read and heard.

Adipose Tissue

The technical name for what is commonly called fat is *lipid.* Lipids are necessary for our lives as humans. There are five major types of lipids: phospholipids, steroids, free fatty acids, sphingolipids, and triacylglycerides. Many scientific researchers (as well as many average people) are concerned with triacylglycerides because these lipids go on to become the fat that can be seen on the human body. Triacylglycerides are formed when there is excess energy in the body, which occurs after the liver has stored all the glucose that it is capable of storing. Triacylglycerides travel through the bloodstream and eventually become stored in adipose tissue. Adipose tissue is made up of many lipids that are deposited in certain key places throughout the body, such as the stomach, thighs, and around lymph nodes. The more triacylglycerides that enter the bloodstream, the more adipose tissue will be created, causing those certain areas of the body to enlarge.

Adipose tissue is essential for life, serving as an energy store, insulation against cold, and protection for vital organs. Though the common person may desire a body without fat, actually a healthy man needs about 20 percent of his body mass to be made of fat, while a woman needs at least 30 percent. Too much adipose tissue, however, can lead to health problems such as heart disease and diabetes. Once adipose tissue is created, it is not significantly destroyed, though it can shrink. This is why it is so difficult to lose weight and so easy to put weight back on after it has been lost.

Lecture: Turning Fat into Muscle

Press Play.

WRITING TASK

You will have twenty (20) minutes to write a response to the following prompt.

Explain how adipose tissue is formed in the body and the effect that it has on our weight.

Understanding the Prompt

When responding to a question of this type, you should keep in mind the relationship between the reading and the lecture. Though you will not know the actual writing prompt as you listen and read, you can be sure that the prompt will ask you to integrate the two texts. Here, the relationship between the two is that the reading explains more formally the function of fats or lipids in the body, while the lecture applies that knowledge to a more common or everyday concern: losing weight. Naturally, the prompt asks you to integrate this information.

Organizing

The question is asking you to explain a process and the effect of this process. You should focus on process and results. It would be appropriate to use process-oriented transition words such as *first*, *second*, and *third*, but you, of course, do not have to choose this format.

Remember that part of your job in this question type is to select information to include, and to do this, you must identify the main idea and supporting details. Notice, for example, that the five types of lipids that are mentioned in the first paragraph of the reading are neither part of the main idea nor part of the supporting details that are important enough to include in your response. They simply serve as introductory material.

The number of scientific vocabulary words might seem intimidating at first, but remember that while paraphrasing, it is acceptable and necessary to use some technical vocabulary.

SAMPLE RESPONSE

Adipose tissue is what the common person thinks of as fat. There are various types of fats, or lipids, in the body. The formation of adipose tissue starts with lipids called triacylglycerides. When a person eats more calories than he or she can burn, the liver stores as much glucose as possible and then releases the rest into the bloodstream as triacylglycerides. These eventually end up becoming adipose tissue, and this is the fat that we see in our stomachs and other areas of the body.

According to the article, adipose tissue serves several important functions in the body, so it is necessary in some amount for the human body to survive. However, excess adipose tissue can be bad for your health. Because of this, many people who are overweight want to lose their excess adipose tissue. This is harder than it seems, however, for a variety of reasons. One reason is that once adipose tissue is created, it cannot really be destroyed. It can only shrink. This means that it is very easy to gain weight back after we have lost it.

The nature of adipose tissue has been studied a lot by scientists, but still the only way to lose weight (or shrink adipose tissue) is to burn more calories than you eat. This is because the body has a natural process of storing energy that it cannot burn, which used to be to our advantage in our hunt for food. Today, however, it is this process of creating and storing adipose tissue that has caused health problems such as heart disease and diabetes in many overweight people.

When you have finished writing, read through your essay and be sure that it is as good as it can be.

- Did the information in your writing accurately reflect the information in the reading and lecture?
- Did you balance information from both the reading and the lecture?
- Did your writing contain facts and inferences from the texts and <u>not</u> your own opinion?
- Is the language different from the language in the reading or lecture (you used your own words)?
- Did you cite your source?

Practicing with a Reading and Lecture on Your Own

Practice 2: Human Sex Determination

You will have five minutes to read the following passage. You may take notes while you read. After you have read the passage, you will hear a short lecture, during which you may also take notes. Finally, you will write a short summary of the main ideas you read and heard.

Human Sex Determination

The sex of a human being—in most cases, either male or female—is determined by the production of hormones. Like other proteins, hormones are produced in response to genetic commands, which are coded into the DNA typically found on certain chromosomes. So, ultimately, humans exhibit chromosomal sex determination. The focus of research into human chromosomal sex determination is on the 23rd pair of chromosomes in the cell. If there are two X chromosomes (XX) at this site, the organism will be female. If the pair consists of one X chromosome and one Y chromosome (XY), the organism will be male.

In a sense, being female is the "default" setting of the human organism.

Every normal human embryo has at least one X chromosome, so most of the protein production triggered by X chromosomes will occur unless it is blocked or overruled by other instructions from the genes on a Y chromosome. This effect is demonstrated in the cases of people who happen to have only one chromosome, an X, at site 23 instead of a pair. These individuals will not develop normally and are unlikely to conceive children of their own, but their appearance is female. The effect is also demonstrated by the cases of persons who are XY but whose Y chromosome fails to produce proteins that would determine certain aspects of maleness. Such individuals look female, because many of the "default" female hormones have been allowed to determine protein production.

 **Lecture: Gender**

Press Play.

> **WRITING TASK**
> You will have twenty (20) minutes to write a response to the following prompt.
>   Use your own words to explain the different types of sex determination.

SAMPLE RESPONSES

Authentic student sample responses to the prompt that you just answered follow.

The reading passage describes human sex determination, but the lecture talks about other types of sex determination, including non-chromosomal. It is important to understand that the prompt is asking you to talk about all types of sex determination mentioned in both the reading and the lecture. In essence, you should write a summary of everything you have heard and read about sex determination.

Remember that you will not be able to see the prompt as you read, so you should take some notes. You should also try to take notes during the listening passage. Remember, too, that you will not know the prompt as you read and listen, so it is best to simply try to write down the main ideas and important supporting details.

The reading passage here is pretty straightforward, and maybe it is information that you already know from an introductory biology class, which makes it easier to understand. However, the information in the lecture is probably new to you. Students in this situation will tend to write much more about the information they already know than about the new information. Another reason for an essay that focuses too much on the passage might be that your listening skills are weaker than your reading skills. Remember, this is not only a test of your writing, but an integrated test of your listening and reading as well.

In this particular passage and lecture, there are some important things to note. As you read the sample responses, you should look for how each writer deals with these issues.

- The lecture is basically *adding* more information about sex determination to the passage.
- The organization of both the passage and lecture is basically this: name a certain type of determination, then give an example of that type and how it works.

In addition, you should note some things about the prompt before you read the sample responses.

- The prompt asks for a summary of the main ideas of *both* the passage and the lecture.
- You must use your own words.

Finally, you should think about these questions before reading the responses. These questions will help you to put yourself into the minds of the writers.

- How should I organize my response?
- What key examples should I include?
- What grammatical structures will I need in order to write my answer?

SAMPLE RESPONSE 1: 5 (high)

The most common type of sex determination is the chromosomal. This means that the information related to our sex characteristics is codified in the DNA contained in the chromosomes, specifically in the 23rd pair in the human beings. These chromosomes are denoted X and Y and, as a rule, individuals who are XX are female and XY are male.

> "Codified" in line 2 is just one example of sophisticated, correctly used, original vocabulary.

> The writer recognizes that the reading and lecture basically add information, and her transitions at the beginning of the second, third, and fourth paragraphs reflect this.

There are also other chromosomal types, for example the one found in some species of birds and butterflies. The so-called WZ presents the characteristic that the repeated chromosome is male and the different type chromosome combination is female.

Furthermore there are non-chromosomal sex determination types. One example is the environmental sex determination as presented in crocodiles. Here the temperatures determine whether an individual will be male or female. Thus, if high temperatures are present during the embryo development, the crocodile will elquire male characteristics; if low temperatures are present the individual will be female. And there is even an intermediate type when temperatures are intermediate!

> In line 5 of the third paragraph, the writer correctly uses a semi-colon, another marker of her sophistication and mastery of English conventions.

Another non-chromosomal type of sex determination is found in fish species. The source of this type is unclear but fish are observed to change their sex during their life's spans. The change can go either way from

175

female to male and vice-versa and some individuals may exhibit mixed characteristics. These latter are called hermafrodyte.

Comments: The writer has provided an excellent response to this question. She not only includes all of the main ideas and important supporting details from both the reading and the lecture, she does so in her own words and with her own clear, logical organizational structure. The writer has very few errors in grammar and vocabulary use (a few misspellings), and in fact uses quite sophisticated, original vocabulary correctly. There can be no argument that this response would receive the highest score.

SAMPLE RESPONSE 2: 4 (high)

People usually know that sex cromozoms determine the different kinds of sex types, such as male and female. Therefore, I can say that sex types are determine by production of hormones. If there are two same cromozoms such as "XX", the person will be female, but when two different cromozoms get together, such as "XY" the person will be male.

In addition to the male and female cromozoms, there could be single cromozoms which can make anormal sex types instead of male and female. For example, if there is only X cromozom the person probably will look like a female, but not all all.

In the third paragraph, the writer signals (besides) that she will also include information from the lecture.

Besides sex cromozoms that produce male or female sex types, there are also some different kinds of sex determination types, such as enviromental sex determination and "WZ" sex determination.

According to the lecture, enviromental sex determination has three kinds of sex types that are male, female and both types. In the enviromental sex determination, high temperature produces females. If there is not enough condition about tempreture, the sex type can have the characteristics of male and female sex types.

In line 1 of the fourth paragraph, the writer references the source of the information, showing that she knows how to paraphrase.

Birds and butterflies are the examples of enviromental sex determination. It also can be named the changing sex types.

Comments: The writer understands the main point of the reading and summarizes it well in the first paragraph. However, she does less well summarizing the lecture. She has the content elements but did not hear (or understand) the relationship between those elements. Note here that the author does have the rhetorical summary down effectively, and decent grammar and vocabulary.

SAMPLE RESPONSE 3: 3 (medium)

There are some types of sex determination on the earth. It depends on species.

The sex of human being is determined by the production of hormones. As everyone knows, every beings have DNA. In human case, the 23rd pair of chromosomes in the cell has influence to human sex. Human being has the X chromosome and the Y one. If the 23rd pair was XX, the human is female. One the other hand, if the pair was XY, the human is male. So the sex of human being is decided by the pair.

Some kinds of fishes can change their own sex after they were born. The mechanizm is unknown, but actually the sex can change from male to female if there were only two males or females. Moreover, the tempareture of water influence to fish's sex. High tempareture bring them to male, low tempareture bring them to female, and middle tempareture bring them both sex.

Some other species, such as birds and bataflies, have totally different chromosomes, W and Z. The mechanizm of sex determination is similar to human being, but of course it is not exactly some as humans because of types of chromosomes.

As I mentioned above, there are some types of sex determination, and we could say that they are amazing!

Comments: The content here is good. The main idea statements at the beginning show that the author understood the prompt and will incorporate the information from both the reading and the lecture. One error (*fish* instead of *crocodilians* in paragraph 3) keeps him from being 100 percent accurate. Some grammar problems are apparent, but nothing so serious that it inhibits understanding.

SAMPLE RESPONSE 4: 2 (low)

When it comes to talk about the different types of sex determination, There three types of sex determination.

One is male who owns human chromosomes sex determination on the 23rd pair of chromosome in the cell which is XY.

Second is Female who has XX at this site or X or XY. The Last one fail to produce protein determine certain aspect of maleness.

The Last one is mix type. But as far as I know, It has XX/XY. WZ at this site.

In a conclusion, sex determination in most cases, There are always XX or XY which will be Female or Male. Either male or female is the production of hormone which responses to genetic commands and it is coded into DNA chromosome in the cell as I talked above.

Line 7 shows the only attempt to incorporate information from the lecture.

Comments: This is a classic example of a low-scoring response because it leaves out information from the lecture. This style of question tests your reading, writing, and listening skills. It is designed to look for your weakness in one or more of these areas, and this student lets his weakness show through. The author gets it wrong when he says, *there are three types of sex determination*. Actually, the reading and lecture talk about various types of sex determination, not all of which are chromosomal, so immediately the reader knows that this summary will leave out key ideas. In addition, the sentence structure is rather simple and often confusing. Strange vocabulary uses, like *owns* in the second paragraph and *as I talked above* in the last paragraph, also bring down the score.

PART 4

Speaking

> ## Four General Test-Taking Strategies for the Speaking Section
>
> A few general test-taking strategies will improve your performance on the speaking section of the 2005 TOEFL®.
>
> 1. Do not attempt to write out a word-for-word response before you speak it. You won't have time, and you won't sound natural.
>
> 2. Take notes during the readings and lectures. This will help you summarize. Try to take notes in English.
>
> 3. Answer the question that is asked.
>
> 4. For integrated tasks, try to balance information from the reading and the lecture in your response. Do not rely too heavily on either one.

In this section, you will learn how to do two kinds of speaking tasks that may be required of you on a multi-skills test: *independent speaking* and *speaking in response to a lecture, a reading, or both.*

In the past, few tests have included speaking assessments. With advances in technology, however, it is easier than ever to record a test-taker's speech for assessment. Speaking for a short time in response to a prompt or a reading or lecture is a very realistic academic task because this is the kind of speaking that you will be asked to do in the classroom. In a university class, it is important to be able to speak fluently and communicate your ideas clearly in a short amount of time. Communicative tests like the TOEFL® Test and other multi-skills tests assess this academic skill.

The speaking section of the 2005 TOEFL® is similar to the writing section in many ways. The two types of questions are very similar (speaking in response to a prompt and speaking in response to a reading, lecture, or both); however, the way that you prepare for and deliver your spoken responses is different from the way you can prepare for your written responses. The main difference is that you will have very little time to prepare and deliver your spoken answers. Unlike the writing section, the speaking section gives you only seconds to prepare and answer.

Speaking is the last skill covered in this book because the work you have done in the previous parts will help prepare you for the things you need to do in the Part 4: Speaking. Some of these skills include *identifying main ideas and supporting details in a reading or lecture* (Parts 1 & 2,

Reading and Listening), *note-taking* (Part 2: Listening), *organizing your ideas* (Part 3: Writing), and *paraphrasing* (Part 3: Writing). If you have not already completed these parts of the book, you should do so before starting Part 4: Speaking.

In this section you will also work on some new skills that are specific to speaking, including *identifying the question type, organizing a spoken response*, and *improving your fluency and overall understandability*. Both independent and integrated question types are worked together throughout this chapter. Finally, you will learn how raters will score your spoken responses.

Building Skills: Responding to Independent and Integrated Speaking Prompts

Basic Skills	Some Related Academic Tasks	Related Tasks on Tests like the 2005 TOEFL®
1. **Speaking in response to a prompt** 2. **Synthesizing information** 3. **Summarizing**	• responding to a prompt on a test • responding to a teacher's question in class • preparing to participate in class discussions • participating in group discussions • preparing presentations • speaking about research you have done • speaking about materials you have read or lectures you have heard • doing a presentation using readings or lectures as support • participating in classroom discussions about readings or lectures • presenting an oral summary to show you understand a reading • taking notes	• independent speaking task • integrated speaking tasks • integrated tasks: reading/speaking, listening/speaking, and reading/listening/speaking • speaking about the ideas in a passage • speaking about the ideas in a lecture

Rhetorical Styles

Because the time that you are given to prepare to speak is so short, familiarizing yourself with rhetorical expectations will make your spoken response more likely to earn a high score. **Rhetorical expectations** are the accepted style of organizing your content and making your point in speaking or writing. Rhetorical expectations vary by genre and culture. For example, when telling a children's story or a fairy tale in English, a native speaker will often start with the phrase, "Once upon a time." This phrase signals to whomever is listening that the following story is fiction, that there will likely be magic involved, and that probably (in North American fairy tales, at least) there will be a happy ending. These are rhetorical expectations. If you started an academic lecture with the phrase "Once upon a time," your listeners would think you were crazy.

Similarly, rhetorical expectations vary across languages and cultures. Some cultures value explaining reasons and examples and letting the listener or reader draw his or her own conclusions, while others value hearing the main idea first, and then reasons and examples to support it. In general, North American Academic style values the latter. You should state the main idea and then support it with examples. North American listeners and test raters will think that a spoken response with this basic rhetorical structure is clear and organized.

EXERCISE 1

Look at the following transcripts of student responses to a typical independent speaking task. For each transcript, circle the main idea and then underline the supporting details. Finally, answer the questions that follow.

Prompt: When students come to a university, most live with a roommate, though some choose to live alone. Would you prefer to live with a roommate or live alone during your university studies? Why?

Transcript 1: Um, when I come to a university I'd like to live with a roommate rather than live alone. The main reason for this selection is mainly come from the economic consideration. As far as you know, as students, we are often poor and it's not, a, likely that we can afford to live alone. With a roommate we can live more affordably and we can have some company.

Transcript 2: I'm not a person who gets along with people well. I am an introverted person—I, umm, I like to be alone a lot so . . . I tend to be less social than other people. I don't want to have roommate because I will lose my privacy.

Questions:

    a. What is the main idea of the first example? Restate it in your own words.

---

b. What is the main idea of the second example? Restate it in your own words.

_____

c. Which example follows North American rhetorical style?

_____

Identifying the Question Type

Just as a fairy tale and an academic lecture have different rhetorical styles and content, so do questions that ask for your opinion and questions that ask for a summary. In both cases, you should state your main idea first. However, if the question asks for a summary of the ideas in a short lecture and you talk about your opinion of the lecture, your score will be lowered because of content. In this case, you have given a spoken response that does not fulfill the rhetorical expectations of the rater and that does not address the question.

Some questions in the speaking section will ask you to simply speak an answer (*independent* speaking tasks). Others will ask you to respond in some way to a reading, lecture, or conversation (*integrated* speaking tasks). In Exercise 2, you will practice determining whether the question is asking you for a summary, for your opinion, or for both a summary and your opinion. You will see examples of both independent speaking tasks and integrated speaking tasks.

EXERCISE 2

Listen to the following questions. Determine whether they ask for your opinion or for a summary or both. Circle the correct answer for each. Press Play.

a. Some people prefer to do homework with a friend, while others prefer to work alone. Which do you prefer and why?

opinion   summary   both

b. What is your favorite season of the year? Why?

opinion   summary   both

c. Briefly explain the problem that the student had and how she solved it. What do you think about her solution?

opinion   summary   both

    d. Explain the problem that the student and professor were discussing. What do you think about the solution?

                opinion   summary   both

    e. What problem is the university having? How would you solve that problem?

                opinion   summary   both

    f. According to the lecture, what is the best method for preventing a flu outbreak?

                opinion   summary   both

You will notice that there are certain key words or phrases in the prompt that signal whether your answer should be a summary, an opinion, or both. Some of them are listed below, but you may be able to think of others.

Summary Key Words	Opinion Prompt Key Words
Briefly summarize *Explain the main idea of* _____ *According to the lecture,* (direct question about content)	*What do you think about . . .* *Give your opinion of . . .* *Tell your ideas about . . .* *What is you favorite . . .* *Which do you prefer . . . .* *How would you . . . .*

    Prompts that ask for **both summary and opinion** will combine these key words and phrases.

    If you are asked to give both a summary and an opinion, try to manage your time so that you can do both.

Managing Your Time

Perhaps the most difficult thing about the speaking section is time management. Even very good speakers (actually, especially those speakers!) can get carried away with a certain part of the prompt and run out of time. Your penalty for running out of time will not be that great if your response has good grammar, vocabulary, and fluidity. However, if you run out of time because you are talking slowly, pausing a lot, or summarizing something in too much detail, you will likely get a low score.

EXERCISE 3

Read the following two student responses to a typical listening/speaking prompt. Do the exercises that follow. Check your answers in the key.

Prompt: Briefly describe the problem that the students discussed in the conversation, and give your opinion about the solution that the two students decided on.

Sample 1 Transcript: The problem is that they couldn't aah keep up with aah profess . . . , they didn't understand professor's lecture so they they think like aah if they didn't get . . . main idea this time they were they are worried about next time, . . . so and also the midterm is coming so they ah they ah think about their . . . they yeah, so they wanted they wanted to meet they wanted to meet their professor but before meet before meeting professor they ah have they have ah . . . ah they have appointment to compare their notes in this evening. And . . . I think their idea is very good because if I don't have if I have something problem, it's the best way to solve the problem is to ask the professor so I think their idea is very good.

Sample 2 Transcript: The two student is talking about their, aah, lecture um the man said like the professor go too far and then it's hard to follow and then um both of them think that aah, no the girl think that she get the main um idea but still not very clear about the lecture, the materials and then um the man decide to go to his ah ah ah ah the professor's office hours . . . and then like they suggest to go together because it would not be so embarrassed and then because they they they ah need to go to the office hour because of the midterm is coming and then the girl suggest to go to suggest they should compare they notes ah before they ah go to find the professor because they can compare the notes and then ah see what they missed. And then yeah . . . And then ah, . . . my opinion of the solution is, ah, pretty good.

a. Is the prompt asking for a summary, opinion, or both?

_____

b. What is missing from sample 2?

_____

c. Which answer do you think would get a higher score?

_____

Bonus! d. If you have access to the Internet, listen to the responses and answer this question. Mark the pauses in both transcripts with a slash (/). Who pauses more and for longer?

_____

It is best to try to keep your summaries brief. First, this will show that you understand paraphrasing. Remember that paraphrases are shorter than in the original, so make them brief. Do not attempt to recount every statement in a conversation. For example, avoid saying, *First, he said _____. Then she said _____. Then he answered with _____. And then she said _____.* This is too tedious. Raters want to see that you can listen, understand, and tell the main idea and important (but not all!) supporting details.

You might think that using a watch during the test will help you to divide your time more successfully. Depending on your personality and your state of mind during test-taking, using a watch may help you, but it may also cause you to panic! A better idea is to practice with a stopwatch while preparing for the test, but to eventually not rely on the stopwatch for your timing.

Stating the Main Idea Clearly

As we have emphasized throughout this section, it is important that your main idea is stated clearly. Just as in writing, your spoken response should have some sort of main idea statement, like a thesis. As you practiced in the writing section, one effective way of stating your main idea is to simply change the prompt into a sentence stating your main idea. This method works better with opinion questions than with summary questions, but it can be done with both.

EXERCISE 4

Match the prompts on the left with the main idea statements on the right. Write the letter in the blank.

Prompt	Main Idea Statement
_____ 1. Describe the problem that the students were discussing and how they decided to solve it.	a. According to the lecture, adipose tissue protects our vital organs, insulates us against cold, and functions as an energy store.
_____ 2. Based on the reading and the lecture, describe the process of photosynthesis.	b. If you were going to visit me in my own country, I would take you to the Mayan ruins because they are the most fascinating place in Mexico.
_____ 3. If I were going to visit you in your country, where would you take me and why?	c. If I had the money, I would buy a new computer because it would help me to do my school work more efficiently.
_____ 4. According to the lecture, what is the function of adipose tissue?	d. The process of photosynthesis is how plants turn sunlight into energy.

_____ 5.	If you had the money, would you buy a new computer or an old used car?	e. According to the reading and the lecture, malaria is spread through mosquito bites, and one effective way to stop it is to reduce the amount of mosquito habitat.
_____ 6.	What is your favorite type of music and why?	f. The two students were roommates whose problem was that their neighbor was playing his music loudly while they were trying to study.
_____ 7.	What is your favorite place on campus to study?	g. The professor's main point about ethnographic research was that the researcher must become a part of the community that he or she is researching.
_____ 8.	Discuss the professor's main points about doing ethnographic research.	h. The most important leader from my country is Simon Bolivar because he helped Venezuela to gain independence from Spain.
_____ 9.	Who is the most important leader from your country, and why is he or she important?	i. My favorite type of music is the folk music from my country because when I hear it, I think of home.
_____ 10.	According to the reading and the lecture, how is malaria spread and what is the most effective way to stop it?	j. My favorite place on campus to study is the coffee shop because I can watch interesting people there, which keeps me from getting bored.

Follow-up question: For each matched pair, notice the words and phrases that stay the same, and those that have been changed. Why has some of the language been changed, while other language remains the same?

On your own: _Use prompts 3, 5, 6, 7, 9 as practice. Read the prompt, prepare for 15 seconds, and speak for 45 seconds._

Supporting and Developing Your Point

Of course, you will want to support your main idea in your spoken response. There is a slight difference between doing this with independent speaking tasks and integrated speaking tasks. In an independent speaking task, you will be using your background knowledge and examples from your life to support your point. In an integrated speaking task, your support will come from what you heard and read.

EXERCISE 5

Read the following sample responses, and then answer the questions that follow.

Prompt: Briefly describe the problem that the students discussed in the conversation, and give your opinion about the solution that the two students decided on.

Response 1:   There are two people, er . . . a man, at there . . . . . . the professor is really fast so they miss the main ideas . . . so they wanna meet their professor at first . . . they kept office hour and then they . . . they wanna to check together, and they want to compare their take notes . . . so they will meet . . . dinner at after dinner at study lounge. . . . . . . It's problem and they resolves that. That's it.

Response 2:   The two student is talking about their, aah, lecture um the man said like the professor go too far and then it's hard to follow and then um . . . both of them think that aah, no the girl think that she get the main idea but still not very clear about the lecture, the materials and then um the man decide to go the ah ah ah the professor's office hours and then like they suggest to go together because it would not be so embarrassed and then because they they they ah need to go to the office hour because of the midterm is coming and then the girl suggest to go to suggest they should compare they notes ah before they ah go ah to find the professor because they can compare the notes and then see ah what they missed. And then yeah . . . And then ah, my opinion of the solution is, ah, pretty good.

1. Circle the main idea in each transcript.

2. Underline the supporting ideas in each transcript. Which response has more supporting ideas?

3. In each transcript, how could the speaker improve the support he or she gives?

Using Transitions

Once you have learned how to determine what the question is asking you to do, you need to have some words and phrases that will help you to organize your response. If you can learn to use these, it will help you to show the raters that you can logically connect and organize your ideas. However, beware! Try not to overuse transition words, and take care to use only the ones that you have mastered.

EXERCISE 6

This chart contains the functions of commonly used spoken transitions. Think of as many transition words for each function as possible.

Function	Signal Words
Adding information	
Listing	
Comparing (expressing similarities)	
Contrasting (expressing differences)	
Explaining a process	
Giving a definition	
Explaining a result	
Giving examples	
Changing ideas, changing topics	
Drawing conclusions	
Repeating a point	
Summarizing/concluding	

Transition words aren't the only way to show organization. In fact, sophisticated speakers will use other types of rhetorical devices to show the relationships between ideas.

EXERCISE 7

Read the transcript. Circle the transitions that the speaker uses.

Prompt: When students come to a university, most live with a roommate, though some choose to live alone. Would you prefer to live with a roommate or live alone during your university studies? Why?

Sample Transcript: Ah, when I think about this question, I would prefer to live with a roommate . . . during my university studies . . . cause I don't want to live . . . just myself in a house or in a room of the dormitory. When I stay with someone . . . in my room, I can talk to him . . . and . . . improve my English skills. And also when I have some trouble or . . . . some sad events, I can talk to my roommate roommate and feel better. In conclusion, I like to have roommates.

1. Circle any transition words or phrases that the speaker uses.

2. What is the relationship between the two ideas that are connected by these transitions?

3. Look at the places where the speaker *does not* use a transition word or phrase. How is the connection between the ideas shown in these situations?

4. What can you conclude about making transitions *without* using transition words or phrases?

As you can see from the transcript, the speaker is not using just simple transition words to show the relationship between ideas.

Practicing with Skills You've Learned

In addition to the speaking skills that you have already practiced, you will need to draw on your previous work in this book to answer questions in the speaking section. Below you will find advice about how to transfer the skills that you have already worked on into speaking skills.

Synthesizing Information

As in the writing section, some questions on the speaking section will ask you to synthesize ideas from a passage and a lecture into a spoken response. The difference in the speaking test is the length and, therefore, difficulty of the passages and lectures. Passages will be only one short paragraph long, and you will have only 45 seconds to read. Listenings will also be short, generally about three minutes long. Because of this, the information included cannot be very complex. In addition, you will have much less time in which to formulate your response. Because of this, most passages and lectures will complement or add to each other.

Using Your Own Words

As in the writing section of the TOEFL® Test, the speaking section will require you to use your own words when paraphrasing and summarizing information that you hear or read. It is easier to paraphrase when you listen because you do not have the temptation of reading off the page. On the speaking section of the 2005 TOEFL®, the passages will remain visible to you as you speak. Be careful not to read information exactly. Instead, use your own words as you learned in the paraphrasing part of the writing section of this book.

Understanding Key Ideas

As you worked through the reading and listening sections of this book, you focussed on determining the main idea and important supporting points of a passage. As you respond in the speaking section, you will need to draw upon these skills. Especially remember these key ways to determine the main idea and important supporting information.

- Listen and read for repeated ideas, especially those that are repeated in both a reading and a listening passage.
- Look for main ideas in the passages in the first few sentences and in the concluding sentence. Listen for main ideas in the lecture in an organizing statement near the beginning of the talk and in a concluding statement near the end.
- Try to figure out the relationship between the ideas in the reading and the ideas in the listening. Does one add information to the other? Do they present contrasting information?

Selecting and Organizing Information

This is related to time management. Since the readings and listenings are so short in the speaking section, there will be less information to sift through as you form your response. Remember to keep your summaries brief if the question asks for both summary and opinion.

Note-Taking

The listening passages on this part of the test are very short, so you might not take many notes at all. Listen for these things to direct your note taking:

- main idea statements and concluding statement
- definitions of key terms
- information that adds to or contradicts information in a reading passage
- the opinion of the speaker

How Your Response Will Be Rated

Just as with your essays, raters will give your speaking a holistic score. The rubric for speaking will focus on language use and content. Responses here are scored between 4 and 1, with 4 being the highest and 1 being the lowest.

In the next section, we will look at responses to each type of speaking prompt: speaking alone, reading/listening/speaking, and listening/speaking. While examining these responses, you will start to notice what increases the scores and what lowers them. To preview, these things are:

- accuracy and completeness of content
- intelligibility (phonological or prosodic features)
- lexical and grammatical complexity and precision
- overall fluency and coherence

Although you probably cannot accurately rate your own speaking, you can get a better understanding of what raters expect and compare your practice responses to the responses to get an approximation of your score.

Grading Criteria

A review of the TOEFL® Test scoring criteria for the independent speaking task shows that raters will highly value:

- clear statement of the main idea
- well-developed supporting ideas
- clear pronunciation
- correct vocabulary use and appropriate range of vocabulary
- fluid delivery
- well-organized response
- accurate, understandable grammar

Responses with these features will receive a lower score:

- many distracting pauses
- pronunciation problems that interfere with understanding
- inaccurate vocabulary use or limited vocabulary range
- rambling, disorganized speech
- poor time management
- frequent, distracting grammatical errors
- content irrelevant or lacking

Independent Speaking Prompts

The first two questions on the speaking section of the 2005 TOEFL® will be independent speaking prompts. These prompts will ask you about your opinion or preference, sometimes asking you to make a choice between two things or situations (as in Question 2 on page 193). Since these are completely based on your own opinion, you should draw on your background and experience to answer the questions.

Listen to the sample test items and respond based on the prompts. Press Play. Pause the audio after Question 1.

QUESTION 1

Choose a favorite holiday from your culture. Explain why it is your favorite.

Preparation time: 15 seconds
Response time: 45 seconds

QUESTION 2

When students come to a university, most live with a roommate, though some choose to live alone. Would you prefer to live with a roommate or live alone during your university studies? Why?

Preparation time: 15 seconds
Response time: 45 seconds

These are fairly simple questions meant to get you speaking easily. You should approach these questions with confidence because there are no wrong answers. The rhetorical expectations for these prompts are very similar. For Question 1, you are expected to state your favorite holiday in a main idea sentence toward the beginning of your response, and then support your answer with concrete reasons why the holiday is your favorite. For Question 2, you are expected to state your preference for living with or without a roommate, and then to support your idea with reasons and examples that justify or explain your preference.

Think about these questions as you listen to the sample responses:

  a. How should I organize my response?

  b. What key vocabulary or phrases might be useful in responding to this prompt?

Sample Responses—Question 1

SAMPLE RESPONSE 1: 4 (high)

Transcript: Umm . . . umm my favorite holiday in my culture from my culture is full moon ah festival day . . . umm . . . . Ah the reason I like this holiday is ah . . . is that it's a really long like ah it's almost fo . . . three or four days so I can take a rest for long time and . . . when we reach ah the this holiday, ah we our relatives and our rela . . . our relative get together so we get together and eat food together and . . . we can go to um we can go to somewhere and then we can play something and also we can um do lots of. . . . (cut off)

Comments: The speaker gives a generally good response here. She changes the prompt into her main idea sentence and then follows this with reasons to support her opinion. She has generally good fluidity and comprehensibility. Her vocabulary is relatively simple, and she uses vague terms such as *go somewhere* and *do something*, which should be avoided. In addition, she uses the phrase *take a rest* unidiomatically. The speaker's pronunciation problems include the /r/ and /l/ distinction and her pronunciation of /w/. To listen to them, you'll need access to the Internet.

To improve, this student should practice with a minimal pair list and a mirror. This will help develop the /r/ and /l/ distinction. Working with a mirror will also be helpful for getting the lip-rounding necessary to pronounce the /w/.

> **Vocabulary Note: Resting**
>
> Many students of English know the meaning of words but have not quite mastered how to use those words together in a phrase. One example is using *take a rest* to mean "have a vacation." If you are talking about stopping work and resting for a short period of time, say, for ten minutes or an hour, you can use the phrase *to take a rest* or *to take a break*, or you could simply use the verb *to rest*. If you are talking about a vacation, then you should use the phrase *to take a vacation* or *to go on a vacation*. For example:
>
> After I read this chapter, I am going to take a rest and watch some TV.
>
> I am going to take a vacation during the Christmas holidays.

SAMPLE RESPONSE 2: 4 (high)

Transcript: Um, my favorite holiday is ah mid-autumn festival. Aah it's a a Chinese festival just like American Thanksgiving. It's a holiday for family re reunion so every year . . . on this holiday my family, um, maybe my fam all the family members just come from all the different places in the country and, ah, we are going to have a big meal and ah talk about what happened a recently. And also, we will enjoy the moon cakea. Um, I love moon cake very ah, very much much, so it is a . . . . (cut off)

Comments: The speaker has a good organizing statement, and she supports her idea well with good examples and explanations. She is very understandable, with excellent grammar. One pronunciation problem is that she tends to add syllables unconsciously. Despite this, she would score well. (To listen to her pronunciation problems, you'll need access to the Internet.)

To improve, this student should record herself and listen for the "extra" syllables that she is adding to the ends of words. This is a problem for many speakers, depending on their first language, and is usually a problem of becoming aware that you are doing it at all. Once awareness has been built, you are halfway to fixing the problem.

Sample Responses—Question 2

SAMPLE RESPONSE 1: 3 (medium to high)

Transcript: I prefer to live with a roommate because aah my um my roommate can help me to can help me study or we can share lots of thing in our university and . . . actually, aah when, when I can when I go to a university, maybe I will feel I feel lonely but if I have a roommate I can share lots of worries or problem so we can solve it together . . . and I can't feel like I don't feel lonely if I have a roommate. Maybe I will. And . . . ah if I have a roommate we can help each other so that's . . . .

Comments: The content of this speaker's response is good. She gives her opinion clearly and follows up with a well-developed set of reasons for that opinion. This speaker has a problem with her /r/ and /l/ distinction and with the *th* as in *that*—it is coming across as a /z/. To listen, you'll need access to the Internet.

To improve, this student should work on her /th/ using a mirror. When forming the /th/ in English (either the voiced or voiceless one), the tongue must touch the top teeth, so it should be visible when the sound is made.

SAMPLE RESPONSE 2: 3 (medium to high)

Transcript: In my opinion I prefer to live with a roommate. When I come to in the USA I have a roommate, an American roommate. It is a little bit different with me because I am a little bit outgoing person but she is a really shy . . . and quiet girl so I don't like her too much but we can share each other we can understand each other so . . . in my opinion it is really important to live with my roommate. And my second roommate also is a little bit different with me but I learned a lot.

Comments: Here, the pronunciation and grammar are good and require little listener effort. The biggest problem is with development. She only has one idea here, really: that she and her roommate did not get along but they can share things anyway. This idea needs to be developed more, rather than repeated, as she does.

To improve, this student should practice development in writing (perhaps reviewng the Using Questions for Development section on pages 130–31 in the Part 3: Writing in this book) to understand what development is and how it can be achieved. Then she can move to oral practice, perhaps beginning by having a friend ask her questions to help her develop the ideas.

Speaking Prompts

As in the writing section of the 2005 TOEFL®, the speaking section will include questions where you must integrate information that you read with information that you hear. There are two prompts like this in the speaking section. One is usually about a problem or issue related to university life, while the other is about an academic topic.

Grading Criteria

A review of the TOEFL® Test scoring criteria for the integrated speaking task shows that raters will highly value:

- ability to incorporate information from both the reading and the listening
- accurate summary
- appropriate rhetorical style
- clear main idea or organizing statement
- good time management
- pronunciation does not cause too much listener effort
- correct vocabulary use and access to a range of vocabulary
- appropriate grammar
- speech without too many distracting pauses

Responses with these features will receive a lower score:

- too much reliance on information from the passage or lecture, rather than a synthesis of both
- inability to accurately summarize
- poor time management (long pauses, distractingly slow speaking)
- misuse of vocabulary; lack of necessary vocabulary
- poor grammar
- pronunciation that requires much listener effort
- disorganized/unexpected rhetorical style

READ, LISTEN, AND SPEAK

The following question describes a problem that is happening on campus and one student's opinion about how to solve that problem. This is a fairly typical question type.

Read and listen to the sample test item. Press Play. Pause the audio to read the passage.

QUESTION 3

Reading time: 45 seconds

The university has had difficulty covering all its expenses lately. The university is considering two possibilities. One is to reduce expenses by cutting some programs and firing some workers. The other is to raise more money by increasing the cost of taking classes at the university.

Restart the audio.

The student gives her own opinion about the best way to solve the university's money problems. Say what her opinion is, and summarize the reasons she gives.

Preparation time: 30 seconds

Response time: 60 seconds

This prompt asks you to read about a problem on campus and then listen to one student's opinion about how to solve the problem. The passage describes the problem in a fairly neutral way and lays out two possible solutions. It should not surprise you that when giving her opinion about how to solve the problem, the student chooses one of these solutions and elaborates on it. She gives reasons why she prefers to solve the problem by raising tuition. Those reasons are important supporting details to remember.

In addition, you should note some things about the prompt itself before you listen to and read about the samples below. This prompt is asking for a summary, not an opinion. Because of this, your time should be focused on summarizing what you heard, not making a judgment about the student's ideas. Also, although the prompt is asking you to summarize the student's opinion and her reasons for it, you should also restate the problem that she is responding to in order to organize your summary effectively.

Finally, you should think about these questions before listening to the responses below. These questions will help you to put yourself into the minds of the speakers.

- How should I organize my response?
- What is the student's main idea?
- What are her reasons for her opinion?
- What key vocabulary might be useful in my response?

Sample Responses—Question 3

SAMPLE RESPONSE 1: 4 (high)

Transcript: Ah the student favors the solution of raising more money by increasing the cost, aah . . . she doesn't favor this . . . , she ah favors raising more money oh sorry she favors raising ah more money, ah because-a she thinks the the university's ah costs of taking classes-ah now is very low. Even if we raise a little bit-a it doesn't hurt-a just the people will still want to go to this ah ah university for its low rate. But if we cut the ah programs-a that will ah hurt the quality of the education and ah people won't-a think the university ah is a respect—respectable a-university anymore thus people will not come to this ah university anymore. So, that hurts ah the university's future. So, ahh . . . so the so the girl, the student think that it is better to raise the money by increasing the cost, ah that's all . . . and . . . aah and also . . . oh my gosh, I still have one minute.

Comments: The speaker has very good vocabulary and grammar. Her pronunciation does hold her back on certain words. She addresses the prompt very well, but she stumbles at the beginning as she summarizes the woman's opinion. The good thing here is the speaker's rhetorical structure. She gives a context to her summary of the woman's opinion by first describing the problem that the woman is talking about. Then she includes the relevant ideas in her response.

> **Stumbling**
>
> If you find that you are stumbling over words, don't let it get you down. The important thing is to keep going and complete your response. If you recover well, your score should not be drastically affected.

SAMPLE RESPONSE 2: 3 (medium to high)

Transcript: umm . . . er. The . . . . She argues that the university raise tuition fee aah because if the if the university um . . . raise aah raise their tuition fee tuition fee maybe students will get a better deal in their program. But if the university cut the budget, cut the program, maybe . . . ah the quality will be worse, will be getting, will be getting worse. So she argues um university have to ah think about ah university university have to raise tuition fee raise tuition rather than um . . . rather than cutting the um rather than reducing expenses by cutting some programs and firing some workers. Umm . . . ah . . . Also she said ah if university, if university raise the tuition fee maybe it's ah it will be good for students because they can take a good program and ah it's it's better um it's good for, it's good for students so she argues, ah she insists that the university have to raise tuition fee.

Comments: Very good summary. It is clear that the speaker understood the student's point and was able to put the ideas in her own words. The speaker also cites her source when she says, *she argues that . . .*, which shows that she knows about the rhetorical conventions of summarizing.

Though in general the speaker has good fluidity, the response is a bit halting here, with many stops, starts, and recasts. Good vocabulary and grammar.

SAMPLE RESPONSE 3: 3 (medium to high)

Transcript: In this question, the problem is about a university which has some financial problems. The speaker. the speaker's opinion is . . . to raise more money by increasing the cost of taking classes at the university because . . . the other possibility, that is, . . . reducing expenses by cutting some programs and firing some workers . . . is not a good idea for the speaker. . . . In my case, . . . I think, I think the same way that, speaker speaker believes. If I were the responsible people, responsible person in the university who will . . . solve the problem, I would raise more money by increasing the cost of taking classes at the university because this is a better solution than reducing expenses by cutting some programs if university cuts its programs and fires some workers, that that would be that would be bad for the university because there is lots of university and people who will think that this school is not good.

> **Recasting**
>
> One (often good) habit of non-native speakers of English is recasting, or repeating a word or phrase, in order to correct it just after you have said it. The above response does this quite frequently. Although it is perfectly fine to correct yourself mid-sentence (and many native speakers do it as well), too much recasting can be distracting. As you can see from these responses, you do not need perfect grammar to get a high score, so it is okay to let some grammar errors go by.

Comments: The speaker starts out very well by stating the problem and the main idea of the speaker. This organizes the response very well according to North American rhetorical style. The pronunciation doesn't require much listener effort, and the grammar is very good overall. The only thing holding this response back is fluidity or speed. In addition, the speaker launches into a whole section giving his opinion, which is not asked for in the question.

To improve, this speaker should practice by talking to himself. It might sound crazy, but a good way to develop speed and comfort in a language is to talk to yourself. This helps develop automaticity, or the ability to make the step between thinking and speaking more automatic.

SAMPLE RESPONSE 4: 3 (medium to high)

Transcript: I think, I think she said ah . . . increasing the cost and keep quality of classes is good. Um I agree, I totally agree with her. Um . . . actually, this is kind of trade-off, aah . . . I mean that cost and quality of class, so we need the minimum quality of classes but umm . . . for this purpose . . . we need to pay some cost for classes so if we can take classes that is that has very high quality we can pay even though this is high cost. So um . . . Actually, nobody wants to pay high cost, . . . but um . . . for getting good education this is necess—, nec— necessary to pay some tuitions or fee or something like that. So . . . ummm . . . this is good to aah increase the cost and keep the quality of classes. That's my opinion. Thank you.

Comments: There is a good argument about the trade-off (and good use of the word *trade-off!*). The main feature holding this student back is the halting nature of his response. He speaks in chunks with pauses in between. This lowers the score. Good features of this response include relatively sophisticated vocabulary and grammar structures. Pronunciation requires a bit of listener effort. To listen, you'll need access to the Internet.

To improve, this student should develop fluidity in speaking. To help develop fluidity in speaking (especially when you are summarizing something or making an argument), try reading a short newspaper article or listening to a short news report and then summarizing it orally and give your opinion about the content.

READ, LISTEN, AND SPEAK ABOUT AN ACADEMIC TOPIC

You should expect to have a question about a fairly academic subject. For these questions, as in the one that follows, the reading and listening will build on or complement each other, and your job will be to summarize all the information that you read and heard. This will require you to synthesize information, as you already practiced in the writing section of this book, into a coherent summary.

Read and listen to the sample test item and then respond according to the prompt. Press Play. Pause the audio to read the passage.

QUESTION 4

Reading time: 45 seconds

The Anomalous Expansion of Water

Almost every substance contracts (takes up less space) as it get older. The same is true for water, until it reaches a temperature of 4 degrees Celsius. At that point, its volume increases as it gets colder, until the point (0 degrees Celsius) where it freezes and becomes ice. This is known as "the anomalous expansion of water."

Restart the audio.

Considering the information you have just received from the reading and the lecture, explain why water is unusual and describe some of the effects of this property of water.

Preparation time: 30 seconds
Response time: 60 seconds

This particular prompt seems difficult because of the word *anomalous* in the passage. You should note, however, that the passage defines the phrase *the anomalous expansion of water,* and so prior knowledge of the meaning of the term *anomalous* is not necessary at all. Try not to let the technical vocabulary disrupt your preparation of the response. Also, the lecture gives examples of some of the results of this odd property of water, so the relationship between the passage and the lecture is that the lecture further elaborates on the passage. This is a fairly typical relationship.

Remember that the prompt is asking you to summarize the information from the passage and the lecture. You will need to be able to synthesize ideas here.

Finally, you should think about these questions as you listen to the sample responses.

- How should I organize my response?
- What is the main idea?
- What are the key supporting ideas that I need to include in my response?
- What vocabulary do I need?
- What grammatical structures would be useful?

Sample Responses—Question 4

SAMPLE RESPONSE 1: 4 (high)

Transcript: In common case things ah become smaller when it-a get-a colder, but water is an an exception. As far as we know, ah water will . . . be ah usually water-a will become smaller . . . when it gets colder but ah when it reaches ah 4 degrees Celsius ah things are different-a, it ah just become bigger. So ah it has some effects on the world such as the road in the colder area got more damages than ah the road in ah warm area because the water just-a gets gets bigger so it crashes road-a and also imagine put some ice cubes in a drink and ah when the ice cube melts-a and maybe the water becomes more so the water just, the drink just overflow from your ah cup-a. And ah also also this is why ice can float on the sea because the ice is ah less dense than water.

Comments: Excellent summary! The speaker obviously understood the lecture and was able to summarize well in her own words, choosing appropriate examples and doing it all within the time allowed. Great work!

SAMPLE RESPONSE 2: 3 (medium to high)

Transcript: The speaker talks about some of the effects of water. . . . What I heard from this conversation is when water gets colder it takes less space. That is a natural event. For example, the water, the water gets when the water gets ah 4 degree celcius at that point its volume increases as it gets colder until the point zero celcius. And zero celcius means . . . it's frozen and . . . it becomes ice. . . . Actually, I heard lots of difficult vocabulary words in this conversation, so . . . it is it is hard for me to explain exact information in this recording. Thank you.

Comments: Besides the fact that he admitted that he didn't understand the more complicated aspects of the lecture, he did pretty well. The speaker is very good at structuring his response, and is very easy to understand. However, it was obvious that he was not able to explain some of the effects of this property of water (*holes in the road,* etc.), and so this lowers his score.

Listening/Speaking Prompts

Two types of integrated listening/speaking items will appear on the speaking section of the 2005 TOEFL®. One asks you to listen to an academic lecture, and one asks you to listen to a more informal conversation. For both, you will need to summarize what you heard. For the informal conversation, you may be asked to also give your opinion.

LISTEN TO AN INFORMAL CONVERSATION

The informal conversations on the test will almost always take place in an academic context. They may be conversations between two students or an informal conversation between a professor and a student, but they almost always deal with issues related to university life.

Listen to the sample test item and then respond according to the prompt. Press Play.

> **QUESTION 5**
>
> Listen to the conversation.
>
> Briefly describe the problem that the students discussed in the conversation, and give your opinion about the solution that the two students decided on.
>
> Preparation time: 20 seconds
> Response time: 60 seconds

As mentioned above, this prompt asks you to listen to an informal conversation and respond to it.

In this particular conversation, there are some important things to note. After you hear the first two lines of dialogue, you should be able to determine that this conversation takes place between two students who are taking a class together because they are talking about the notes that they took at today's lecture. As the conversation proceeds, you should be able to understand that the two students are making a plan or deciding something. One clue to this is that they often respond to each other by saying, *Good idea.*

In addition, you should note some things about the prompt before you listen to and read about the samples below. The prompt is asking you to summarize the conversation (*Briefly describe . . .*) and then to give your personal opinion about the decision that the students ultimately make (*. . . and give your opinion about . . .*).

Finally, you should think about these questions before listening to the responses below. These questions will help you to put yourself into the minds of the speakers.

- How should I organize my response?
- What was the main topic of the conversation?
- What did the students ultimately decide to do?
- What is my opinion about their decision?
- What grammatical structures will I need in order to speak my answer?

Sample Responses—Question 5

SAMPLE RESPONSE 1: 3 (medium to high)

Transcript: There are two students and they both have a problem . . . about one of their classes. The problem is basically about a professor cause they had difficulties to understand the professor. . . . They know that they should understand . . . now what they, what they heard in this class so they are, they are deciding how how can, how how they can learn . . . this lecture . . . for their, for their next exams. They just have got an idea, which is just going to professor's office and . . . ask, ask the professor about their questions. But before do that, before they do that, they need to prepare their questions and get ready for talking.

> Good clear statement of the main idea right at the beginning.

> Notice how he rephrases after making a grammatical mistake in lines 5 and 8. This shows that he has awareness of his own errors and should not reduce his score.

Comments: This student's biggest problem is time management. Though he gets out a very good summary of the conversation, he hesitates so much and talks so slowly that he doesn't have enough time to get to the part of the question that asks him to express his opinion. His grammar is sufficiently correct and complex, with correctly used vocabulary as well. His pronunciation is certainly easy to understand, though he does have some errors in stress and intonation and vowel quality (he tends to front and round his vowels). To listen, you'll need access to the Internet.

In order to improve, this student should practice orally summarizing something that he has heard, like a short news report or even a phone conversation with a friend.

SAMPLE RESPONSE 2: 2 (low to medium)

Transcript: They got some problems in their class cause their professor give lecture very faster so they . . . they were hard to follow the lecture so they talked about that and they got some solution about that . . . umm . . . . They wanted to go to the professor's office but before that . . . they, they will meet together and compare their notes and ready to ask questions to profess . . . the professor. I think the solution is very good cause we have to prepare for anything, I mean . . . for asking question or for giving presentation or something like that. So this effort is kind of required for us. . . . Um . . . So I think this is very good and professor probably think good.

Comments: The student responds appropriately to the prompt. It is clear that he understands that the prompt is asking him to summarize and then give his opinion, which he is able to do, more or less. His opinion about the solution is too general, and begins to sound like he is generally commenting about what is good and right rather than commenting on the solution specifically. The student's biggest problems are in grammar and pronunciation. His grammar gets in the way of comprehensibility because expected grammatical elements are missing, for example, some forms of *be*. His pronunciation problems are also very obvious, including distinguishing between /r/ and /l/, that require lots of listener effort to understand. What happens as a result is that you wonder what that word is. To listen, you'll need access to the Internet.

In order to improve, this student should:

- work with a mirror and minimal pair lists
- watch television and notice the mouths of the people as they speak
- for grammar, record, transcribe, and look for errors, then make a list of his common errors

---

Grammar Point: Expressing the Difficulty of Something

One mistake that is very common among English learners is the misuse of verbs expressing difficulty. In this response, the student says, *They were hard to follow the lecture.* This is a very common mistake! It is helpful to know the collocations of the words **difficult** and **hard** in order to avoid this mistake. Here are some things to remember.

- **Difficult** and **hard** are both adjectives. As adjectives they can describe nouns. However, they can't just describe any noun. Depending on the type of noun, the meaning of these adjectives changes. When describing a person with one of these adjectives, you are talking about the personality of that person. For example:

  My brother is difficult. = *My brother is not easy to get along with or relate to; his personality causes problems for other people.*

  Note that in this use, you do not use the verb *to* **feel**. The sentence "My brother feels difficult" does not mean the same thing as "My brother is difficult." In fact, native speakers will not understand you if you say this sentence.

- Most errors occur when an English learner wants to describe a situation as being difficult or hard. The appropriate way to express this meaning is using a regular descriptive construction, just like you would with any noun and adjective:

  [noun] + **be** + **difficult/hard.**

  OR

  Difficult/hard + [noun].

  Here are some example sentences:

  That was a really hard test!

  Living in the U.S. is difficult.

  Remember: **difficult** and **hard** are not feelings. You cannot feel **difficult** in English!

LISTEN TO AN ACADEMIC LECTURE

The final question will ask you to listen to an academic lecture and summarize the contents.

Listen to the sample test item and respond according to the prompt. Press Play.

QUESTION 6

Listen to the lecture given in a freshman sociology class.

Using points and examples from the talk, explain the two strategies for conflict resolution presented by the professor.

Preparation time: 20 seconds

Response time: 60 seconds

In this particular lecture, there are some important things to think about. The lecture is about social conflict, and it defines two ways of resolving social conflict. You may have never heard the terms *contending* and *yielding* before. Again, there is no need to panic when you encounter unfamiliar terms. In fact, you should expect to hear terms in a lecture that are specific to the field of study that the lecture is about. Learning how to listen for definitions is one of the skills necessary for understanding an academic lecture.

In addition, note that the prompt asks you to summarize the lecture, not to give your opinion about its content.

Finally, think about these questions before you listen to the response below:

- How should I organize my response?
- What is the main idea of the lecture?
- What important supporting ideas do I need to include?
- How can I explain the examples given in the lecture?
- What vocabulary do I need to form my response?
- What grammatical structures would be useful?

Sample Responses—Question 6

SAMPLE RESPONSE 1: 4 (high)

Transcript: Um . . . If you have a, if we have a conflict it usually means ah people ah just don't agree ah at the same time on one thing or topic. Um . . . Usually there are two strategies to solve to solve this problem. One is called contending and another is called yielding. Um . . . As for contending, ah we just ah we . . . we usually force the other the other party ah or hurt the other parties um . . . benefit-a and let us win, let ourselves win. And as for yielding, maybe we just-a step back forward and-a sit down to the ask what we want and hope we can achieve ah to some ah level . . . agreement. . . . Both can solve the problem and ah same as in global. . . . (cut off)

Comments: This speaker has a very good organizing statement. It is truly a great summary, even though she runs out of time on the last sentence. She has very strong grammar and vocabulary and is able to express the complicated concepts in the lecture relatively well.

SAMPLE RESPONSE 2: 3 (medium to high)

Transcript: The professor aa just suggesting two strategy for conflict resolution. The first method is um contending, is try to force the solution to ah the other parties. ah she gives a example is um if I and my brother go out for or want to go out after the evening, and then, but one of us need to stay at home and then baby-sit our five-years-old ah brother . . . and then what I going to do is, like um [?] to go and and also tell my parents that my brother failed the math test and ask him to stay at home and then punish him and then I can go out this is one of this is the method of ah . . . so-called contending. And then ah other one is the . . . yield. It's like I wanted to stay at home and hope my parents, ah will get, will let me go out next time. This two things is sim . . . ah simple but is ah true in most of the families and groups or global.

Comments: Overall, this is a very good summary. The speaker obviously heard every detail and was able to summarize it well. Pronunciation problems hold this response back a bit. There are also quite a few pauses that are distracting. However, the content is very good. To listen, you'll need access to the Internet.

SAMPLE RESPONSE 3: 3 (medium to high)

Transcript: The lecture that the professor talked about is social conflict. The professor taught the students the ways that people can solve . . . the social conflicts. One way to solve the social conflict is named contending . . . and the other one is named yielding. . . . Contending means try to force the solution. . . . For example, . . . the professor talked about . . . two brothers, brothers, they have a problem whether they will go to dinner or not. . . . They can force the solution to solve. And then the other . . . way is yielding. Yielding means to be volunteer to sit home, like one of the brother does. And then the next time the oth- . . . (cut off)

Comments: The speaker communicates clearly and organizes the response well. He does need to work on time management, however. This has to do with the speed of the response, which does really need to be increased if he is going to accomplish the task in time. Also, his definitions are not quite correct, and he fails to provide examples from the lecture, which indicates that there are some parts of the lecture which he misunderstood.

SAMPLE RESPONSE 4: 2 (low to medium)

Transcript: When we had a conflict, social conflict, we have two solution, two strategies for resolve this. One is contending and the other is yeild- yielding. The former one is force the solution. It is kind of negotiation I think, . . . um, yes, the latter one is kind of volunteering . . . If we took later one for solution the conflict um we need . . . oh, sorry . . . no, no . . . no, anyway . . . this is similar to, the conflict is similar between individuals and group and individuals.

Comments: Very good organizing statement followed by definitions. It seems that the speaker understood the lecture, however, she was not exactly able to express the definition of *yielding*. This is an example of a response with poor development. It is unclear whether this is a problem with speaking or with listening/understanding. If she had more time (or if she took more time), she should give more of an explanation of each term. Very basic pronunciation problems require some listener effort, as do basic grammar errors. To listen, you'll need access to the Internet.

To improve, this student should:

- try working with mirror and minimal pair lists (lists of words like *rice/lice*, which you could find on the Internet or in a pronunciation textbook)
- watch television and notice the mouths of the people as they speak
- for grammar, record, transcribe, and look for errors, then make a list of common errors

Summary of Advice

Below is a chart of the advice given to improve certain speaking problems, for your reference.

Problem	How to Improve
Pronunciation	• Try working with mirror and minimal pair lists (lists of words like *rice/lice,* which you could find on the Internet or in a pronunciation textbook). Notice how your mouth must change to form the different sounds. • Watch television and notice the mouths of the people. How do they form the sounds? What shapes do their lips make? Can you see their tongues? • To work on the /th/ sound, use a mirror. When forming the /th/ in English (either the voiced or voiceless one), the tongue must touch the top teeth, so it should be visible when the sound is made. • Record yourself and listen for the "extra" syllables that you are adding to the ends of words. This is a problem for many speakers, depending on their first language, and is usually a problem of becoming aware that you are doing it at all. Once awareness has been built, you are halfway to fixing the problem.
Grammar	• Record, transcribe, look for errors. Then make a "top ten" list of your common errors.
Fluidity/speed	• Practice listening to conversations and then summarizing the main idea orally. • Practice orally summarizing something that you hear on TV, like a short news report. • Practice by talking to yourself. It might sound crazy, but a good way to develop speed and comfort in a language is to talk to yourself. This helps develop automaticity, or the ability to make the step between thinking and speaking automatic.
Support/development	• Practice development in writing (perhaps reviewing the Using Questions for Development section in Part 3: Writing in this book) to understand what development is and how it can be achieved. Then move to oral practice, perhaps beginning by having a friend ask you questions to help you develop the ideas.

A COMPLETE MULTI-SKILLS PRACTICE TEST

The following can be used as a complete multi-skills practice test, like the 2005 TOEFL®. It can also be used as further practice for specific skills. Answers can be found in the answer key. Be sure to take a ten-minute break after Section 2.

Although you practiced the writing before speaking in this book, the order in the practice test has been switched to be consistent with the actual 2005 TOEFL® Test.

Section 1: Reading
Passage 1

(1)   John Muir's exuberant descriptions of the "fresh unblighted, unredeemed wilderness" that he found in his explorations of the Sierra Nevada mountains of California popularized an ideal that has shaped American thinking about the value of wilderness and the importance of preserving it. They reflect a revolution in sensibility influenced by English romantic writers and American transcendentalists, most notably Henry David Thoreau, by which wilderness came to be seen as desirable, even as a manifestation of the *sublime*. Δ1 William Bradford's famous characterization of the Cape Cod found by the settlers who arrived on the Mayflower as "a hideous and desolate wilderness, full of wild beasts and wild men," reflects a much older sense of wilderness, going back to the desert wildernesses of the Old Testament, as an inhospitable and dangerous place. In his story "Young Goodman Brown" Nathaniel Hawthorne captured the Puritan sensibility in which the dark forest, the wilderness of the early settlers, became a frightening and disorienting place of evil, haunted by demonic Indians and the devil himself.

sublime: extreme beauty, beyond what humans can see

(2)   By the time Muir wrote, in the later nineteenth century, the appeal of wilderness as a distinctive feature of the American landscape was firmly established. Muir could see the Sierra as a "range of light" and a vibrant, pure, "divine wilderness" ordered and given life by a benevolent God. If Muir's particular religion of nature is no longer so likely to be shared, he nonetheless remains a cultural icon, widely quoted and celebrated as the prophet of

wilderness preservation and the first president of the Sierra Club. △2 His writing, along with that of such other famous defenders of wilderness as Thoreau and Aldo Leopold and Edward Abbey, can be found in the *Trailside Reader* of the Sierra Club, a pocket-sized book of inspirational reading for backpackers. Reading Muir and others who have meditated on the meaning of wild places has become a part of the American experience of wildness.

(3)   For all the popular fascination with wilderness, which increased dramatically in the later twentieth century, "wilderness" has in recent years become a contested and hence problematic term. Wilderness has long seemed an alien concept to Native Americans, a European import that served white culture as a way of signaling the strangeness of a natural world that indigenous peoples found familiar and sustaining, in fact regarded as home.

(4)   More recently, Third World critics have attacked the notion of wilderness as an embodiment of a peculiarly American set of attitudes symbolized by a national park ideal that they see as inappropriate for countries in which intense human pressures on available land make preservation seem a luxury. △3 In India and Brazil, for example, critics have advocated "social ecology," a theory of conservation based upon preserving the living patterns of indigenous peoples, in opposition to the emphasis of conservation biologists upon preserving biological diversity.

(5)   Another important critique of the idea of wilderness has come from environmental historians and others who profess support for preserving wild areas but object to what they see as a pervasive habit of opposing nature and culture and consequently neglecting the role of humans in shaping and continuing to live with the natural world. I am thinking particularly of William Cronon's influential "The Trouble with Wilderness; or, Getting Back to the Wrong Nature" and other essays in the collection he edited, *Uncommon Ground: Toward Reinventing Nature* (1990). Michael Pollan's *Second Nature* (1991) contributed to the reconsideration of the contemporary American attraction to wilderness, which he sees as supported by a "wilderness ethic" deriving ultimately from Thoreau and Muir and "a romantic, pantheistic idea of nature that we invented in the first place." △4 Recent books by Susan G. Davis on the version of "nature" presented by theme parks like Sea World and by Jennifer Price on such phenomena as the vogue of the plastic pink flamingo and the greening of television offer revealing

commentaries on the ways in which we invent versions of nature that serve our various purposes.

Adapted from John R. Knott, *Imagining Wild America* (Ann Arbor: University of Michigan Press, 2002).

1. Which of the following best states the main idea of the reading?

   a. Mainstream American ideas about the wilderness conflict with those of American Indians and people in poorer countries.

   b. Americans now tend to admire the wilderness, but this attitude has been criticized for several reasons.

   c. American would not admire the wilderness if John Muir had not revolutionized the nation's thinking about wild places.

   d. The wilderness, though once considered a frightening place, is now thought of in the United States as a place of purity and beauty.

2. The author mentions the story "Young Goodman Brown" in order to

   a. show that the wilderness of Puritan times was more dangerous than today's wilderness

   b. name a work of literature in which Puritan attitudes about nature were described very well

   c. give an example of how literature influenced Puritan attitudes toward the wilderness

   d. explain that, by Hawthorne's time, attitudes toward the American wilderness had changed

3. In Paragraph 2, this passage implies that a cultural icon is

   a. no longer popular

   b. a famous symbol

   c. a benevolent God

   d. a defender

4. According to Paragraph 4, which of the following statements would a "Third World critic" be most likely to agree with?

   a. American national parks take up too much usable land, which should be farmed in order to help reduce worldwide poverty and hunger.

   b. American attitudes toward conservation have helped preserve traditional lifestyles and biological diversity.

   c. Americans are able to preserve a lot of land in national parks only because the U.S. is rich and has more land than it needs.

   d. If Americans practiced "social ecology," the U.S. would be able to preserve more of its land in national parks.

5. The word alien in this passage is closest in meaning to

   a. foreign

   b. threatening

   c. familiar

   d. useful

6. Which of the following best expresses the main idea of the boxed sentence in Paragraph 5?

   a. Some critics think the United States has made a mistake by conserving wild areas that should be put to use.

   b. Some critics think American ways of preserving wild places reflect an unrealistic view of nature and human culture.

   c. Some critics think humans have neglected nature as they have interacted with their environment.

   d. Some critics think it is impossible to preserve land that humans have shaped and lived on.

7. According to this passage, John Muir's beliefs about the wilderness included all of the following except

   a. the wilderness is worth preserving

   b. the wilderness was created by God

   c. the wilderness is inhospitable

   d. the wilderness is prophetic

8. The word deriving in this passage is closest in meaning to

   a. coming

   b. copying

   c. separating

   d. jumping

9. Which of the following can be inferred from Paragraph 5 about Susan G. Davis's view of animal-related theme parks?

   a. She considers them a good way of preserving parts of nature.

   b. She considers them romantic and pantheistic.

   c. She considers them to be a revealing commentary on how we invent versions of nature.

   d. She considers them socially valuable.

10. Look at the four triangles in the passage, numbered 1–4. Which triangle shows the best place to insert (add) the following sentence?

> *Prior to this, the American wilderness was generally seen as more a threat than as a blessing.*

The sentence could best be added at

  a. △ 1

  b. △ 2

  c. △ 3

  d. △ 4

Schematic Table

Directions: *Complete the table below by classifying each of the answer choices. According to the reading, is it (1) an image of the wilderness from a time before the "revolution of sensibility" mentioned in Paragraph 1, or (2) an image of the wilderness from a time since that "revolution." Two of the statements will <u>not</u> be used. Write the letter of each of your choices in the proper blank.*

Images of the wilderness from before the "revolution of sensibility"	_____ _____ _____
Images of the wilderness since the "revolution of sensibility"	_____ _____ _____

  a. The wilderness is hideous and desolate.

  b. The wilderness is no longer so likely to be shared.

  c. The wilderness is haunted by the devil himself.

  d. The wilderness is a manifestation of the sublime.

  e. The wilderness should be preserved.

  f. The wilderness is like the deserts mentioned in the Bible.

  g   The wilderness is influenced by English romantic writers and American transcendentalists.

  h. The wilderness is not the romantic, pantheistic place that Thoreau and Muir imagined.

Passage 2

(1) The AEC study of nuclear workers at the Hanford site had been prompted, in 1965, by public concern over atomic weapons and the expansion of the nuclear industry. Mancuso had been chosen to head it because he had designed and conducted several long-term epidemiological studies of cancer hazards in industries. He had pioneered a way of using Social Security records for tracking the deaths of workers that made it possible to trace deaths that occur much later than the termination of employment and far from the place of work. Since cancer can have a latency period of up to thirty to forty years, and since companies usually destroy worker records after ten years, Mancuso's Social Security method represented a breakthrough in investigating cancer cause and effect. △ 1 He was well-known for having used this method to link brain tumors to industrial chemicals in a study of rubber workers in Ohio.

(2) Mancuso had been a protege of Dr. Wilhelm Hueper, a brilliant researcher and a pioneer in occupational cancer whose discovery of links between cancer and industrial pollutants earned him the reputation of a troublemaker. Head of research on chemical carcinogenesis at the National Cancer Institute (NCI), he'd had his funding frozen and his publications censured by the NCI, which did not want to hear the bad news about the *toxins* industries were producing, since the good will of industry was important to its funding. △ 2 Mancuso was soon to follow his mentor into similar disfavor.

toxins: poisons

(3) But at the time Mancuso was put in charge of the AEC study, he was reputed to be one of the foremost occupational epidemiologists in the world, a reputation that would lend the study the authority it needed. No one really thought the study would turn up anything. The official story was that radiation at low dose was negligible. Most health physicists in the new field of radiation biology accepted this: the AEC, which was paying their salaries, was energetically promoting a massive development of nuclear power that depended on public confidence.

(4) The official story came out of the Atomic Bomb Casualty Commission's (ABCC's) studies of the Hiroshima and Nagasaki survivors, the most lavishly funded and extensive research on the health effects of radiation ever conducted, which assured that a threshold existed beneath which radiation exposure incurred no risk. △3 This position was upheld by the medical establishment—health physicists, researchers, radiologists—in the United States and United Kingdom. Since Hanford workers were well below the determined limit, it was assumed that Mancuso's study would confirm that nuclear work was safe and worker standards were adequate.

(5) The only previous study that had turned up evidence of damage at low dose was the Oxford Survey of Childhood Cancer (OSCC).

(6) By 1973, Mancuso and his research team had been at work for more than a decade, collecting data on thirty-five thousand people. He was looking at records going back to 1946, following the workers' health through more than twenty-five years. But it was slow work, partly because of the huge size of the task. He'd had to travel to Tennessee, Washington, New Mexico, and elsewhere to track down records of the workers who'd died, the causes of death, job histories, and radiation exposures. Then he had to work out a system for collating the data and analyzing it. △ 4 It was slowed further because he kept encountering roadblocks. He reported that data about past workers was systematically destroyed, supposedly "to save file space." Mancuso forced Hanford to end this practice.

Adapted from Gayle Greene, *The Woman Who Knew Too Much: Alice Stewart and the Secrets of Radiation* (Ann Arbor: Univesity of Michigan Press, 2001), 131–32.

1. Which of the following best expresses the main idea of the passage as a whole?

   a. Mancuso's study carried on a tradition established by Dr. Wilhelm Hueper.

   b. In the AEC study, Mancuso discovered that industrial chemicals had caused cancer in rubber workers.

   c. In conducting his study of nuclear workers, Mancuso challenged prevailing beliefs about the effects of low-level radiation.

   d. Mancuso invented the only effective method of linking cancer deaths to their real causes.

2. In this passage, head is closest in meaning to

   a. lead

   b. go toward

   c. prevent

   d. start

3. According to Paragraph 1, Mancuso's Social Security method was significant because

    a. it helped detect industrial chemicals

    b. it helped reduce the latency period of cancer

    c. it helped make connections that were hard to make in other ways

    d. it was a long-term epidemiological study

4. In Paragraph 2, the word he refers to

    a. Hueper

    b. Mancuso

    c. the NCI

    d. the protégé

5. Which of the following best describes the relationship between Mancuso and Hueper, according to the passage?

    a. Hueper caused trouble for Mancuso.

    b. Hueper was one of Mancuso's employees.

    c. Hueper led the AEC study before Mancuso did.

    d. Hueper taught Mancuso many things.

6. The author mentions the studies of Hiroshima and Nagasaki in order to

    a. explain one way in which the Hanford workers were exposed to radiation

    b. explain one reason why most experts believed that low doses of radiation were harmless

    c. explain one way in which Mancuso decided which nuclear workers to study

    d. explain one of Mancuso's reasons for thinking that nuclear workers were harmed by low-level radiation

7. In the passage, collating is closest in meaning to

    a. finding

    b. protecting

    c. taking apart

    d. putting together

8. All of the following are reasons why Mancuso was put in charge of the AEC study <u>except</u>

   a. He had a lot of experience in investigating industrial causes of cancer.

   b. The AEC wanted a leader who would help make their study respectable.

   c. He was a leading epidemiologist.

   d. He had been the protégé of Dr. Wilhelm Hueper.

9. We can infer from the passage that the author believes

   a. the conclusions of the AEC study were wrong

   b. the conclusions of the NCI study were wrong

   c. the conclusions of the ABCC study were wrong

   d. the conclusions of the OSCC study were wrong

10. Look at the 4 triangles (△) in the reading (numbered 1–4). Which triangle shows the best place to insert (add) the following sentence?

    It was finally possible to establish that a cancer victim had indeed been exposed to a certain chemical or dose of radiation at work.

    The sentence could best be added at

    a. △ 1

    b. △ 2

    c. △ 3

    d. △ 4

Prose Summary

An introductory sentence for a brief summary of the passage is provided below. Complete the summary by selecting the <u>three</u> answer choices that express the most important ideas in the passage. Some sentences do not belong in the summary because they express ideas that are not presented in the passage or are minor ideas in the passage. In each blank, write the letter of one of your choices.

> The AEC study headed by Mancuso investigated whether nuclear workers at the Hanford site had developed cancer from radiation in the workplace.
>
> •
> _____
> •
> _____
> •

a. The AEC paid the salaries of many health physicists who worked in the area of radiation biology.

b. In conducting his study, Mancuso had to overcome great difficulty in collecting records, some of which had been destroyed.

c. Mancuso was a leading epidemiologist who had developed an effective technique for linking cancer to its causes.

d. Mancuso eventually proved that low-level radiation at Hanford had caused cancer in several workers.

e. At the time the study started, most experts believed that low levels of radiation posed no health risk.

f. The National Cancer Institute was unwilling to blame industry for cancer cases.

Passage 3

(1) Politically, the 1994 Dietary Supplements Health and Education Act (DSHEA) marked a victory for advocates of increased access to vitamins, minerals, herbs, amino acids, and other dietary supplements, while it marked a defeat for those who believed in strict regulatory controls on dietary supplements. Philosophically, the DSHEA represented a compromise between two poles: extreme medical paternalism, on the one hand, and radical patient autonomy, on the other. Δ 1

(2) Paternalism involves interference with autonomous choices. Medical paternalism refers to the notion of the physician as a benevolent parent making decisions for dependent, ignorant children. In cases of extreme medical paternalism, patients' choices are overridden despite their making voluntary and autonomous choices based on information available to them from a variety of sources, including but not limited to information printed on the labels of goods. Extreme medical paternalism holds that majoritarian medical consensus, based on existing medical orthodoxy or the views of a government agency, such as the FDA, should dictate consumer access to products and substances. At the other extreme, supporters of radical consumer autonomy assert that patients should have unlimited access to goods whether or not their decisions are informed or even volitional. $\triangle$ 2

(3) Traditionally, health care regulation in general and food and drug law in particular have tilted the balance toward extreme medical paternalism. In food and drug law, the FOCA provides that no new drug may be introduced into interstate commerce until the manufacturer has proven, to the FDA's satisfaction, that the drug is "safe and effective" for its intended use. Today it is almost unthinkable that the law would change to allow manufacturers to introduce a drug into interstate commerce without proving its effectiveness as well as safety.

(4) The policy is justified from a paternalistic perspective of patient protection. Yet safety and effectiveness are judged by the FDA; the focus is on FDA approval rather than consumer access. Thus, even if the patient wants to use the drug, understands that it has not been proven safe and effective to the FDA's satisfaction, and makes a knowing, intelligent, and voluntary choice to assume all known and disclosed risks of the product, as well as those that cannot be disclosed because they are unknown, the patient still cannot have access to the drug.

(5) In recent years, the policy has been softened in certain situations. $\triangle$ 3 One example involves the case of a boy named Dustin, who, at the age of two, was diagnosed with a brain tumor. Oncologists gave him only a few months to live and offered radiation treatment, which would have left him "*a vegetable.*" Through a process we will detail later, his parents gained unusual access to medicines that had not yet gone through the full gantlet of FDA scrutiny. His mother described his condition on unapproved treatments: "Dustin . . . is a happy, healthy four-year-old who has outlived his prognosis—

"a vegetable": a patient who is alive but unable to move or communicate

219

there is no [FDA-approved] treatment that would have kept him alive with such good quality of life." This provides a concrete, human example of the effect of defining patient protection from a paternalistic vantage.

(6) Counterexamples are far easier to find. One comes from litigation in the late 1970s during which patients sought to establish a constitutional right to freedom of access to medical treatments—a right to select the treatment of choice, whether or not such treatments have been approved by the FDA. In *United States v. Rutherford,* the U.S. Supreme Court rejected efforts by terminally ill cancer patients to obtain laetrile, a compound made from the pits of apricots. The Court concluded that Congress reasonably could have intended to protect terminal patients from such drugs as laetrile, which had not been proven safe, and effective, and that it was not the court's function to overturn a "longstanding administrative policy [by the FDA] that comports with the plain language, history, and prophylactic purpose" of the FDCA.

(7) On remand, the Tenth Circuit Court of Appeals held that a patient's decision to have treatment or not is a constitutionally protected right but that the patient's "selection of a particular treatment, or at least a medication, is within the area of governmental interest in protecting public health" and is not encompassed by the constitutional right to privacy. Thus, *Rutherford* rejected the claim patients made, based on a constitutional right to privacy, to greater autonomous decision making; the courts instead rested on the medical paternalism inherent in the FDCA and the statutory grant of authority to the FDA. △ 4

(8) Both sides probably would agree that the DSHEA represented a marked departure from historical legal strictures on patient access to nontraditional treatments and remedies. Reasonable minds have differed and will continue to differ on whether this departure constituted an evolutionary leap in federal health care regulation or a reckless unlocking of a Pandora's box of unresolved regulatory problems.

1. Which of the following best expresses the main idea of this passage as a whole?

    a. The DSHEA has resolved the conflict between paternalism and autonomy.

    b. In the conflict between paternalism and autonomy, the government has usually supported paternalism.

    c. The courts have traditionally opposed the paternalist tendencies of the FDA and other government agencies.

    d. Although paternalism traditionally received more official support than autonomy, the opposite is now true.

2. According the passage, an extreme medical paternalist would probably agree with all the following <u>except</u>

    a. Doctors should make most decisions for patients.

    b. A doctor should not prescribe a medicine for a patient unless it has been approved by the FDA.

    c. A patient's right to decide about whether to have treatment is constitutionally protected.

    d. It was wrong for Dustin's parents to get access to unapproved medications for him.

3. The word its in Paragraph 3 refers to

    a. the law's

    b. the manufacturer's

    c. the drug's

    d. the commerce's

4. According to Paragraph 5, Dustin's mother believes

    a. Dustin would not have lived so long if he had been given an FDA-approved treatment.

    b. Dustin has lived so long only because he had an FDA-approved treatment.

    c. With an FDA-approved treatment, Dustin might be alive but in worse health.

    d. With an FDA-approved treatment, Dustin would still have to use a prognosis.

5. The word assume in Paragraph 4 is closest in meaning to

    a. think about

    b. reduce

    c. reveal

    d. accept

6. Which of the following best expresses the most important information in the boxed sentence in Paragraph 6?

   a. In the late 1970s, the government sued patients who had been using unapproved treatments.

   b. In the late 1970s, the regulations against unapproved treatments became stricter.

   c. In the late 1970s, a constitutional amendment gave patients the right to seek unapproved treatments.

   d. In the late 1970s, patients sued to make unapproved treatments easier to get.

7. According to Paragraph 6, which of the following did the Supreme Court give as one reason for its decision in *United States v. Rutherford*?

   a. The Court had no right to take this case.

   b. The Court had a responsibility to clarify the complicated wording of the FDCA.

   c. The Court believed Congress did not give any reasons for protecting patients from such drugs as laetrile.

   d. The Court had no right to interfere with the FDA's handling of this matter.

8. In this passage, rested on is closest in meaning to

   a. based its position on

   b. argued against

   c. stopped working on

   d. was biased toward

9. According to Paragraph 8, some reasonable people believe the DSHEA

   a. supports traditional legal limitations on patient access

   b. opens the way for a large number of regulatory problems

   c. opens the way for changes to the Constitution

   d. was modeled on similar legislation in Pandora and other countries

10. Look at the 4 triangles (△) in the reading (numbered 1–4). Which triangle shows the best place to insert (add) the following sentence?

    Although true believers on both sides are outspoken and sincere, the two views are hardly equal in their power and social influence.

The sentence could best be added at

a. △ 1

b. △ 2

c. △ 3

d. △ 4

Schematic Table

Complete the table below by classifying each of the answer choices. According to the reading, is it a real-life case or event that has (1) caused an increase in medical paternalism, or (2) caused an increase in patient autonomy. Two of the statements will <u>not</u> be used. Write the letter of each of your choices in the proper blank.

Has caused an increase in medical paternalism	_____ _____ _____
Has caused an increase in patient autonomy	_____ _____ _____

a. the 1994 Dietary Supplements Health and Education Act

b. the law allowing manufacturers to introduce a drug into interstate commerce without proving effectiveness as well as safety

c. the FOCA

d. research in other countries into the safety of laetrile

e. the decision in *United States v. Rutherford*

f. the decision by the Tenth District Court of Appeals

Section 2: Listening

Conversation: A Teaching Assistant and a Student

Listen to the following conversation adapted from the MICASE transcripts of the University of Michigan. Answer the questions that follow by circling the best response. Restart your audio for Question 4 (it is a new track on the audio). Press Play.

1. What is the main topic of the talk?

    a. a poem

    b. art classes

    c. high school

    d. a student's writing classes

2. What did the student focus on in high school?

    a. sports

    b. art

    c. drama

    d. writing

3. What kind of grades has the student earned in her English classes?

    a. the highest

    b. pretty good

    c. below average

    d. failing

4. *Start the audio.* Listen again to a part of the lecture. Then answer the question.

   Why is the student taking these two English classes now?

   a. Introductory classes are the easiest.

   b. American literature and poetry are considered literary art.

   c. The credits are required for her degree.

   d. She missed them when she was in high school.

5. How does the student feel about her study of English?

   a. She is mildly interested.

   b. She wants to make it her major.

   c. She is irritated and discouraged by past experiences.

   d. She is curious because she has little experience.

Conversation: An Advisor and a Student

Listen to the following conversation adapted from the MICASE transcripts of the University of Michigan. Answer the questions that follow by circling the best response. Restart the audio for Question 10 (it is a new track on the audio). Press Play.

6. What is the main topic of discussion?

   a. how many credits the student needs in order to graduate

   b. which class the student should take next

   c. when to start looking for a job

   d. what other majors interest the student

7. The student sees benefits and drawbacks to her pre-business major. List the following issues in one of the three columns.

   a. Pre-business majors often work with numbers.

   b. The coursework has a lot of reading.

   c. Business majors end up in desk jobs.

   d. Many business careers involve travel.

   e. Business studies limit interaction with people and ideas.

   f. Business topics are often black and white.

   g. Most business majors ultimately need an MBA.

   h. Business experience can get you a better job than a business major.

Benefits	Drawbacks	No information
•	•	•
•	•	•
•	•	•
•	•	•

8. What other majors has the student considered? (Choose two answers.)

   a. paleontology

   b. biology

   c. astronomy

   d. history

9. Why does the advisor ask, "Have you done any digs or anything like that?"

   a. to encourage the student to do more research

   b. to learn about the student's hands-on experience

   c. to imply that the student needs to do more research

   d. to ask about professors' opinions from other departments

10. *Start the audio.* Listen again to part of the lecture. Then answer the question:

    What does the advisor mean when she says "geology and biological anthropology will 'lead you that way'"?

    a. the courses can take you into that field

    b. the courses will take you away from your goal

    c. the courses are required for graduation

    d. the courses will determine your major

11. What course does her advisor recommend?

    a. dinosaurs

    b. music

    c. politics

    d. geography

Lecture: Midwestern Geography

Listen to the following segment from a lecture originally given by Dr. Catherine Yansa, Assistant Professor of Geography at Michigan State University. Answer the questions that follow by circling the best response. Press Play.

12. What is the topic of the lecture?

    a. a flood

    b. belts and other leather goods

    c. a section of the United States

    d. agricultural exports

13. What is the physical environment in the Corn Belt?

    a. dry

    b. humid

    c. tropical

    d. marine

14. How tall were the highest native grasses?

    a. several inches

    b. up to a foot

    c. several feet

    d. several yards

15. What is corn?

    a. a flower

    b. a fruit-bearing tree

    c. a kind of moss

    d. a grass

16. Why did Native Americans burn the forests? (Choose two answers.)

    a. to cultivate the land

    b. to attract deer

    c. to worship forest gods

    d. to scare Euro-Americans

Lecture: Cyrus the Great

Listen to the following lecture segment from a history class. The professor is discussing Cyrus the Great. Answer the questions that follow by circling the best response. Press Play.

17. What lands did Cyrus the Great control?

    a. The Mediterranean to India

    b. India to China

    c. Syria to France

    d. Iran, Saudi Arabia, and Egypt

18. How did Cyrus gain control over conquered people? (Choose 2 answers.)

    a. fear and force

    b. tolerance

    c. emphasizing a tribal connection

    d. enslavement

19. What was the "pax Achaeminica"?

    a. return of the Jews to Palestine

    b. sufficient food for the empire

    c. civilization of nomadic tribes

    d. community through liberation

20. Why did Cyrus let the Jews go to Palestine? (Choose 2 answers.)

    a. He was Jewish.

    b. They fought for him as mercenaries.

    c. He accepted various religions.

    d. To strengthen his western border.

21. What was the basis for Cyrus' laws and constitution?

    a. natural law

    b. ethical values

    c. old Median texts

    d. his personal goals

 **Lecture: Economics**

Listen to part of an economics lecture. The professor is discussing the Gross Domestic Product. Answer the questions that follow by circling the best response. Restart the audio for Question 27 (it is a new track on an audio). Press Play.

22. Why does the student ask about Gross National Product?

    a. Comparing the two figures tells us more about the economy.

    b. Combining the two figures yields the relevant total.

    c. He thinks that the lecturer has made a mistake.

    d. He's trying to figure out the connection between GNP and GDP.

23. What time period is counted in the Gross Domestic Product?

    a. one presidential term

    b. one fiscal year

    c. one calendar year

    d. one company's lifetime

24. What new item is included when calculating GDP?

    a. technology

    b. intermediate goods

    c. taxes

    d. information

25. Why does GDP count only final output?

    a. because the final product has the most value

    b. because final output is the same as the sum of intermediate goods

    c. so exports can be seen in relation to imports

    d. to make sure that nothing is counted twice

26. If a Japanese company produces cars in the United States, which GDP is credited?

    a. only the U.S.

    b. only Japan's GDP

    c. half and half: Japan-U.S.

    d. the GDP of any country where the assembled cars are sold

27. *Start the audio.* Listen again to part of the lecture. Then answer the question.

    What does the lecturer mean when she says, ". . . that's six thousand, nine hundred-something thousand dollars."

    a. She doesn't know the exact number.

    b. The money was spent in many different ways.

    c. The currency is dollars in the U.S., but it is quoted in local currencies in other countries.

    d. She can't remember if the number is hundreds, thousands, millions, or billions.

28. What is the basis of the U.S. economy?

    a. production

    b. research and development

    c. spending

    d. investment

29. Each box describes a specific component of the GDP. Write the letter of each component in the space where it belongs. Use each letter only once.

a. personal consumption expenditures

b. investment

c. government spending

d. net exports

19% of GDP (Figure has been stable)

Household spending (2/3 of GDP)

Relationship between goods shipped into or out of the U.S. (Negative figure)

Business spending (15% of GDP)

 **Lecture: Plants**

Listen to the following segment from a lecture originally given by E. David Ford, Professor in the Department of College and Forest Resources at the University of Washington. Answer the questions that follow by circling the best response. Restart the audio for Question 32 (it is a new track on the audio). Press Play.

30. What defines "autotrophic" plants?

    a. They produce their own food.

    b. They can exist in their own eco-system.

    c. They have both male and female reproductive capacity.

    d. They eat themselves.

31. According to the lecturer, how do plants relate to soil?

    a. Plants maintain soil.

    b. Plants destroy soil.

    c. Plants convert soil to energy.

    d. Plants create carbon dioxide in the soil.

32. *Start the audio now.* Listen again to part of the talk. Then answer the question.

    What does the professor imply when he says, "I'm not going into it, I assume you know it."

    a. Students should realize that he will not enter the room.

    b. Discussing the given topic has no value.

    c. The professor will not talk about details because students already know the information.

    d. Students are responsible for remembering about paper assignments and due dates.

33. What is the relationship between autotrophs and heterotrophs?

    a. They compete for light.

    b. Their production and consumption of nutrients are linked.

    c. They can co-exist because they consume different organic materials.

    d. They produce inorganic compounds.

34. What would happen if there were no heterotrophs?

    a. Soil composition would improve.

    b. Fungi and bacteria would disappear.

    c. Decomposition would accelerate.

    d. Nothing would decompose.

35. Why does the professor mention peat bogs?

    a. as an example of a place where there are no autotrophs

    b. to prove that hydrogen ions can preserve organic matter

    c. as an example of a place with few heterotrophs

    d. to show that photosynthesis requires light

Section 3: Speaking

Listen to the test items and then respond according to the directions given in each prompt.

Press Play.

QUESTION 1

Choose a favorite place in your hometown. Explain why it is your favorite.

Preparation time: 15 seconds
Response time: 45 seconds

Press Play.

QUESTION 2

When students come to a university, most live on campus in a dormitory, while some choose to live farther from campus in an apartment. Would you prefer to live in an on-campus dormitory or an off-campus apartment during your university studies? Why?

Preparation time: 15 seconds
Response time: 45 seconds

QUESTION 3

Reading time: 45 seconds

> Current university policy requires undergraduate students to take two credits of physical education. The university is considering changing this requirement. One option is to eliminate it completely. Another is to create a required two-credit "Introduction to University Life" course that would teach students about study skills and how to survive in the university. The final option is to keep the physical education requirement.

Press Play.

The student gives her own opinion about the physical education requirement. Say what her opinion is, and summarize the reasons she gives.

Preparation time: 30 seconds
Response time: 60 seconds

QUESTION 4

Reading time: 45 seconds

Human Genetics

Human genes are the blueprints for the body. A person's genetic code is unique and is determined at conception as a combination of the mother and father's genetic material. The genes in the cells of the zygote, or fertilized egg, multiply and make up all the cells of the entire body.

Press Play.

Considering the information you have just received from the reading and the lecture, explain the function of genes in the body and how specialized cells are created.

Preparation time: 30 seconds

Response time: 60 seconds

QUESTION 5

Press Play.

Briefly describe the problem that the student and the professor discussed in the conversation, and give your opinion about the professor's advice.

Preparation time: 20 seconds

Response time: 60 seconds

QUESTION 6

Press Play.

Using points and examples from the lecture, explain the formation of the Lesser Antilles as presented by the professor.

Preparation time: 20 seconds

Response time: 60 seconds

Section 4: Writing
Integrated Writing Task

You will have five minutes to read the following passage. You may take notes while you read.

A dispute, or argument, usually starts when one person or group of people makes a demand on another person or group of people, who reject it. There are three basic elements in every dispute: interests, rights, and power. The parties might try to resolve the dispute by pursuing one of the three elements: by reconciling interests, determining who is right, and/or by determining who is more powerful.

The different parties in the dispute have certain interests that are at stake. These interests might be physical, like a loss of money, but could also be social, like a loss of face or social position if the dispute is not resolved in their favor. In addition, one of the parties may be more right or wrong in the given situation. In any dispute there is also the element of power. The power relationship between the two parties may profoundly affect how the dispute is resolved. Imagine how differently a dispute between a peasant and a wealthy landowner might be resolved compared to a dispute between two wealthy landowners. The power of a certain party in a dispute is not relegated only to finances, however. Power may come from age in certain cases, such as when there is a dispute between mother and daughter.

Sociologists are concerned with looking at how these three aspects of a dispute, interest, rights, and power, factor into disputes at all levels of society.

 ## Lecture: A Dispute

Listen to the lecture about a dispute at an amusement park. Press Play.

> **INTEGRATED WRITING TASK**
>
> You will have twenty (20) minutes to write a response to the following prompt.
>
> Use an example from the lecture to explain the three basic elements of every dispute, according to the reading.

INDEPENDENT WRITING TASK

You will have thirty (30) minutes to plan, organize, and write a response to the following prompt. Use specific reasons and examples to support your answer.

Agree or disagree with the following statement:

The most important lessons in life are learned in school.

AUDIO SCRIPT, PART 2: LISTENING

The audio script only contains text that is not included elsewhere in the book.

Building Skills: Listening for Main Ideas
Practice 1 (with Answer Analysis) (pages 84–87)
Lecture: Economic Conditions

We are not sure if the U.S. economy is in a recession because there are mixed indicators. The unemployment rate fell from 5.9 percent to 5.7 percent from July to August, which is good news. Unfortunately, this is not sustainable job growth because the new jobs were mostly the result of a one-time increase in government jobs. Personal consumption climbed 1 percent in July, which is good because it comprises two-thirds of GDP. However, people were spending more and the savings rate dropped to 3.4 percent, as personal income remained unchanged. The U.S. has the lowest savings rate of any developed economy.

Factory orders rose 4.7 percent in July after falling 2.5 percent in June, though most of these orders were in the aircraft sector. Productivity in the second quarter grew at an annual rate of 1.5 percent, which is very low. Ideally, productivity should grow at 2 percent to 3 percent, so we experience growth in per capita income. Still, productivity grew at 4.8 percent for the year that ended in June, which is very good news. These are mixed signs about the economy, so we cannot tell if we are in a recession right now. In any case, we are in a period of slow growth.

Practice 2 (pages 87–88)
Conversation: Two Students

Female student [F]: That lecture really tired me out.

Male student [M]: (laughs) Yeah, same here. My hand is tired from writing so much.

F: She really covered a lot of material . . . .

M: Yeah, well, like she said, um, we missed those snow days last week. We had to make it up somewhere.

F: Did you get everything?

M: Man, I doubt it. I mean, I was taking notes as fast as I could, but there are all these gaps. I ended up with probably 5, 6 pages. All those facts, dates, tables . . . .

F: Plus the handouts.

M: Yeah, it was a lot. I'm definitely going to have to review this stuff tonight, or it'll be gone forever.

F: That's a good idea. I'd like to go over it too.

M: If you want, we could study together. Between us, we probably got most of the major ideas written down.

F: Sure. Might as well.

M: I'll probably be heading over to the library after dinner . . . .

F: Oh, no, I just remembered, I think I have choir practice tonight.

M: What time?

F: Seven, I think. But it's just an hour. Is that too late for you?

M: No, that's fine. We could meet around 8 or 8:30 . . . whenever you get there.

F: Great.

M: I'll be on the third floor. I'll try to get us a room, you know, back on the, um, the, those rooms on the west wall.

F: Yeah, I know them. I'll see you then.

Question 4, page 87. Listen again to part of the talk. Then answer the question.

M: Yeah, well, like she said, um, we missed those snow days last week. We had to make it up somewhere.

Exercise 4 (pages 90–93)
Lecture: Gathering Information

Let's talk about a few types of data. Actually, there are many types of data. First, let's talk about clinical interviews.

The video we saw the first day of the woman with bipolar disorder was a *clinical interview*. We focused on what she said and how she said it. It was an unstructured clinical interview and takes a lot of skill to do. They are good because you can see many different sides of the person. The downside is that, if you have different clinicians, they might take completely different paths and come up with different assessments—there is low inter-rater reliability. In structured interviews, clinicians just ask questions from a questionnaire. These are valuable because they have much better inter-rater reliability. However, they are very constrained and answer only specific questions.

Another type of data comes from *psychological testing*. There are different types: personality inventories, intelligence or cognitive tests, and projectives. The MMPI is a commonly used personality inventory with about 400 questions. Each question empirically correlates with different levels of psychological functioning. The inventory was created purely empirically. Depressed people, for example, will systematically answer a certain way on certain questions. It is hard for the subject to tell what each question is telling. There are scores on nine different scales, such as depression, mania, sociopathy, and so on. Each scale corresponds somewhat to something in the DSM so it can help in diagnosing. The higher score you get on each scale, the more of that trait you have. You would not want to base the entire assessment on this graph, however.

Intelligence or cognitive tests, such as IQ tests, can be useful in diagnosing learning disorders. Does the child have a learning disorder due to an information processing deficiency? If there is a discrepancy between IQ and level of achievement, then there may be a learning disorder. The only way to find this is to measure IQ and then measure achievement and see if there is a big discrepancy.

A third class is *projectives*. The Rorschach inkblot test is an example of this. There is an assumption that, if one looks at a neutral stimulus and talks about what he sees, it can say something about their unconscious mental process. Another is the TAT (thematic apperception test). The subject sees pictures of people doing things together, and the subject tells stories about the pictures. However, there is debate whether these tests say more about what clinicians believe about the subject or whether they truly talk about what is going on in the unconscious. Inter-judge reliability is not too good. Do these tests really have incremental utility to the assessment process?

Next, I'll talk about *behavioral measures*. Sometimes, you want to get more concrete information. We can do this by measuring behavior. We can measure behavior in many ways. We can simply observe the child in his environment (a child in a classroom). One can then make inferences based on behavior. We can also use third-party reports—give the parents or teacher a checklist. There are not many third-party reports used for adults. They are used commonly for children.

Last today, I'll talk about *biological measures*. These include neuroimaging techniques as well as neuropsychological tests. Neuropsychological tests gather samples of behavior to make inferences about functioning in different parts of the brain. If the child had a head injury, neuropsychological testing can help pinpoint where any brain damage may have occurred. Children with cancer who undergo radiation therapy can have some neurological damage. If tests are given before and after, we can tell if the radiation does damage. There are other purposes of neuropsychological tests, as well.

Practice 3 (pages 93–94)
Lecture: Gender

Prof: Yeah, so there's XY sex determination, like humans have. But I want to point out that the chromosomal type of sex determination is by no means universal. This XY sex determination that humans have isn't the only way. So what other types of sex determination are there other than XY sex determination? Yeah?

Student: Environmental.

Prof: Yeah, so there's environmental sex determination, and, an example of that? Environmental sex determination, this is known to be the case in both crocodilians and turtles. In crocodilian nests, nests that are incubated at high temperature produce males; nests that are incubated at low temperatures produce females, and intermediate temperatures produce a mixture of sexes. So in crocodilians, sex is not at all produced by chromosomes.

What about other forms of chromosomal sex determination other than XY? Does anybody know about that? There are other forms, it's often called a "WZ sex determination scheme." And in this case where . . . as in XY sex determination, females are the so-called homogametic sex, they have two X chromosomes. In WZ sex determination, males are the homogametic sex. And in WZ sex determination, we have organisms like birds, for example, or butterflies.

So, XY sex determination isn't the only chromosomal sex determination system out there, and chromosomes aren't the only way sex is determined anyway, it can be determined environmentally as well.

Building Skills: Listening for Details

Practice 1 (with Answer Analysis) (pages 96–98)
Lecture: Mental Illness

We talked about the DSM-IV and its five axes last time. It is important to remember these because much of what we will talk about will fit into the framework of the five axes. Before we go on, I want to point out a few things about the DSM-IV:

First, the DSM-IV is a categorical taxonomy—you either do have or do not have a mental illness. You either have or do not have depression or schizophrenia. A lot of us are familiar with things like depression and sadness. It is universal to experience some sadness and anxiety. However, the taxonomy is categorical, and certain diagnostic criteria must be met in order to have a mental illness. Even though the taxonomy is categorical, there are many gradations. There may be someone who is so depressed that he cannot get out of bed, and there may be someone who can function in daily life.

Another very important point to remember is that mental illnesses carry stigma. The act of labeling somebody with a mental disorder can harm someone. We need to find a balance between the harm of labeling someone as someone with a mental illness and the benefits of the treatments that he or she can get after diagnosed.

Third, we should ask, is the DSM-IV totally correct? As we go through all the different disorders, we will talk about them as if they are individual entities. For many disorders, there is a great chance that someone will have more than one disorder. Some disorders occur together commonly. If people systematically tend to have the same disorders together, is our taxonomy correct?

Culture is another important thing to think about. There are culture-bound syndromes. In Latin America, there is a disorder called *nervios*. This disorder is not in the DSM-IV but occurs with regular frequency in the Latin American context. Is the DSM-IV comprehensive enough? Is it universally relevant? Can that disorder be found regardless of culture? We also have to keep in mind that there are cultural variations within particular syndromes defined in the DSM-IV.

The DSM-IV has weaknesses, but there are advantages of a taxonomy. With a taxonomy, we can speak the same language when talking about mental illness. This allows us to build a science of mental illness and psychotherapy. It allows us to do research and clinical intervention.

Anticipating Information
Exercise 1 (pages 99–100)
Conversation: A Professor and a Student

Student [S]: I'm Andrew Zodorsky, I was in your poli sci class.

Professor [P]: Come in, come in. Yes, Andrew. What brings you in today?

Narrator [N]: *Stop the audio to answer the first question.*

P: Come in, come in. Yes, Andrew. What brings you in today?

S: Well, actually, it's about my grade in poli sci . . . .

P: Which quarter are you referring to?

S: Oh, oh yeah. Um, it was last quarter. Fall quarter. I was in 101.

P: And . . . You're not happy with your grade.

N: *Stop the audio to answer the second question.*

P: And . . . You're not happy with your grade.

S: Well, actually, um, that's right. I mean, I attended all of the classes, I took notes.

P: Let me pull that up here. "Zodorsky," Z-O-D-O-R . . . . Yes, here it is. You earned a B minus.

S: As I was saying, I attended all of the classes, I took notes.

P: Let me talk about these two areas—uh, attendance and note-taking. And this was in my syllabus from day one. Attendance is a very small part of your grade.

N: *Stop the audio to answer the third question.*

P: Let me talk about these two areas—uh, attendance and note-taking. And this was in my syllabus from day one. Attendance is a very small part of your grade. But note-taking is not. Taking notes itself does not affect your grade.

S: I turned in all of my written assignments and I got As on most of them, a couple of Bs.

P: I calculate grades according to a formula, and the whole thing is on this computer here. So, unless there's been some kind of glitch, a B minus should accurately reflect your work in this class. It looks like you were missing one homework assignment, on October 9th. That would count as a "zero."

N: *Stop the audio to answer the fourth question.*

P: It looks like you were missing one homework assignment, on October 9th. That would count as a "zero."

S: Actually, that homework was just late. I turned it in on Monday . . . . I finished it over the weekend, so that would have been the 12th, or no, that 12th was a holiday. But anyway, I turned it in late.

P: Do you have that homework with you?

S: Let me look. It's in my notebook. Yes, here it is . . . .

P: It's graded, too. Okay, the T.A. must have forgotten to mark that. I'll add it in here. But that's not a lot. It's just one homework, late, half credit. But it's something. Let's look on here. Your mid-term exam . . . . a C plus.

S: But then on the final, I got an A–.

P: An A–, good for you. You must have put in some extra effort in that second part of the quarter.

N: *Stop the audio to answer the fifth question.*

P: An A–, good for you. You must have put in some extra effort in that second part of the quarter.

S: Actually, well, I did. I mean, after the mid-term, I knew I had to get a little more serious about this class. So I joined a study group, and I started doing each reading twice, sometimes three times.

P: I don't see any extra credit points . . . .

S: Actually, though, I mean, I did some. I mean, it wasn't a lot. But I was part of that team, remember, the presentation of the war in overseas newspapers. Covering the war . . . .

P: Yes, yes. Forgive me. Yes. That was a splendid presentation. You put the images into the computer, that was fantastic. You got some really good quality.

S: Thank you, um, yeah, I like that kind of stuff. Computers and stuff. It's my major.

P: I see. Well, I'm glad you came in today. Clearly, there are some gaps in our records . . . . who was your T.A.?

N: *Stop the audio to answer the sixth question.*

P: Well, I'm glad you came in today. Clearly, there are some gaps in our records . . . who was your T.A.?

S: Coleman.

P: Coleman. Let me send her an e-mail so we can review this grade. By any chance, do you have copies of your written work and tests?

S: I do, but they're just in a big pile in this notebook.

N: *Stop the audio to answer the seventh question.*

P: By any chance, do you have copies of all your written work and tests?

S: I do, but they're just in a big pile in this notebook. If you just give me 20 minutes or so, I can put them in order.

P: Fine. Please do that. Then, would you put them in my box? I've got to run now—meeting—but I do want to straighten out this grade thing.

S: Thank you, Professor Wall.

P: Of course. Will we see you again this quarter?

S: Actually, I'll probably spend more time in computer classes from now on . . . .

P: (laughter) Okay, then, good luck.

Repeat of conversation: A Professor and a Student (no interruptions) (page 99)

S: I'm Andrew Zodorsky, I was in your poly sci class.

P: Come in, come in. Yes, Andrew. What brings you in today?

S: Well, actually, it's about my grade in poli sci . . . .

P: Which quarter are you referring to?

S: Oh, oh yeah. Um, it was last quarter. Fall quarter. I was in 101

P: You're not happy with your grade.

S: Well, actually, um, that's right. I mean, I attended all of the classes, I took notes.

P: Let me pull that up here. "Zodorsky," Z-O-D-O-R . . . . Yes, here it is. You earned a B minus.

S: As I was saying, I attended all of the classes, I took notes.

P: Let me talk about these two areas—uh, attendance and note-taking. And this was in my syllabus from day one. Attendance is a very small part of your grade. But note-taking is not. Taking notes itself does not affect your grade in my course.

S: I turned in all of my written assignments and I got As on most of them, a couple of Bs.

P: I calculate grades according to a formula, and the whole thing is on this computer here. So, unless there's been some kind of glitch, a B minus should accurately reflect your work in this class. It looks like you were missing one homework assignment, on October 9th. That would count as a "zero."

S: Actually, that homework was just late. I turned it in on Monday . . . . I finished it over the weekend, so that would have been the 12th, or no, that 12th was a holiday. But anyway, I turned it in late.

P: Do you have that homework with you?

S: Let me look. It's in my notebook. Yes, here it is . . . .

P: It's graded, too. Okay, the T.A. must have forgotten to mark that. I'll add it in here. But that's not a lot. It's just one homework, late, half credit. But it's something. Let's look on here. Your mid-term exam . . . a C plus.

S: But then on the final, I got an A–.

P: An A–, good for you. You must have put in some extra effort in that second part of the quarter.

S: Actually, well, I did. I mean, after the mid-term, I knew I had to get a little more serious about this class. So I joined a study group, and I started doing each reading twice, sometimes three times.

P: I don't see any extra credit points . . . .

S: Actually, though, I mean, I did some. I mean, it wasn't a lot. But I was part of that team, remember, the presentation of the war in overseas newspapers. Covering the war . . . .

P: Yes, yes. Forgive me. Yes. That was a splendid presentation. You put the images into the computer, that was fantastic. You got some really good quality.

S: Thank you, um, yeah, I like that kind of stuff. Computers and stuff. It's my major.

P: I see. Well, I'm glad you came in today. Clearly, there are some gaps in our records . . . who was your T.A.?

S: Coleman.

P: Coleman. Let me send her an e-mail so we can review this grade. By any chance, do you have copies of your written work and tests?

S: I do, but they're just in a big pile in this notebook. If you just give me 20 minutes or so, I can put them in order.

P: Fine. Please do that. Then, would you put them in my box? I've got to run now—meeting—but I do want to straighten out this grade thing.

S: Thank you, Professor Wall.

P: Of course. Will we see you again this quarter?

S: Actually, I'll probably spend more time in computer classes from now on . . . .

P: (laughter) Okay, then, good luck.

Organization Signals

Exercise 2
Lecture: Poverty (pages 101–02)

At "We the People's Forum," which was the follow-up of the declaration for a culture of peace, six factors were discussed under the rubric of peace: poverty, disarmament, equity, justice, diversity, human rights, sustainable development, and democratizing international organizations (including the United Nations itself). Notice these formulations all expand the definition of violence from direct forms of violence, which are designed to produce harm and kill people, to another type of violence called structural violence. Structural violence is the unintended consequences or by-products of institutional activities. The goal of this kind of violence is not to kill, harm, or maim people but, nevertheless, people are harmed as a result of these practices.

A classic example of this would be the International Monetary Fund, with its structural adjustment policies under the neo-liberal development, which we will talk about more later in this course. There is great documentation and proof that, as a result of this privatization, deregulation, and cutting back on public spending (all these various parts that are required for countries to become creditworthy to the international organizations and private banks), people are harmed quite severely in terms of poverty, diseases associated with poverty, access to healthcare, and these types of things. These repercussions should all be considered kinds of violence.

On this point, for instance, more people die each year from hunger than from war. This is the point that prompted Mohandas Gandhi to say, "Poverty is the most deadly form of violence." We have approximately 2 billion people in the world living off of less than two dollars a day. Also, as a result of malnutrition and lack of healthcare access, about one child dies every four minutes. These are preventable deaths (unlike, say, an earthquake). When you look at countries, we see the same thing. We can see there is structural violence when we look at a country whose average lifespan is 30 years because we know that, in other countries, it is possible to live beyond that. What can explain this kind of discrepancy? That kind of question is the kind of thing that gets talked about in discussing preventable deaths.

Practice 3
Lecture: Modern Social Change (pages 106–07)

Time has trumped space. In class the other day, someone asked how far LA is, and I said 45 minutes; I answered with a flight time because it will be 45 minutes for me on Thursday. For others, it is six and a half hours or less. How far is Tokyo? You give me hours again. No one knows how many miles. The key is the time it takes to get there, and that time is decreasing. Thus, we are getting the sense that the world is getting faster and smaller. Because we can reach points and move things so much faster, it seems that the world has become smaller and faster. Everything is sped up, and this consequently speeds up the interconnectedness of everything. That is what I was talking about in terms of **flows**, which I will talk about more later on.

Scapes are about landscapes depending upon the perspective of the person looking at the landscape. Consequently, everyone who looks out on a landscape does not see the same thing. It depends upon where they are standing and their participation. We live in a multiperspectival world today, in which there are different ways of looking at the same thing. We have landscapes, and we have technoscapes. Some people see technology and see a smiley face: "Wow, this is good stuff." Others see technology as a threat. Where you are in relation to this is critical. The one thing we know is that technology is an accelerating force, traveling around the world and greatly changing how we live.

In a book called *Turbulence and World Politics*, James Rosenthal points out that human beings have lived on the earth for 800 lifetimes and, in the last two lifetimes, they have seen more technological achievement than the first 798 put together. What does this mean? For one thing, it means that the world of the 1960s was one-fiftieth the size of the world of the 16th century because of time overcoming spatial distances. Jet aircraft travels over 50 times what steam engines traveled in the 16th century. They were traveling the earth at ten miles an hour, and people and messages, thus, traveled only ten miles an hour—so it took awhile. When you got to the 1960s, things could travel 50 miles an hour, which made the world move faster.

This brings us to the present time, with fiber optics and satellite communication. How small is the world today? How intensified are our interconnections by the simultaneity of the fact that we can experience things here as they are happening elsewhere? What effect does that have in viewing "us and them"? "Them" can look really threatening to us because what they do can greatly impact us. What does "us and them" really mean anymore? We can begin to communicate with "them" through the Internet, we can fly at cheaper rates, and we can call people on telephones. All of this causes us to question these distinctions between boundaries— boundaries between cultures and between people. Because we are so interdependent in terms of our risk factors with one another, we come to know that we have, in some sense, a common fate. Thus, it would make some sense to understand the person who may be threatening you. How do they see it? What is their perspective in this **conflict scape**?

There are also **finance scapes**: money crossing borders, the capital that moves through currency markets (which is basically 1.2 trillion dollars a day). There has always been trade and people that loan money across borders, but now it has reached an exponential rate. We also have commodity speculations, moneys from drug propagation, and international crime crossing borders and becoming an issue for huge conflict in terms of violence and possibilities for peace. We also have another factor of moneys that are sent to countries of origin: money sent back to Mexico by Mexican citizens working in the U.S.

We also have **ethnoscapes**. People move around the world more and more. Who are these people? Some are tourists, some are immigrants, some are exiles, and some are refugees. Some are Diaspora people—people who have left a homeland but are still very much connected to their homeland, which is made possible by technoscapes. These people are able to be constantly connected to their homelands by Internet, phone, and television. Many people say we should talk today about migration not as a one-way flow, but as circulation; many people are circulating. People are moving often back to their countries of origin from the countries where they are working. Often times, these people engage in the politics from afar, which greatly shifts political activity in interesting ways. Cultures are not these distinct identities connected to geography, so it has become difficult today to locate culture in geography. Culture is more and more at a virtual level, where people that consider themselves part of the same nation can live in different places.

Building Skills: Pragmatic Understanding
Practice 1 (pages 109–10)

Narrator [N]:   1. Listen again to a part of the lecture. Then answer the question.

In class the other day, someone asked how far LA is, and I said 45 minutes; I answered with a flight time because it will be 45 minutes for me on Thursday. For others, it is six and a half hours or less. How far is Tokyo? You give me hours again. No one knows how many miles. The key is the time it takes to get there, and that time is decreasing

N: Stop the audio.

N: 2. Listen again to a part of the lecture. Then answer the question.

We live in a multiperspectival world today, in which there are different ways of looking at the same thing. We have landscapes, and we have technoscapes. Some people see technology and see a smiley face: "Wow, this is good stuff."

N: *Stop the audio.*

N: 3. Listen again to a part of the lecture. Then answer the question.

How small is the world today? How intensified are our interconnections by the simultaneity of the fact that we can experience things here as they are happening elsewhere? What effect does that have in viewing "us and them"? "Them" can look really threatening to us because what they do can greatly impact us. What does "us and them" really mean anymore?

N: *Stop the audio.*

N: 4. Listen again to a part of the lecture. Then answer the question.

We also have ethnoscapes. People more around the world more and more. Who are these people? Some are tourists, some are immigrants, some are exiles, and some are refugees.

N: *Stop the audio.*

Reading between the Lines

EXERCISE 1 (PAGE 111)

1. The class limit is 25 students, because there are only 25 desks in that room. But I'm looking at my roster, right here in front of me, and there are 28 names—three tacked on at the end: Quinlan, Jean; Steiner, Nathaniel; and Vance, Annie. Who are these people?

2.

Student 1: Did you see that religious group down by the Union Building . . . ?

Student 2: Yeah. They were handing out flyers and calling from a bull horn . . . .

Student 1: One of them walked right up to me put his hands on my shoulders, then he . . . .

Student 2: He touched your shoulders?

Student 1: Physically stopped me with his hands on my shoulders and . . . .

Student 2: Phew. . . . Who are these people?

3. We have fossil remains dating back to 6,000 B.C. We find arrows, so we know they were hunters. They have the same broad, angled forehead as central African dwellers of the same time period. But the arms and fingers are much shorter. Who are these people?

4.

Student 1: They walked straight into my dorm room.

Student 2: Without knocking?

Student 1: No, well, I mean, actually, they knocked, and I opened the door. But as I was opening the door, the dorm resident manager was taking out a huge ring of keys . . . .

Student 2: Do you think they would have come in if you didn't answer?

Student 1: Of course they would have come in. In addition, they had a checklist of places to search.

Student 2: Did they search your room?

Student 1: Every square inch. They asked me to stay there while they did it, but to be quiet. And in the end, they made me sign their list . . . .

Student 2: Who are these people?

Student 1: I couldn't believe it was for real, but later Toni told me that we all signed some agreement before we moved into the dorms, giving them the right to inspect rooms at random . . . .

Student 2: Geez. Nobody ever reads those things.

Practice 2 (pages 112–13)
Lecture: Genes

Most behaviors in humans are affected by multiple pairs of genes. We know that behavior is affected by multiple genes, but we do not know which genes correspond to behaviors. One day we might be able to know exactly which genes are responsible for being talkative or shy. Every once in a while a researcher isolates one gene that has something to do with a specific type of behavior, but we really have a long way to go in mapping genes. Right now all we can do is make guesses about how much most behaviors are influenced by genes. Psychologists have a term called *heritability,* which is an estimate of the variance within population that is due to heredity. Most of the time when people think, what percentage of my intelligence comes from my genes and what percentage comes from my environment? You cannot answer that type of question. You cannot say half my intelligence comes from my genes, and half from the way my family raised me. Heritability is an estimate of the variability within a population that is due to heredity. You are not looking at one person, you are looking at a whole population, where everyone's intelligence varies along a distribution, and there is a certain percentage of that variability that could be explained by people's genes. This is what we call heritability. You cannot talk about one person; you are talking about the variability on a population level.

In order to get estimates of heritability of behaviors, psychologists do a lot of different studies: twin studies, family studies, and adoption studies. This is all based on the premise that monozygotic twins, identical twins, share all the same genes, whereas dizygotic twins, fraternal twins, share half the same genes, and people who are even less related to each other than dizygotic twins, share even less genes.

In this graph, you do not have to memorize the numbers, but understand the concept that identical twins share 100 percent of their genes; fraternal twins, or brother and sister, or parent and child, share half the same genes; grandparents, grandchildren, uncles, aunts, nieces, nephews, half brothers, and half sisters share 25 percent of their genes; first cousins share 12.5 percent of their genes; second cousins share 6.25 percent of their genes; and unrelated people share none of the same genes. The point is that if you were to look at who is related to you, there is a spectrum of what percentage of genes you share depending on how closely related to you they are. Psychologists use this tract in order to make heritability estimates.

Specifically in a twin and family study, researchers are looking to see if people who are more related tend to resemble each other more than people who are less related. For example, if you were looking at monozygotic twins, identical twins, if they are more similar in how talkative they are compared to dizygotic twins, then researchers might conclude that genetic factors probably influence talkativeness in some way. This is the same idea as in adoption studies. Researchers might look at children who have been adopted from birth, to see if the adopted children are more like their adopted parents, with whom they share no genetic material, but presumably share the same environment, as compared with their biological parents with whom they share genetic material. You would assume that if children were more like their biological parents than their adopted parents in a certain trait, then you would think genes have to do with that trait.

Researchers might also look at monozygotic twins raised apart in two different families and see if they turn out similar. In fact, this is one of researchers' favorite things to do, and there is a big project in Minnesota where they look at twins who have been separated at birth, and they do not even know that their twin existed. Some time in adulthood they are reunited. Researchers like to look at the adults and how similar they are. This is from one of the famous studies. Researchers found monozygotic twins who were raised apart and reunited at 40 years old. They found that both had married a woman named Mary, both drove black Ford Mustangs, both loved to play tennis, and both loved to shop at garage sales. Both were salesmen, loved spicy foods, and had similar, undisclosed sexual fantasies. Now are you convinced? No, why?

Narrator: 3. Listen again to the statement made by the professor. Then answer the question.

In this graph, you do not have to memorize the numbers, but understand the concept that identical twins share 100 percent of their genes; fraternal twins, or brother and sister, or parent and child, share half the same genes.

N: Why does the professor tell the students that they do not have to memorize the graph?

N: 4. Listen again to a part of the lecture. Then answer the question.

Researchers might also look at monozygotic twins raised apart in two different families and see if they turn out similar. In fact, this is one of researchers' favorite things to do, and there is a big project in Minnesota where they look at twins who have been separated at birth, and they do not even know that their twin existed. Some time in adulthood they are reunited. Researchers like to look at the adults and how similar they are.

N: What does the professor imply when she says that "this is one of researchers favorite things to do"?

N: 5. Listen again to a part of the lecture. Then answer the question.

Researchers found monozygotic twins who were raised apart and reunited at 40 years old. They found that both had married a women named Mary, both drove black Ford Mustangs, both loved to play tennis, and both loved to shop at garage sales. Both were salesmen, loved spicy foods, and had similar, undisclosed sexual fantasies. Now are you convinced? No, why?

N: What does the professor imply when she says, "Now are you convinced? No, why?"

Listening for Attitude
Exercise 2 (pages 113–14)
Conversation: Two Students (pages 114–15)

Student 1: So, our main ideas for the new club are kendo and flower arranging?

Student 2: Those are your and my ideas. We also had the one submission, for a club that teaches Thai cooking.

S1: Okay. Well, first, I think that the cooking thing is out. You can't even buy seaweed in Oklahoma, let alone Japanese rice.

S2: (laughs) I heard in San Francisco, you can buy all that stuff. They have these huge Asian import stores, and you can buy miso, pickled radishes, sushi-grade fish . . . .

S1: Fine. But that's San Francisco. What are we going to do, drive to San Francisco every time the club meets?

S2: Okay, you're right. I mean, it's not very practical. We'd end up cooking from our own private stashes . . . .

S1: Speaking of which, I'm completely out of rice wine. Do you have any?

S2: Sorry . . . .

S1: Anyway, okay, okay, so look, the only practical options are flower arranging and kendo.

S2: I hope we can do the flower arranging.

S1: What's so great about flower arranging?

S2: Everybody knows Japanese flower arranging. People like it. They'd be willing to sign up for a flower arranging class. They'd have flowers for their houses . . . .

S1: I disagree. The way I see it, college students don't need flowers for their houses. They need to get their laundry off the floor . . . .

S2: (laughter) I meant, they don't have to put the flowers in their houses. We could donate them, to the faculty room, I mean, or a hospital . . . .

S1: I just feel like flower arranging is so slow. It's boring.

S2: Well, lots of American people know about Japanese flower arranging. That's all I'm saying. I think there'd be a lot of interest, and we'd end up with . . . .

S1: What about kendo?

S2: It's the opposite of flower arranging. Nobody has ever even heard of it. I'd rather have a full club of boring flower arrangers than two people with their kendo equipment . . . .

S1: For me, kendo is active. It's energizing. You can bring an audience. You can have competitions.

S2: Have you asked any other Americans about kendo?

S1: Even my roommate has heard of kendo—she once saw a tournament on cable . . . .

S2: Do you know anybody who can teach kendo?

S1: There's a senior here from Yokohama who used to be the head of her high school club. I talked to her, and she said she'd be willing to participate . . . .

S2: But how many students do we need to get the funding? Student Activities gave us that sheet . . . where is it . . . look, yeah, see, I mean, we need at least six active members to get the matching funds from Student Activities.

S1: I just prefer a sport to an art. Americans love sports.

S2: Yeah, that's probably true. Well, how are we going to generate interest? Are you going to stand in the quad in your kendo uniform? The police will probably come . . . .

S1: I'd rather do that than run around with a rose between my teeth . . . .

S2: (laughter) Okay, okay. Look, if you think we can find enough students, I'll go with the kendo . . . .

S1: No, no, I don't want this whole decision on my shoulders. I mean, I'm guessing folks will be interested. But maybe we should ask around some more. Just to see.

Narrator: 6. Listen again to a part of the talk. Then answer the question.

Practice 3 (page 115)

S2: Have you asked any other Americans about kendo?

S1: Even my roommate has heard of kendo—she once saw a tournament on cable . . . .

Narrator: What does the woman imply when she says, "Even my roommate has heard of kendo"?

Identifying Purpose (pages 115–17)

EXERCISE 3 (pages 116–17)

1. For this weekend, I'd like you to look at Chapters 6 and 7 in the book. Six, you really need to understand. Look through it a couple of times, and answer the questions at the end of the chapter. Seven isn't so important, but

it would be good if you had a general idea. Oh, and the weekend reading includes a photocopied handout. You can pick that up in the copy center in the basement of the McBrain Building, you know where that is.

2.

Student 1: First, we have to read Chapters 6 and 7. For six, we're supposed to answer the questions at the end of the chapter.

Student 2: That's no big deal . . . .

Student 1: But don't forget, the outline for your final paper is due on Wednesday, too.

Student 2: Oh man, I completely forgot about that. Well, there goes the game . . . .

Student 1: And listen to this. The weekend reading includes a photocopied handout. We have to go buy some packet in McBrain by 5:00 today. I mean, man, this is unbelievable.

3.

Professor: Are there any questions about the homework? Yes . . . .

Student: I see that the weekend reading includes a photocopied handout . . . . (trailing question intonation)

Professor: Yes. That handout is about six pages. You can get it in the copy center . . . .

4.

Professor: Now, don't forget your homework. We had a lot of questions today that were material that was already covered in the book. *In your reading.* You gotta do the reading if we're gonna' get through this stuff. So, take a look at the syllabus. For Monday, you need to read Chapters 6 and 7. Oh, and the weekend reading includes a photocopied handout. Okay? You got that? Any questions?

Practice 4 (pages 117–18)
Lecture: Politics and Resources

Professor: Last Friday, I had a meeting with the facilitators. I walked in, and I had this orange. Some conflict broke out because two people asked for the orange almost simultaneously. Here we have this orange, and the question becomes how we resolve the issue of having one orange and two claimants?

Student: Just cut it in half.

Professor: That is usually the step—just cut it in half—or, actually, the more traditional step is to let them fight over it. As a resource in the world, the traditional way of dealing with this conflict is to let them fight it out; that is called Realism, and it is the dominant theory of international relations. We live in an anarchical context where you can forget about community or construct morality in issues where resources are at stake—it basically comes down to a struggle.

Professor: Hans Morgenthal, in a book called *Politics of All Nations*, writes that the purpose of politics is to get power, keep power, and maximize power because that is all you can rely on in the world. The bottom line of power is armed force. This is exactly what happened with countries. Both parties said that they needed this orange. A lot of people say it is futile to discuss negotiation and, basically, what it comes down to is the notion that the UN should get out of the way—that you have to fight to get over conflict, and the UN is just standing in the way of that. You let them fight it out, you get it over with, then someone comes out the winner, and they impose peace. I did not want them to fight it out, but neither of them were happy with a compromise, so what else might be possible?

Student: We can expand the resources by planting oranges.

Professor: The problem with that is the time factor. Neither party wants to wait to get the resource.

Student: Determine which one has more nutritional deficiencies and, thus, needs the orange more.

Professor: I am going to do a little report and measure their nutritional levels somehow to determine which one is more deficient. But, after I have done all that, it is still not going to work. Are we sure we have the right issue? The issue is that they are both hungry. That is an assumption. That may not be right.

Student: Maybe you could open the dialogue and ask them why they want the orange and, through dialogical terms, we can see exactly what the problem is.

Professor: Did you hear that? Do you want the orange? You get it? Notice what she said: "Open the dialogue." We have tried everything but have not thought of this. We have ignored them and tried to keep them out of it, but we have not asked them why they want the orange. When we ask them why they want the orange, watch what happens.

Professor: When I asked them last Friday, I said, "Krissy, could you tell me why you want the orange?"

Krissy: I need the orange for the juice so I can make a tequila sunrise.

Professor: This is Friday afternoon, so, Laura, do you want to make a tequila sunrise?

Laura: No. I need the peel to make a cake for my mom.

Professor: You want the juice, and you want the peel. I think we have a solution. They can both be happy because what we have done is reframe the conflict and redefine the problem. Consequently, through dialogical process, we can look at the relationship that exists to find out what exactly is the problem and find a solution to the problem.

Student: What if they both wanted the same resource?

Professor: Then we would have another kind of problem but, still, through dialogue, we would be able to figure out whether or not they would be able to reach some sort of solution that could be compatible. You, of course, recognize that that did not happen. It is all a set up, but there are actually land issues where you find out the conflict is about different things: access to a warm water port or a matter of identity or security. There are different reasons for wanting the land and, through the dialogue, you can reconstruct the conflict and determine the possibilities for resolving the conflict without some kind of inadequate compromise that neither party will be happy with (as well as future generations). You might get some parties that are so tired that they will accept a compromise, but what about the testosterone-filled generation coming up? They are learning about history and conflict and still not having what they feel they deserve.

Narrator: 5. Listen again to a part of the lecture. Then answer the question.

I am going to do a little report and measure their nutritional levels somehow to determine which one is more deficient. But, after I have done all that, it is still not going to work. Are we sure we have the right issue? The issue is that they are both hungry. That is an assumption. That may not be right.

Narrator: What is the lecturer's purpose in asking, "Are we sure we have the right issue?"

Narrator: 6. Listen again to a part of the lecture. Then answer the question.

There are different reasons for wanting the land and, through the dialogue, you can reconstruct the conflict and determine the possibilities for resolving the conflict without some kind of inadequate compromise that neither party will be happy with (as well as future generations). You might get some parties that are so tired that they will accept a compromise, but what about the testosterone-filled generation coming up? They are learning about history and conflict and still not having what they feel they deserve.

Narrator: Why does the lecturer mention "the testosterone-filled generation coming up"?

AUDIO SCRIPT, PART 3: WRITING

Building Skills: The Integrated Writing Task
Lecture: Poverty (page 166)

At "We the People's Forum," which was the follow-up of the declaration for a culture of peace, six factors were discussed under the rubric of peace: poverty, disarmament, equity, justice, diversity, human rights, sustainable development, and democratizing international organizations (including the United Nations itself). Notice these formulations all expand the definition of violence from direct forms of violence, which are designed to produce harm and kill people, to another type of violence called structural violence. Structural violence is the unintended consequences or by-products of institutional activities. The goal of this kind of violence is not to kill, harm, or maim people but, nevertheless, people are harmed as a result of these practices.

A classic example of this would be the International Monetary Fund, with its structural adjustment policies under the neo-liberal development, which we will talk about more later in this course. There is great documentation and proof that, as a result of this privatization, deregulation, and cutting back on public spending (all these various parts that are required for countries to become creditworthy to the international organizations and private banks), people are harmed quite severely in terms of poverty, diseases associated with poverty, access to healthcare, and these types of things. These repercussions should all be considered kinds of violence.

On this point, for instance, more people die each year from hunger than from war. This is the point that prompted Mohandas Gandhi to say, "Poverty is the most deadly form of violence." We have approximately 2 billion people in the world living off of less than two dollars a day. Also, as a result of malnutrition and lack of healthcare access, about one child dies every four minutes. These are preventable deaths (unlike, say, an earthquake). When you look at countries, we see the same thing. We can see there is structural violence when we look at a country whose average lifespan is 30 years because we know that, in other countries, it is possible to live beyond that. What can explain this kind of discrepancy? That kind of question is the kind of thing that gets talked about in discussing preventable deaths.

Lecture: Genes (page 168)

Specifically in a twin and family study researchers are looking to see if people who are more related tend to resemble each other more than people who are less related. For example, if you were looking at monozygotic twins, identical twins, if they are more similar in how talkative they are compared to dizygotic twins, then researchers might conclude that genetic factors probably influence talkativeness in some way. This is the same idea as in adoption studies. Researchers might look at children who have been adopted from birth, to see if the adopted children are more like their adopted parents, with whom they share no genetic material, but presumably share the same environment, as compared with their biological parents with whom they share genetic material. You would assume that if children were more like their biological parents than their adopted parents in a certain trait, then you would think genes have to do with that trait.

Researchers might also look at monozygotic twins raised apart in two different families and see if they turn out similar. In fact, this is one of researchers' favorite things to do, and there is a big project in Minnesota where they look at twins who have been separated at birth, and they do not even know that their twin existed. Some time in adulthood they are reunited. Researchers like to look at the adults and how similar they are. This is from one of the famous studies. Researchers found monozygotic twins who were raised apart and reunited at 40 years old. They found that both had married a women named Mary, both drove black Ford Mustangs, both loved to play tennis, and both loved to shop at garage sales. Both were salesmen, loved spicy foods, and had similar, undisclosed sexual fantasies. Now are you convinced? No, why?

Lecture: Turning Fat into Muscle (page 171)

Today we're going to talk about a common myth: that fat can be turned into muscle. TV ads for diet medication hawk this as the truth, but in fact, it is completely false.

First of all, when you get on the scale, it is impossible to determine what kind of weight you are losing. The scale is measuring the weight of everything in your body: fat, muscles, bones, water—everything. So, you might think that you are losing fat, when actually you are losing water.

This problem is complicated by the make-up of fat and muscle tissues. Fat and muscle are two different types of tissue. Fat, or adipose tissue, is made up of lipids. Muscle tissues, on the other hand, are made up of proteins. Therefore, muscle tissue is more dense than adipose tissue. You might think that because you get on the scale and you weigh less that you are "replacing" fat with muscle, but actually this is counter-intuitive. If you were really replacing fat with muscle, you would weigh more.

Nevertheless, people in many developed countries are desperate to figure out how to lose weight and become more lean. While scientists are focussing on this area to try to find a "miracle drug," and while many companies claim to have that "miracle diet," the only way to really lose weight is to burn more calories than you take in. We can't fight nature in that respect. Here's how it works: When you *don't* burn more calories than you take in, your body has a natural process of storing that extra energy for use later. The excess glucose becomes triacylglycerides in your bloodstream that are later deposited as adipose tissue, or fat. This process really helped us out when we didn't know where our next meal would come from. It was to our biological advantage at that time to be able to eat a lot when food was available, and to store whatever our bodies couldn't burn for later. This actually helped us to survive.

Today, though, for those of us who live in a country where there is a fast food restaurant on every corner, this process actually is beginning to harm us. If the body has too much adipose tissue, health problems can occur.

Lecture: Gender (page 174)

Professor: A bit about sex determination because it has a bearing on how we predict patterns of inheritance for genes that are linked to sex chromosomes, that are found on sex chromosomes.

But before I talk about sex determination in humans um, I just want to point out that the chromosomal type of sex determination is by no means universal. So what other types of sex determination are there other than this XY sex determination that humans have? Yeah?

Student: Environmental.

Professor: Yeah so there's environmental sex determination, and, an example of that? Environmental sex determination, this is known to be the case in both crocodilians and turtles. In crocodilian nests, nests that are incubated at high temperature produce males, nests that are incubated at low temperatures produce females and intermediate temperatures produce a mixture of sexes. So in crocodilians, sex is not at all produced by chromosomes.

Besides environmental, what are some other types of non-chromosomal sex determination? Well, some species of fish, for example, actually change sex during the course of their life. Tropical teleosts, the colorful fish that live in coral reefs, are of this type. The majority of reef fish change sex at some point in their life. In fact, reef fish that remain as the same sex for their life span are the minority. These fish change sex in different ways—some start out as males and become females, some start as females and become males, and some are hermaphroditic, that is, they are both male and female simultaneously. Regardless, scientists are not exactly sure how this sex change occurs, whether it is the result of hormones, or what. Maybe it is somehow genetic, but the cause has yet to be determined.

What about other forms of chromosomal sex determination other than XY? Does anybody know about that? There are other forms, it's often called a "WZ sex determination scheme." And in this case where . . . as in XY sex determination, females are the so-called homogametic sex, they have two X chromosomes. In WZ sex determination, males are the homogametic sex. And in WZ sex determination, we have organisms like birds for example, or butterflies.

So, XY sex determination isn't the only chromosomal sex determination system out there and chromosomes aren't the only way sex is determined anyway, it can be determined environmentally as well.

AUDIO SCRIPT, PART 4: SPEAKING

Building Skills: Responding to Independent and Integrated Speaking Prompt

Question 3 (pages 197–200)

The university should definitely raise the cost of tuition. Costs at this university are already lower than at most places, so even with higher fees, students will be getting a good deal. And if the university cuts out some programs, the quality of the education here will suffer. I mean, people will stop respecting us.

Question 4 (pages 200–02)

You probably know that water expands when it freezes. This odd property of water has a lot of everyday consequences. For one thing, it means that roads in cold regions suffer more damage than those in warm areas, because moisture in the surface expands during winter and cracks the road. For another, it allows you to let ice cubes melt in a drink. Imagine what would happen if the water in ice cubes expanded as the ice melted. Soon, the volume of an unfinished drink might increase so much that the drink would pour out over the rim of your cup or glass. It's also the reason why ice floats. The ice, expanded as it is, is less dense than the water around it.

Question 5 (pages 202–04)

Student 1: OK, so, how are your notes from today's lecture?

Student 2: Not too good. I just felt like the professor was going too fast today . . . ya know, she was really hard to follow.

Student 1: I totally agree. I think that I got her main ideas, but there was a lot that I missed.

Student 2: What do you think about going to her office hours tomorrow before class? I'm just afraid that if we didn't get this week's lecture, well, next week's lecture might not make sense. And you know that the midterm is coming up soon.

Student 1: That's a good idea, and if we go together I won't feel embarrassed asking a lot of questions. But let's get together tonight and compare our notes first. That way we can go to her office hours with a list of questions ready.

Student 2: Of course, that's a great idea. Can we meet in the lounge after dinner?

Student 1: Perfect.

Briefly describe the problem that the students discussed in the conversation and give your opinion about the solution that the two students decided on.

Question 6 (pages 205–07)

Today we are going to talk about social conflict and how those conflicts begin to get resolved. In the context of sociology, *conflict* means the perception or belief that the desires of the parties involved cannot be achieved simultaneously. There are many different ways that social conflict might be resolved. We'll start by exploring two of these strategies: contending and yielding. *Contending* means that you try to force the solution that you want on the other parties. To take an easy example, let's say you and your brother both want to go out for the evening, but your parents have told you that one of you has to stay home and baby-sit your 5-year-old sister. You might tell your parents that your brother failed his math test this week and is keeping it a secret from them, hoping that they'll punish him and let you go out. Or you might simply yell and scream, hoping that your parents will tell you to go out just to get you out of the house (that's unlikely to work, right?). Both are forms of contending.

Another way to solve a conflict is, of course, to yield, to settle for less than you wanted. In the case of you and your brother, this would simply mean that you volunteer to stay home for the night and baby-sit, perhaps with the hopes that next time it will be his turn.

These examples might sound overly simple, but actually conflict between individuals or within a family is very similar to conflict between groups in a community, or even between nations on a global scale. And the resolution strategies are similar, too.

MULTI-SKILLS PRACTICE TEST AUDIO SCRIPT FOR SECTION 2: LISTENING

Conversation: A Teaching Assistant and a Student (page 224–25)

Listen to the following conversation adapted from the MICASE transcripts of the University of Michigan. Answer the questions that follow by circling the best response.

TA: Alright . . . okay first, tell me wh- wh- what your experience has been in writing classes in the past?

Student: Okay, um you mean from like high school?

TA: No, m- mostly here

Student: Or just in college well I've tak-

TA: Well where did you go to high school?

Student: I went to uh are you familiar with the area?

TA: *mhm*

Student: I lived in Wyandotte.

TA: *okay*

Student: and I went to Roosevelt High School.

TA: okay

Student: the public school there wasn't uh, there was it was pretty much in high school it was just like the basic English classes. I didn't really get any farther in that cuz my my main thing was art. and uh, with all the classes I had to take it was like the English classes kinda like suffered a little bit. which I kinda regret now.

TA: right

Student: But in college I took uh English 125 and uh, did pretty well in there, I got like a B-plus I think.

TA: Who was the instructor?

Student: The instruc- it was a graduate student I uh I, don't remember her name. She was, Romanian I don't know if that really rings a bell. I don't know.

TA: No

Student: Yeah I didn't think it would but uh, it was a it was like that night class so like it was it was I just liked it, it was a good class. And then, I needed to take uh, like in my requirement for art and design you need to take six credits of English. So right now I'm taking American Lit, Intro to American Lit, and Intro to Poetry.

TA: okay

Student: and uh, that's, that's pretty much, that's it,

TA: okay

Student: really. So I'm uh

TA: And how are you doing in that other course?

Student: uh

TA: Have you done much writing?

Student: It's pretty, it's pretty decent cuz uh it's really not too bad you, you take, I think the the grading scale is attendance is like a fifty percent of your grade and you get like these writing assignments every class, where you pretty much write like, uh three quarters to a page, um about a question that he's asked from the previous class so you pretty much you, you think about it and then you write about it in class and then, uh the tests are are pretty uh, if you read the book you should know what you're doing so I think I'm doing pretty well in there.

TA: okay

Student: um, well enough to like I mean I'd probably I'd probably have to say somewhere around a B area.

TA: okay

Student: But uh, and that's that's pretty much pretty much the English extent right there. So

TA: Okay and who's teaching that course?

Student: Uh it's uh, it's um, Boeching or how do you say

TA: Beechum

Student: Beechum that's it.

TA: okay

Student: Yeah.

QUESTION 4 (page 223)

1. Listen again to a part of the lecture. Then answer the question.

> I needed to take uh, like in my requirement for art and design you need to take six credits of English. So right now I'm taking American Lit, Intro to American Lit, and Intro to Poetry.

Conversation: An Advisor and a Student (pages 225–27)

Listen to the following conversation adapted from the MICASE transcripts of the University of Michigan. Answer the questions that follow by circling the best response.

Advisor: So. I see that you're from Hartland Michigan.

Student: yes

Advisor: This is, right up the road.

Student: Mhm, like forty minutes from here.

Advisor: yeah

Student: mhm

Advisor: Okay, and uh, you say that you're interested in prebusiness and economics.

Student: I was, I don't think that I am anymore.

Advisor: Okay cuz you write a lot about international business.

Student: I I'm interested in the um, international aspect, like the international, business I was gonna do, you know like all that stuff but I don't, think that that's what I wanna do anymore

Advisor: Okay so what, what changed your mind and what has it been changed to?

Student: Um, I, don't know if I wanna experience like you know, cultures and the world and

Advisor: mhm

Student: everything and business but I don't know if I wanna spend all my time behind a desk, not really enjoying where I am, you know, like having to work with numbers all the time and like, not really being out, doing something a little more interesting maybe like flavorful I have lots of other interests like um, that are a little bit more like, paleontology or astronomy or

Advisor: oh

Student: international relations, so, those things I wanna don't think I wanna do the business.

Advisor: Have you done any digs or anything like that?

Student: No like dinosaurs fascinate me, like that stuff fascinates me, but I don't know if that's like a career choice yet but I, was looking through the course book and I know they offer like a half a term class or something, that I could, like, take and see if I, if it was worth it

Advisor: mhm

Student: you know, more depth

Advisor: Both geology and biological anthropology, will lead you, that way.

Student: mhm

Advisor: um, geology has got this one course called I think Dinosaurs and Other Failures

Student: mhm

Advisor: is that the

Student: mhm

Advisor: one that you noticed? yeah, that's a very, it's kind of a fun course actually

Student: right

Advisor: and I think, you know we're all interested in triceratopses and woolly mammoths

Student: right

Advisor: you know and it talks about what, all of the various theories about why it is that they

Student: mhm

Advisor: you know

Student: mhm

Advisor: became extinct and why they no longer exist we've heard all of the, big uh, meteors coming from outer space

Student: Right. Yeah I find it, like, absolutely fascinating and that's, one of the things. I don't know if I would wanna be in a career or studying a major that, is not that interesting to me. I'm just doing it because I could be successful, or whatever, I think I'd rather, stick with something that's more, um I could be more involved in,

Advisor: mhm

Student: and that's why, also looking at like um, foreign relations and foreign affairs like

Advisor: mhm

Student: dealing with, people

Advisor: mhm

Student: more and um, issues that I can like be involved in and like controversial things that, you know debatable topics not just something that's like, like doing math, like a you know, plugging in numbers type of a thing all the time so

Advisor: Being an accountant

Student: Yeah I could not be an accountant

QUESTION 10 (page 227)

Listen again to a part of the lecture. Then answer the question:

Student: I, was looking through the course book and I know they offer like a half a term class or something, that I could, like, take and see if I, if it was worth it

Advisor: mhm

Student: You know, more depth

Advisor: Both geology and biological anthropology, will lead you that way.

Lecture: Midwestern Geography (pages 227–28)

Professor: Okay, we were talking about the Corn Belt . . . so I went through identifying the area and I was talking about the physical environment. Remember what I last talked about in class? It was . . . .

Students *(in chorus)*: The flood.

Professor: . . . the flood. The big flood of 1993 on the Mississippi River. So, I need to finish that up, and then go on to land use and then economy. Okay.

So as far as physical environment, we know that this is humid-continental. Continental-humid. We're not into an arid climate yet. The native vegetation—there's some deciduous trees, but we're starting to get into um, areas that, uh, that had the tall grass prairie. And we haven't talked about that yet. We haven't talked about that yet as a vegetation type. So we're in the situation where it is still fairly humid, but when you get to the western edge of this area, you're getting into a prairie vegetation which, of course, is the dominant vegetation on the Great Plains, which we're gonna talk about next. And when I say tall, I mean 4 to 6 feet tall: grasses, and not just grasses, but also lots of flowers. Very tall-growing flowers. Like, the Euro-Americans when they arrived, they were just floored with how tall the grasses were. They reported that a man on horseback going across the prairie couldn't see where he was going, cause the grasses were taller than a man on horseback. So, at least six feet, sometimes maybe 8 feet tall, so I mean, really tall. So, what have we replaced this tall grass prairie with?

Student: Corn.

Professor: Corn . . . which is, corn is a really tall grass . . . it is a grass, even though you don't think of it, but if you take your botany, corn is a grass. Kind of a weird grass, but it is. So is bamboo, is another weird grass. So we replace this really tall grass, the native grass, of course, and replace it with another native grass, which, of course, is corn.

And this is a remnant of it. It's the Chiwaukee Prairie, it's in eastern Wisconsin. And it's not the tallest as what it got, because this is an area of Glacial Lake Chicago, and it's very sandy soil, and sandy soil is not as good for vegetation. So, this is a wimpy . . . or this is a relatively short, tall-grass prairie. But you get . . . there's an idea of a person. And you can still see that some of the, some of the plants are taller than the person. And you can see in this area fire was used to keep the trees back. And so before the Europeans arrived, there was a lot of reports of Native Americans lighting fire to have open area . . . more diverse habitat . . . open area . . . open area for what? Why would they do that? Light fires. There are lots of reports if you . . . the Europeans, when they first came across, they go "Oh, the plains are on fire!" Why would they do that?

Student: To regrow.

Professor: Yes, to kill the trees. To keep the trees back. Or less trees. But why would they do that? Now some are accidental, the campfires get out of control. But they deliberately set fires. Okay, what animals like kind of open areas?

Student: Deer.

Professor: Deer. Yes. That's why deer do so well in Michigan, because we have lots of patchwork landscape with lots of open area—edges. So for deer. Also, re-member the native Americans were also cultivating areas . . . you know, the, uh, like the Mississippian culture, they were planting corn, and so cul-tivating land.

So again, the corn replaced the tall grass prairie. And you know, most of this corn is not used for sweet corn, right? Only a small production of the corn is sweet corn. Most of it is, uh, of course, used for cattle, for feed lot. And you guys know all this, cause we're all from here, we know this. And you should know that the United States produces half the world's corn. And that's a lot, when you think about it. And most of it comes from the Corn Belt.

And a lot of this corn is of course exported, and you don't have to know the countries, but just remember that a great chunk of . . . one of the major consumers is Japan, and a lot of countries in the Orient—Korea, Tai-wan, and other countries. So, it's a major commodity for export.

Lecture: Cyrus the Great (page 229)

Professor: So, did you do the reading? Did you get to that? I'm telling you, this his-tory is interesting stuff. So where are we now . . . we have a full day here and we're still trying to catch up. Sooooo, yes, yes. Cyrus the Great. Cyrus the Great. Who was this man, and where did he come from? Did you get to the reading . . . I'm assuming that you did. So, who was Cyrus the Great? What do we know about Cyrus the great? Anybody . . . anything, what do we know?

Student: He was the king of the Persian Empire.

Professor: Okay, good. He was a king of the Persian Empire. The Persian Empire, or really, more accurately, what would we say? Which empire did he found?

Student: The Acha . . . the Ekayme the . . .

Professor: Right. Good. The Achaemenid Empire. Achaemenid. Good. Cyrus the Great united the two original Iranian tribes, the Medes and the Iranians. So, he founded this empire, which, up until that time in history was one of the largest empires on earth. Where's our map? Where did the map go? No map today.

Student: [laughter]

Professor: Anyway, where was the Achaemenid Empire? Cyrus was a great military leader. Who knows the general boundary of Cyrus's state?

Student: Iran . . .

Professor: Yes, it included modern-day Iran. What else?

Student: India.

Professor: Yeah. It went all the way to India. We aren't sure, I mean, we can't be sure exactly how far east he penetrated. He did invade India, what is modern-day India. We know that. But it seems that he may have stopped short of the Indus Valley itself. What I'd give for a map right now. But anyway, yes, Cyrus took lands from India to . . . ?

Student: The Mediterranean.

Professor: That's right. The Mediterranean Sea. He was an amazing military leader. He overthrew the Medes, the Lydians—we talked about the Lydians—the Babylonians. He took over modern-day Turkey, Syria, Palestine. But he stopped short of Egypt. There is no evidence that Cyrus himself entered Egypt. He left that work to his son. So it was a vast empire. And it was governed by vassal kings called "satraps."

Student: Didn't he conquer Khazakhstan?

Professor: To the east, yes. And in that conquest, he lost his life. In 530. B.C. 530 B.C. But let's back up a little here. Not just any local king can rise up and ac-quire lands like that. What was going on here?

Student: Well, wasn't there the marriage thing?

Professor: "The marriage thing," <laughs>, yeah, and that was a big "thing," right? It wasn't uncommon, as you know. Cyrus was born in about 580 B.C. There is some evidence that Cyrus's father was married to a Mede, to the daughter of a Median king. So that would have encouraged the Medes to accept his rule. Intertribal marriages were not uncommon.

Student: Did they marry on purpose, I mean, to unite the tribes?

Professor: That's a good question. Did they foresee the political convenience of an intermarriage? Or, another question whose answer we really don't know for sure, is did they marry at all? Some historians believe their marriage was just a story, created after the fact, to justify Cyrus's rule.

Student: You mean, they weren't married at all?

Professor: It's possible. It's possible that Cyrus didn't have a single Mede anywhere in his family, but that after he conquered the Median people, they claimed the Mede connection. But it doesn't really matter. It's not the central key to his success. What was the key to Cyrus's success?

Student: He was so tolerant.

Professor: What do you mean by that?

Student: I mean, he was tolerant. He was, like, flexible. He accepted other cultures. He was more, uh, more . . . humanitarian than other leaders.

Professor: He was. We'll read later this quarter, no, I mean, actually, later this week, it's part of our assignment, part of Richard Frye's book, *The Heritage of Persia*. He talks about the new policy of reconciliation, a kind of "pax Achaeminica . . . ." And what does this mean? Cyrus presented himself as a liberator. Not as a conquerer, but as a liberator. He had no hopes of forcing conquered people into a single mold. No.

He had respect, forbearance, for other religious beliefs and cultural traditions. People respected him. His subjects admired him. Now this was a big shift. Because what was the paradigm, up until then? Usually, what did a conqueror do?

Student: They tried to wipe out the local civilizations. They tried to control people.

Professor: And Cyrus changed that. He didn't gallop in and slaughter the heathens. He didn't burn the cities that he conquered. He was a military leader, and he fought, to be sure. But he didn't flaunt his victory. He didn't try to dominate the local identity. The people. Most of his subjects, they admired him.

Student A: He's in the Bible a lot. He's considered a hero by the Jews. He allowed the Jews to return to Palestine.

Professor: Good. The Jewish community saw him as a liberator. That was exactly how he wanted to be seen. What do you know about that?

Student A: Well, he let the Jews return to Palestine. From Babylon.

Professor: What else did he do? What were some of his concrete methods for running a fair and equitable empire?

Student: Well, he had a constitution.

Student: And a judicial system.

Professor: Good, right. A constitution and a judicial system. And they were based on values. He had high ethical values. Like what, what other features defined this empire?

Student: Freedom of where you could live. People could choose their residence.

Professor: Good.

Student: Jobs. Freedom of occupation.

Professor: Good. Freedom of jobs.

Student: Religious tolerance. Like somebody mentioned, the Jews.

Professor: Tolerance. He was tolerant. But he was also shrewd. The Jews, for example, had been exiled to Babylon. And he let them go back to Palestine.

This way, he gained their respect. And *at the same time,* he succeeded in fortifying his western border against possible invasion by the Egyptians. So, it was a win-win political maneuver. What else?

Student: He didn't allow slavery.

Professor: He didn't allow slavery. And think about this. 250 years later, Aristotle shows up. And what did he think about slavery?

Student: It was normal.

Professor: Natural law. He called slavery "natural law." That was almost three centuries after Cyrus's rule. Good. Now, I'm going to read to you. Cyrus wrote a decree on his aims and policies. It was inscribed on a clay cylinder, and it's now at the British Museum. What's important here is that this document, if you will, is considered the first declaration of human rights known to man. And let's read this now. Just listen. Close your eyes, if you want to. You need to get this, what this man is actually saying, in the sixth century before the Common Era.

Lecture: Economics (pages 230–32)

Professor: So, now we're gonna get into a new concept, Gross Domestic Product. Most of you have heard of Gross Domestic Product. G.D.P. Let me give you the exact definition of GDP: It's the market value of all final goods and services and information produced within the United States in one calendar year. That's the definition of the Gross Domestic Product.

Student: Is it, um, is it the same as Gross National Product?

Professor: Aha! Gross National Product. You see, there . . . you date yourself. GNP. Some of you may have taken introductory economics a few years ago. Then, we used the term *Gross National Product.* Gross National Product is essentially the same beast as Gross Domestic Product. But the definition has changed slightly, so we don't say GNP anymore. You won't really hear that. Instead, we now talk about Gross *Domestic* Product. That was, let's see, back in 1992 . . . we shifted to Gross Domestic Product.

Okay. Now, the Gross Domestic Product in the United States is the market value of all final goods that are made, and services, within our economy. When we talk about GDP, we're talking only about the final output. We are not talking about intermediate goods. For example, this podium. Let's look at this high-quality podium that I'm using here. This podium is the final output. That goes into GDP. This podium also has lots of what are called "intermediate goods." These are things that are produced in the process. For example, there's wood in this podium. Or, is this plastic? Anyway, it's like a synthetic wood. But none of the wood is counted in the Gross Domestic Product. It's got nails, or screws, but none of that is counted in the Gross Domestic Product. It's got a lot of other raw materials, steel, and labor even, but none of that is counted in the Gross Domestic Product.

What we count in the United States is the podium itself. When the school buys the podium, GDP goes up. The reason we don't count the intermediate components—the wood, and the hardware, and the labor that manufactured it—is that we would be counting it twice. If we first count the intermediate components, and then we count the final output, we're counting each item twice. That wouldn't be accurate. So, we only measure the *final* goods and services.

GDP—it's the final goods and services and information. Let's look at this next part of the definition: Information. That's a new item in the GDP, is information. We are moving into the Information Age. So information is counted in the GDP.

And this is all produced within one year. *One year.* That's very important. So, the GDP is measured in one calendar year.

When we figure GDP, everything is counted that is produced within the United States. This is a big change from before. Back in the days when it was Gross National Product, when you took economics the first time, Gross National Product was figured differently. It was defined as all goods and products produced domestically by domestic firms. So that if Japan had an auto plant in the United States, the profit incomes earned from the production here, were not part of the GDP. But that's different now. Now, we don't really care anymore, who owns the company. If it's a Japanese company such as Nissan or Toyota, and they're producing in the U.S., that's *our* GDP. If it's Ford Motor Company producing in Germany, that's Germany's GDP. So now everybody counts only what takes place physically within the United States. The fact that Ford Motor Company would produce automobiles in Germany contributed to jobs and incomes in Germany, not the United States. And Toyota's production of automobiles in the U.S. contributes to our GDP, not theirs. So, that's why we've shifted, so that ownership doesn't matter, physical location does.

Now the next thing we'll talk about are the components that make up GDP itself. There are four components. Let's run through these, then we'll talk about each one in more detail over the next few days. They are personal consumption expenditures. That's the biggest one. Personal consumption makes up the majority of Gross Domestic Product. Then there's Investment. Government. And last is net exports. So, four areas.

The very first one is the biggest: personal consumption expenditures. Personal consumption expenditures are spending by the household sector. This makes up approximately two-thirds of the Gross Domestic Product of the United States. This is a huge number. Let's look at the year 2002. The GDP of the United States in 2002 was ten thousand three hundred and eighty three billion dollars. Ten *thousand* three hundred, eighty three billion dollars. Two-thirds of that GDP is you and I. Spending by you and me.

So, for household expenditures alone, that's six thousand, nine hundred-something thousand dollars. Thousand-*billion* dollars.

Our economy is based on spending. Everybody knows it. The more we spend, the higher the level of GDP.

The next element is called "Investment." Investment makes up about 15 percent of the GDP. Investment is spending by the business sector, and we'll look at what they spend on.

Thirdly is government. The level of government expenditures in the United States is about 19 percent of the Gross Domestic Product that we have. And that figure's, interestingly enough, been stable for many, many years.

The last area that we'll look at is called "net exports." And with net exports, we're looking at the relationship between our imports and our exports, away from and into the United States. And you'll notice, the figure is negative. About one percent of the GDP is negative. And if you add all the numbers up, that calculates to 100 percent of what we produce and distribute—goods, services, and information—in the United States, in one calendar year. A huge amount of money.

QUESTION 27

Two-thirds of that GDP is you and I. Spending by you and me. So, for household expenditures alone, that's six thousand, nine hundred-something thousand dollars. Thousand-*billion* dollars.

Lecture: Plants (pages 233–34)

Professor: I want to just have some, have some have some discussion now, have some discussion as to how plants are essential to the existence of life as we know it. Anybody think plants are not essential to life as we know it? Okay, so plants are essential to life as we know it. Why? They're autotrophic? Remember this word "autotrophic"? Okay. Anybody want to define autotrophic for me? They produce their own food from simple chemicals and energy. In this case, most plants use what? Professor Bradshaw told you. Okay, light and CO_2. And from that, they make all sorts of fancy steps, and as far as we're concerned, we eat them. If they didn't do it, we couldn't eat. All right. Next thing, plants maintain the chemistry of the atmosphere. After they use light and carbon dioxide to make, make chemical compounds, what else do they do? What's the other feat of the CO_2 equation? Of the photosynthesis equation? They produce oxygen, right? All right. We'll go into that in a little more detail later. They produce oxygen. We breathe the oxygen they produce.

One more thing that I want to talk about briefly. Plants are essential for creating, developing, and maintaining soil. How many of you knew that? I would guess none. We use soil. These three things I just want to go through briefly just to remind you of this equation um professor Bradshaw gave you. I'm not going into it, I assume you know it, if it's a question on the paper, I assume you will have remembered that. All right?

Let's look at these two plants. In this case, these plants are both autotrophs: They use energy to make carbon dioxide. Autotrophs and heterotrophs. This is all on the Web, if you don't want to take notes at the moment. Photo-autotrophs are what plants are. They take energy from the sun, they produce materials. And here are the heterotrophs, consumers of organic materials such as fungi, such as bacteria. I know they're organisms you would see, and these are essential for taking the material which is produced by plants and breaking it down and sometimes releasing nutrients again from it. It's a nutrient-cycling link between the autotrophs and the heterotrophs. Any questions about this? Everybody got this basic idea?

You've got these photo-autotrophs producing all this material, you've got the heterotrophs living on it. If there were no heterotrophs, what would happen? If there were no heterotrophs, but there were photo-autotrophs, what would happen?

Student: Nothing would decompose.

Professor: Nothing would decompose. We'd be over our ears very quickly, and in some cases there are no heterotrophs. Anybody know where there are very few or no heterotrophs? Yeah?

Student: A bog.

Professor: A bog, a bog, a peat bog. All right, we'll talk about peat bogs. You will see the plants that grow in peat bogs. All right, a peat bog produces peat, there's peat, peat, peat, in which people die and get buried and get dug up thousands of years later, and they're completely pickled and not decomposed. There's a lot of those plants that also produce hydrogen ions that keep the place very acid. So heterotrophs are essential, an integral part of the ecosystem that you see between autotrophs and heterotrophs.

QUESTION 32 (page 234)

These three things I just want to go through briefly just to remind you of this equation that Professor Bradshaw gave you. I'm not going into it, I assure you know it, if it's a question on the paper, I assure you will have remembered that. All right?

MULTI-SKILLS PRACTICE TEST AUDIO SCRIPT FOR SECTION 3: SPEAKING

QUESTION 3 (page 235)

Student: The university should definitely get rid of the physical education requirement. I came to college to study, not to do exercise. In fact, I exercise on my own time, and so do most of my friends. I don't think I want the "Introduction to University Life" course to be a requirement, either. I'd rather be able to take something that is related to my field of study.

Narrator: The student gives her own opinion about the physical education requirement. Say what her opinion is and summarize the reasons she gives.

QUESTION 4 (page 236)

Professor: You probably know that each one of your cells contains genes, which are unique to you. If this is true, then how do cells perform different functions in the body, if they all have at their center the same material? How does a red blood cell become a red blood cell and a skin cell a skin cell? Well, in multi-celled organisms, cells have developed specialized roles in the body. So, every cell contains the same genetic information, but only part of that genetic information is actually used. Some genes are always "on," but others are switched on and off depending on the function of the cell. For example, the cells of the pancreas produce insulin, so in those cells, the gene that codes for insulin production is switched on.

Narrator: Considering the information you have just received from the reading and the lecture, explain the function of genes in the body and how specialized cells are created.

QUESTION 5 (page 236)

Listen to the conversation.

Student: Hi, Professor Foster. Do you have a minute to answer some questions about the exam?

Professor: Sure. You're in my morning section, right?

Student: Yea, English 302.

Professor: Right, then. What can I do for you?

Student: Well, I did worse on the exam than I thought, and I was just wondering what I can do to make sure that I improve my grade on the next exam.

Professor: OK, let me just take a look at your exam . . . umm-hmm . . . Well, you can see here that most of the problems that you missed were related to phonology. It's hard for some of the students to grasp. One thing that should make you feel a little better is that phonology won't be on the next exam, and it won't be on the final either, so you shouldn't worry about that too much, except to try to understand where you went wrong.

Student: OK. That's a relief.

Professor: As for the other area where you lost points, it was the essay. Remember that you need to go into detail—don't just make broad assumptions and generalizations. I'm looking to see that you know and understand the material that we read.

Student: Of course, right. Well, I guess I didn't pay much attention to the readings. I really focused on your lecture notes.

Professor: OK, well, that's something. My lectures highlight important parts of the material, but the readings fill in the rest of the important information, so, for the next exam, you should take notes on the readings and study those notes. Also, when we get closer to the exam, if you have any questions, please come to see me in my office hours again.

Student: OK, great. Thanks.

Professor: No problem.

Narrator: Briefly describe the problem that the student and the professor discussed in the conversation and give your opinion about the professor's advice.

QUESTION 6 (page 236)

Today we're going to talk about the geography of the Caribbean region. Specifically, today's lecture is about the formation of the Lesser Antilles, a chain of small islands in the eastern Caribbean Sea.

To understand how these islands were formed, you need to know about what geographers call "plate tectonics." Basically, the earth's crust is made up of a large number of plates, or pieces that can move around. The movement of these plates is called "plate tectonics." It just means plate movement.

The area where two plates collide is called a *zone of convergence*. Basically what happens is that the one plate is forced under another plate. This movement of one plate under another can cause a number of complex things to happen.

For one thing, earthquakes might occur where one plate is descending. Earthquakes indeed occur in the Lesser Antilles. Another possibility is the formation of an island arc, or curved chain of islands. The Lesser Antilles clearly form such an arc, which stretches from the Anegada fault down toward South America. The island arc was formed like this: as one plate descended under the other, it took with it various sediments from its crust that collected in the trench where the plates hit. The sediments were dragged down, folded under, and crushed. Finally they melted, producing magma that forced its way back up to the surface through fractures caused by the collision of the plates. This resulted in an arc of small volcanic islands that are known today as the Lesser Antilles.

Narrator: Using points and examples from the lecture, explain the formation of the Lesser Antilles as presented by the professor.

MULTI-SKILLS PRACTICE TEST AUDIO SCRIPT FOR SECTION 4: WRITING

Lecture: A Dispute (page 237)

Today's lecture is going to examine the dynamics of a dispute between parties. The parties could be people or groups—even nations. Let's look at an example in detail.

Imagine that a family goes to an amusement park for vacation. They bring their $500 digital camera with them. They decide to ride a roller coaster. Although there is a sign posted at the entrance to the ride that guests should leave their cameras in a locker at the entrance to the ride, the family doesn't pay attention to the sign and brings their camera along. As the father is taking a picture, the roller coaster swerves and the camera flies out of the father's hands and falls to the ground. (Thankfully, no one is hurt!)

The father goes to the manager of the ride and complains, saying that the amusement park should replace the camera. The manager says, politely, "I'm sorry, sir, but warning signs were posted. The amusement park is not responsible for items that are lost or stolen in the park." The father is furious and starts to yell and scream, causing other people in the park to feel uncomfortable. He threatens to launch a media campaign against the park and tell all of his friends, many of whom are regular patrons of the park, to boycott the place.

Now let's analyze this situation in terms of three dynamics to the dispute: interests, rights, and power.

First, what are the interests of the father and the manager? Well, the father's interest is getting his camera replaced. Remember, he is now out $500. The interests of the manager are a little more complex. He probably doesn't care about the amusement park paying the father $500. After all, it's not *his* $500. His interests include doing his job, in other words, enforcing the rules and policies of the amusement park. He has another interest, though, right? Another part of his job is to make sure that guests of the park are happy, and that they leave the park with a good image of the place so that they will come back again and spend money there, and encourage their friends to do the same.

Second, let's look at who is right in this situation. Certainly the amusement park has fulfilled its legal obligation by warning the public of possible damage to cameras on the ride (which is something that should be obvious anyway). So, it's the fault of the father that he didn't pay attention to the warning.

Finally, let's talk about power. The manager has power because he is the keeper of the rules, and the representative of the amusement park, which has power by virtue of owning the ride and being able to make the rules. The father has power, though, too, right? He has power because he can stop going to the park, and, depending on his social connections, he might be able to decrease the park's revenue by virtue of a boycott.

So, how do you think this dispute got resolved?

ANSWER KEY

Part 1: Reading

Building Skills: Identifying Main Ideas and Understanding Content (pages 2–42)

Exercise 1 (page 4) these, biometrics, they, biometric security systems

Exercises with Short Passages

Exercise 1 (page 5)   1. d,   2. a,   3. b,   4. c

Exercise 2 (page 7)   1. b,   2. b,   3. a,   4. a

Exercise 3 (page 8)   1. c,   2. a,   3. a,   4. b

Exercise 4 (page 9)   1. c,   2. b,   3. a,   4. a

Exercise 5 (page 11) 1. a,   2. d,   3. b,   4. c

Exercise 6 (page 12) 1. a,   2. b,   3. b,   4. d

Exercise 7 (page 13) 1. c,   2. d,   3. c,   4. a

Review: Identifying Main Ideas and Understanding Content (pages 30–42)

Main Idea Review Passage 1 (page 31) 1. b,   2. a,   3. d,   4. c,   5. a,   6. b

Scematic Table (page 34)

Images from long ago	b. a killer that dishonorably plays with its victims f. a sneaky animal
Images from recent times	a. a fortunate animal e. a poised and elegantly detached animal g. a graceful animal

Main Idea Review Passage 2 (page 35) 1. d, 2. c, 3. a, 4. d, 5. a

Prose Summary (page 38)

Efforts to regulate the use of dietary supplements have sometimes been difficult or unpopular.
a. Herbs and other supplements often have cultural implications beyond their pharmacological properties, so regulators risk violating religious or cultural rights of herb users.
c. Some elements of U.S. law, particularly the DSHEA of 1994, specifically aim to give consumers easy access to dietary supplements and would likely conflict with a strict regulatory program.
e. Some herbal formulas have effects that are not yet well understood, so it's difficult to evaluate their risks and benefits.

Main Idea Review Passage 3 (page 39) 1. c, 2. a, 3. a, 4. c, 5. d

Schematic Table (page 42)

Make it easier to adopt a child	b. Gay and lesbian couples are increasingly winning the right to become adoptive parents. f. As an outgrowth of in vitro fertilization technology, researchers have created embryo adoption.
Make it harder to adopt a child	a. The adoptee search movement began to demand the opening of adoption records. e. There is a dearth of healthy U.S. infants for adoption. d. State laws govern such things as who may adopt, who may be adopted, and who must consent to the adoption.

Building Skills: Vocabulary (pages 43–80)

Practicing with Short Readings (pages 48–57)

Exercise 1 (page 48) 1. d, 2. a, 3. b

Exercise 2 (page 49) 1. b, 2. d, 3. a, 4. d

Exercise 3 (page 51) 1. b, 2. d, 3. b, 4. a

Exercise 4 (page 52) 1. c, 2. b, 3. a, 4. d

Exercise 5 (page 53) 1. c, 2. a, 3. b, 4. a

Exercise 6 (page 55) 1. c, 2. a, 3. b, 4. a

Exercise 7 (page 56) 1. b, 2. d, 3. b, 4. c

Review: Vocabulary (pages 67–80)

Vocabulary Review Passage 1 (page 68)
1. a, 2. a, 3. d, 4. c, 5. a, 6. b, 7. d, 8. d, 9. c, 10. c, 11. a, 12. b, 13. a

Vocabulary Review Passage 2 (page 72)
1. d, 2. d, 3. a, 4. b, 5. c, 6. a, 7. a, 8. c, 9. d, 10. b, 11. d, 12. c

Vocabulary Review Passage 3 (page 76)
1. b, 2. d, 3. b, 4. a, 5. d, 6. c, 7. c, 8. a, 9. c, 10. a, 11. d, 12. c

Part 2: Listening

Building Skills: Listening for Main Ideas (pages 82–94)

How to Find Main Ideas (pages 83–85)

Practice 1 (with Answer Analysis) (page 84)
Lecture: Economic Conditions
Exercise 1 (page 85)

Answers may vary. Some suggested answers are:

  1   "We are not sure . . ."

  3   "The unemployment rate . . ."

  3   "Unfortunately this is not sustainable . . ."

  3   "Personal consumption climbed . . ."

  3   "However, people were . . ."

  0   "The U.S. has the lowest . . ."

  3   "Factory orders rose . . ."

  3   "Productivity in the second . . ."

  3, 2   "Ideally, productivity should grow . . ."

  3   "Still, productivity grew . . ."

  5   "These are mixed signs . . ."

  5   "In any case, we are in . . ."

Exercise 2 (page 86)

You can expect to hear the main idea in this talk at **a**, the beginning and end of the talk.

Exercise 3 (page 86)

First sentence: *We are not sure if the U.S. economy is in a recession because there are mixed indicators.* Last two sentences: *These are mixed signs about the economy, so we cannot tell if we are in a recession right now. In any case, we are in a period of slow growth.*

Practice 2 (page 87)
Conversation: Two Students

1. c, 2. a, 3. d, 4. b

Organization and Note Taking (pages 88–94)

Exercise 4 (page 90)
Lecture: Gathering Information
Answers may vary.

    I. Clinical Interview (bipolar video)

        A. Unstruct.

            1. skill

            2. ++ Many sides of person

            3. –– <u>low inter-rater reliability</u>

        B. Structured

            1. higher inter-rater rel.

            2. <u>constrained</u>

    II. Psychological Testing

        A. Personality Inventory: MMPI

            1. 400 questions

            2. empirical

dep, mania   3. 9 scales rel. to DSM

            4. ↑ score, ↑ trait

        B. <u>Intel/Cog Tests</u>

            1. ++ = diagnose learning disorders

        C. <u>Projectives</u>

            Ex. Rorschach: neutral stim shows unconscious thought

            Ex. TAT picture stories

                1. Neg points

                    ––??Really show unconscious?

                    ––<u>Lower inter-rater rel.</u>

III. _Behavioral measures_

    A. Observe

    B. Make Inferences

    C. Third-party reports

        1. esp. children/classroom

IV. Biological Measures

    A. Neuroimaging

    B. _Neuropsychological_

        —Sample behavior shows brain function

        —Before/after measurement

Questions about the Lecture (pages 91–93)

1. a.

2.

a. Clinical Interviews
Structured discussion Unstructured consultation

b. Psychological Testing
Personality inventories Projectives

d. Biological Measures
Neuroimaging techniques Neuropsychological tests

c. Behavioral Measures
Observation Third-party reports

3. a

4. c

Practice 3 (page 93)
Lecture: Gender
1. d, 2. a, 3. d, 4. a

Basic Skills: Listening for Details (pages 95–107)

How to Listen for Details (pages 95–98)

Practice 1 (with Answer Analysis) (page 96)
Lecture: Mental Illness

Topic: DSM-IV

1. <u>DSM-IV = categorical: do/don't</u>

   <u>Dprsn, schiz.—unvsl. flngs.</u>

   <u>Diag crit defs. illness</u>

   <u>Gradations</u>

   ♀ <u>in bed = depressed</u>

   ♀ <u>w/Normal life = depressed</u>

2. Mental ill. has stigma

   <u>Label harms person</u>

   <u>Seen as weakness</u>

   Balance harm vs. benefits of treatment

3. <u>Is DSM-IV correct?</u>

   <u>Indvdl. disorders</u>

   <u>Disorders that occur together</u>

4. <u>Culture-Bound Syndromes</u>

   <u>Nervous Impact Syndrome</u>

   <u>Not in DSM-IV</u>

   <u>Latin Amer.</u>

   <u>Is DSM-IV universal, comprehen?</u>

5. <u>DSM-IV: ++</u>

   <u>speak one lang.</u>

   <u>Build science</u>

   <u>Do research & intervention</u>

Anticipating Information (pages 99–100)

Exercise 1 (page 99)
Conversation: A Professor and a Student
Predictions may vary. Accurate predictions are:
1. b,   2. d,   3. a,   4. c,   5. c,   6. d,   7. b

Organizational Signals (pages 101–103)

Practice 2 (page 103)
Lecture: Poverty
1. b,   2. a and c,   3. c,   4. d,   5. b

Abbreviations and Symbols in Note-Taking (pages 104–07)

Exercise 3 (page 105)
Notes from Exercise 4 (Lecture: Gathering Information, pages 90–91)

Topic: Types of Data

I. Clinical Interview (bipolar video)

    A. (Unstruct.) UNSTRUCTURED

        1. skill

        2. (++) Many sides of person ADVANTAGES

        3. (−) low inter-rater reliability DISADVANTAGES

    B. Structured

        1. higher inter-rater (rel.) RELIABILITY

        2. constrained

II. Psychological Testing

    A. Personality Inventory: MMPI

        1. 400 questions

        2. empirical

    dep, mania 3. 9 scales (rel.) to DSM RELATES

        4. (↑)score, (↑)trait

        INCREASE

    B. Intel/Cog Tests

        2. (++ =)diagnose learning disorders ADVANTAGES/ARE

    C. Projectives

        Ex. Rorschach: neutral (stim) shows unconscious thought STIMULUS

        Ex.   TAT picture stories

1. (Neg) points NEGATIVE

—(??) Really show unconscious? QUESTION

—Lower inter-rater (rel.) RELIABILITY

III. Behavioral measures

A. Observe

B. Make Inferences

C. Third-party reports

1. (esp.) children/classroom ESPECIALLY

IV. Biological Measures

A. Neuroimaging

B. Neuropsychological

—Sample behavior shows brain function

—Before/after measurement

Notes from Practice 1 (with answer Analysis) (Lecture: Mental Illness, pages 96–97)

Topic: DSM-IV

1. DSM-IV = categorical: do/don't

(Dprsn, schiz.—unvsl. flngs.) DEPRESSION, SCHIZOPHRENIA, UNIVERSAL, FEELINGS

(Diag crit defs.) illness DIAGNOSTIC CRITERIA DEFINES

Gradations

(♀) in bed = depressed PERSON

(♀) w/Normal life = depressed PERSON

2. Mental (ill.) has stigma ILLNESS

Label harms person

Seen as weakness

Balance harm (vs.) benefits of treatment VERSUS

3. Is DSM-IV correct?

(Indvdl.) disorders INDIVIDUAL

Disorders that occur together

4. Culture-Bound Syndromes

Nervous Impact Syndrome

Not in DMV

Latin (Amer.) AMERICA

Is DSM-IV universal, (comprehen?) COMPREHENSIVE

5. DSM-IV: (++) BENEFITS

   speak one (lang.) LANGUAGE

   Build science

   Do research (&) intervention AND

Exercise 4 (page 105)

1. Thursday
2. decrease
3. because
4. speed up
5. interconnectedness
6. landscape
7. participation
8. technology
9. ten miles an hour
10. communicate
11. telephone
12. threaten
13. thus
14. money
15. international
16. Mexican
17. circulation
18. politics
19. identity
20. geography

Practice 3 (page 106)
Lecture: Modern Social Change

1. d, 2. a and b, 3. a and b

4.

Ethnoscape	Finance Scape	Conflict Scape
b.	c.	f.
d.	g.	h.

5. b

Building Skills: Pragmatic Understanding (pages 108–18)

How to Listen for Pragmatic Understanding (pages 109–10)

Practice 1 (page 109)
1. c and d, 2. b, 3. d, 4. c

Reading between the Lines (pages 110–13)

Practice 2 (page 112)
Lecture: Genes
1. b, 2. c, 3. b, 4. d, 5. c

Listening for Attitude (pages 113–16)

Exercise 2 (page 113)
Conversation: Two Students
Answers may vary but could include the following.

1. I think
2. You're right
3. practical
4. Like
5. I disagree. The way I see it
6. I just feel like
7. slow
8. boring
9. interest
10. I'd rather
11. for me
12. active
13. energizing
14. even
15. she'd be willing
16. I just prefer
17. love
18. I'd rather
19. I don't want this
20. interested

Identifying Purpose (pages 116–18)

Exercise 3 (page 116)

1. a 2. c 3. d 4. b

Practice 4 (page 116)
Lecture: Politics and Resources

1. d, 2. b, 3. a, 4. d, 5. c, 6. a

Part 3: Writing

Building Skills: The Independent Writing Task (pages 119–44)

Generating Ideas (pages 122–23)

Exercise 1 (page 123)
Answers will vary.

Organizing Your Ideas (pages 123–26)

Exercise 2 (page 124)
Suggested answers for Prompts 1 and 2.

Prompt 1: Would you prefer to live in the country or the city? Why?

I prefer the city

There are lots of things to do ■

Museums, restaurants, shopping ■

Don't need a car ✓

Good public transportation ✓

Cultural centers are in city ■

~~My work is in art, there's more access to art in the city~~

~~Energy from people~~

More job opportunities *

~~Easy to travel to and from, lots of flights~~

Easy to meet people because there are so many ■

Job and social life is close to apartment ✓

Prompt 2: *Agree or disagree:* For learning English, it is better to live in a small town than in a big city.

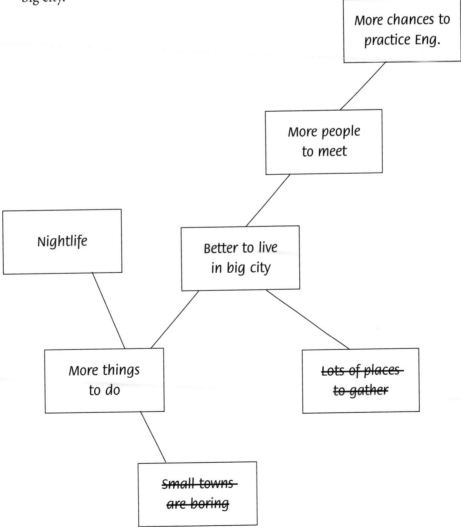

Exercise 3 (page 126)
Answers will vary.

Stating Your Opinion Clearly (pages 126–29)

Exercise 4 (page 127)
Prompt 1: c,   Prompt 2: b

Exercise 5 (page 128)
Answers will vary.

Exercise 6 (page 129)
Prompt 1: a; Prompt 2: b

Exercise 7 (page 132)
Answers may vary. 2, 5, 1, 7, 4, 6, 3

The original paragraph read like this:

Teachers can learn from students because students bring a fresh perspective to the topics that are being taught. Some teachers have been working with the same subject for so long that they have already formed opinions about it that are not easily altered. For example, a student may interpret a piece of literature in a completely new way that is informed by the perspective of his or her generation. The teacher may have never formed that interpretation with the help of the student. Realizing this makes for a much richer learning and teaching environment. A richer learning environment means that more learning will take place, and in a more satisfying way. The result is that teachers and students operate in a reciprocal relationship with each other, giving and taking and learning together. This creates a community of scholarship that is more like the ideal educational institution.

Follow-up Questions, Exercise 7 (page 133)
Answer will vary.

Exercise 8 (page 133)
Answers will vary.

Connecting to a Larger Issue (pages 134–36)

Exercise 9 (page 134)
1. c, 2. a, 3. b, 4. e, 5. d

Example 10 (page 136)

1. The author is connecting her ideas to issues of power and language. Other possible answers include dying languages, the importance of language diversity, the importance of language to humans, dominance of languages.

2. She connects to the larger issue in each paragraph.

Formatting (pages 136–38)

Exercise 11 (page 137)

1. Each sentence starts on a new line.
2. The reader may think that each sentence is about a new idea. To fix this problem, the author would need to indent the first line of the paragraph and then connect all the sentences together without putting each on a new line.

Building Skills: The Integrated Writing Task (pages 145–78)

Paraphrasing (pages 146–53)

Exercise 1 (page 148)

a. paraphrases 1 and 3
b. paraphrases 1 and 3
c. paraphrase 3
d. paraphrase 3
e. Your choices may vary, but the best paraphrase here is number 3. Although the first one is shorter and simpler than the original, it just copies sections of the original passage and strings them together. The second paraphrase simply uses the same grammatical structures as the original and substitutes synonyms for the content words. The final paraphrase, number 3, uses the author's own words and the grammatical structure. Also, it meets the criteria for a good paraphrase because it captures the main idea, and is simpler and shorter than the original.

Exercise 2 (page 149)

1. a, 2. c, 3. a, 4. c, 5. b

Exercise 3 (page 150)

Answers will vary.

Part 4: Speaking

Building Skills: Responding to Independent and Integrated Speaking Prompts (page 180–208)

Rhetorical Styles (pages 181–82)

Exercise 1 (page 181)

Answers may vary.

a. I prefer to live with a roommate because it is cheaper and it provides companionship.
b. I am not very social so I want to live alone.
c. Transcript 1.

Identifying the Question Type (page 182–83)

Exercise 2 (page 182)

a. opinion

b. opinion

c. both

d. both

e. both

f. summary

Managing Your Time (pages 183–85)

Exercise 3 (page 184)

a. both

b. Sample two does not include very much opinion.

c. sample 2

d. sample 1

Stating the Main Idea Clearly (pages 185–86)

Exercise 4 (page 185)

1. f, 2. d, 3. b, 4. a, 5. c, 6. i, 7. j, 8. g, 9. h, 10. e

Supporting and Developing Your Point (page 187)

Exercise 5 (page 187)

Answers may vary.

1. For response 1, the entire first sentence may be the main idea. For response 2, the main idea is, "The two student is talking about their, aah, lecture um the man said like the professor go too far and then it's hard to follow"

2. Response 2 has more supporting ideas.

3. Both speakers could be more concise in their summaries and then add more supporting ideas to their opinions.

Using Transitions (pages 188–90)

Exercise 6 (page 188)

Answers may vary.

Exercise 7 (page 189)

1. Transition words include: "And also," "In conclusion."

2. "And also" adds information. "In conclusion" summarizes.

3. Between the first and second sentence the speaker does not use a specific transition word. Instead, the clause that begins, "When . . ." repeats the idea stated in the first sentence. The clause that begins, "I can talk to him . . ." then adds more information that explains and supports the first idea. Here, the pronoun *him* also acts as a cohesive device.

4. Sometimes it is more effective to use a clause that links the previous idea to the next idea by repeating or building on what has already been stated.

ANSWER KEY FOR A COMPLETE MULTI-SKILLS PRACTICE TEST

Section 1: Reading (page 209–23)

Passage 1 (page 209)
1. b, 2. b, 3. b, 4. c, 5. a, 6. b, 7. c, 8. a, 9. d, 10. a

Schematic Table (page 213)

Images of the wilderness from before the "revolution of sensibility"	a. The wilderness is hideous and desolate. c. The wilderness is haunted by the devil himself. f. The wilderness is like the deserts mentioned in the Bible. h. The wilderness is not the romantic, pantheistic place that Thoreau and Muir would have imagined.
Images of the wilderness since the "revolution of sensibility"	d. The wilderness is a manifestation of the sublime. e. The wilderness should be preserved.

Passage 2 (page 214)
1. c, 2. a, 3. c, 4. a, 5. d, 6. b, 7. d, 8. d, 9. c, 10. a

Prose Summary (page 218)

The AEC study headed by Mancuso investigated whether nuclear workers at the Hanford site had developed cancer from radiation in the workplace.
b. In conducting his study, Mancuso had to overcome great difficulty in collecting records, some of which had been destroyed. c. Mancuso was a leading epidemiologist who had developed an effective technique for linking cancer to its causes. e. At the time the study started, most experts believed that low levels of radiation posed no health risk.

Passage 3 (page 218)
1. b,   2. c,   3. c,   4. c,   5. d,   6. d,   7. d,   8. a,   9. b,   10. b
Schematic Table (page 223)

Has caused an increase in medical paternalism	c. the FOCA e. the decision in *United States v. Rutherford* f. the decision by the Tenth District Court of Appeals
Has caused an increase in patient autonomy	a. the 1994 Dietary Supplements Health and Education Act

Section 2: Listening (pages 224–34)

Conversation: A Teaching Assistant and a Student (page 224)
1. d,   2. b,   3. b,   4. c,   5. a

Conversation: An Advisor and a Student (page 225)
6. d,   7. Benefits—d, Drawbacks—a, c, e, f, No Information—b, g,   8. a, c,   9. b,   10. a,   11. a

Lecture: Midwestern Geography (page 227)
12. c,   13. b,   14. c,   15. d,   16. a, b

Lecture: Cyrus the Great (page 229)
17. a,   18. b, c   19. d,   20. c, d,   21. b

Lecture: Economics (page 230)
22. d,   23. c,   24. d,   25. d,   26. a,   27. a,   28. c,   29. c, a, d, b

Lecture: Plants (page 233)
30. a,   31. a,   32. c,   33. b,   34. d,   35. c

Section 3: Speaking (pages 235–36)

Answers will vary.

Section 4: Writing (pages 237–38)

Answers will vary.

DISK 1 (69:19)

Part 2: Listening

1: Copyright statement/Practice 1: Lecture, pp. 84–85 (2:35)

2: Practice 2: Conversation, pp. 87–88 (1:54)

3: Exercise 4: Lecture, pp. 90–93 (5:52)

4: Practice 3: Lecture, pp. 93–94 (2:00)

5: Practice 1: Lecture, pp. 96–98 (3:42)

6: Exercise 1: Conversation (segments), pp. 99–100 (6:29)

7: Exercise 1: Conversation (without interruption), p. 100 (4:47)

8: Exercise 2: Lecture, pp.101–02 (3:20)

9: Exercise 4, p. 105 (1:42)

10: Practice 3: Lecture, pp. 106–07 (7:04)

11: Practice 1, pp. 109–10 (2:30)

12: Exercise 1, p. 111 (2:36)

13: Practice 2: Lecture, pp. 112–13 (9:27)

14: Exercise 2: Conversation, pp. 113–14 (4:31)

15: Practice 3: Conversation, pp. 114–16 (:27)

16: Exercise 3, pp. 116–17 (2:41)

17: Practice 4: Lecture, pp. 117–18 (7:33)

DISK 2 (77:19)

Part 3: Writing

1: Writing in response to a lecture, p. 166 (3:26)

2: Practicing writing in response to a lecture, p. 168 (2:45)

3: Writing in response to a reading and lecture, p. 171 (3:40)

4: Practicing with a reading and lecture on your own, p. 174 (3:16)

Part 4: Speaking

5: Exercise 2, pp. 182–83 (1:03)

6: Independent speaking prompts, questions 1 and 2, p. 193 (:46)

7: Independent speaking prompt, question 3, p. 197 (:48)

8: Independent speaking prompt, question 4, p. 200 (1:20)

9: Listening/speaking prompt, question 5, p. 202 (1:25)

10: Listening/speaking prompt, question 6, p. 205 (2:27)

Practice Test

11: Conversation, pp. 224 (3:41)

12: Question 4, p. 225 (:25)

13: Conversation, pp. 225–27 (4:39)

14: Question 10, p. 227 (:32)

15: Lecture, pp. 227–28 (7:42)

16: Lecture, p. 229 (10:10)

17: Lecture, pp. 230–32 (9:27)

18: Question 27, p. 231 (:38)

19: Lecture, pp. 233–34 (4:50)

20: Question 32, p. 234 (:29)

21: Speaking Question 1, p. 235 (:25)

22: Speaking Question 2, p. 235 (:32)

23: Speaking Question 3, p. 235 (:59)

24: Speaking Question 4, p. 236 (1:35)

25: Speaking Question 5, p. 236 (2:21)

26: Speaking Question 6, p. 236 (2:36)

27: Integrated writing task, p. 237 (5:05)